Visions for the Future of Continuing Professional Education

Visions for the Future of Continuing Professional Education

Ronald M. Cervero
John F. Azzaretto
and
Associates

The University of Georgia
Department of Adult Education, College of Education
Georgia Center for Continuing Education

Library of Congress Cataloging in Publication Data

Visions for the Future of Continuing Professional Education / Ronald M. Cervero, John F. Azzaretto, and Associates.

    p. cm.

A collection of papers from a landmark 1988 symposium held at The University of Georgia, sponsored by the Dept. of Adult Education and by the Georgia Center for Continuing Education.

Bibliography: p.
ISBN 0-9619031-2-0: $14.95

1. Professional education--United States--Congresses.
2. Continuing education--United States--Congresses. I. Cervero, Ronald M. II. Azzaretto, John F.
III. University of Georgia Adult Education Dept. IV. Georgia Center for Continuing Education.

LC1072.C56V57 1988   89-11863
378.013--dc20   CIP

Published and distributed by

Georgia Center for Continuing Education
The University of Georgia
Athens, Georgia 30602

Published in the United States of America

Contents

Part 2: The Process of Continuing Professional Education

Preface

In 1980, Cyril O. Houle took a sweeping look at the undefined field of continuing professional education. The result, *Continuing Learning in the Professions*, was powerful and far-reaching. In it he stated:

> The plans to establish basic educational programs for those entering the professions were thought in the first quarter century to be visionary, but they have now been realized at levels far beyond those of the original dreams. Continuing education will follow the same pattern of growth; what we hardly dare prophesy today will be seen by later generations as efforts to achieve a manifest necessity. (p. 302)

This book is a response to Houle's challenge to shape the future of continuing professional education. In it we have offered many visions for creating the manifest necessity he describes.

Today, continuing professional education is a fragmented field involving many actors and organizations, often serving differing goals. Most professions are characterized by loosely structured systems of education. However, leaders in the field foresee the growth of more extensive systems in the next quarter century. We understand a system to be a complex unity formed of many diverse parts and serving a common purpose. This book offers one view for a future system of continuing professional education and pays particular attention to both the contexts and the processes in our field. It describes the ways in which we must renew and redirect continuing professional education.

The chapters in this book have a special origin. They were created in a spirit of collegial inquiry and discovery at the symposium "Renewing and Redirecting Continuing Professional Education," held at the Georgia Center for Continuing Education, on The University of Georgia campus in June, 1988. Participating authors were challenged to identify ways to renew and redirect systems of continuing professional education for the future. An open symposium provided opportunities for creativity and breadth of vision for each paper. Roundtable discussions among the invited authors following the symposium energized the group, enabling synergy and creative thinking to flourish. Among the authors, a commitment to a shared vision for the future of continuing professional education grew. Part of that commitment was to continue such conversations about our sprawling field. And in this spirit, *Visions for the Future of Continuing Professional Education* is offered.

Many people deserve our thanks and appreciation for their efforts in producing the symposium and this book. At The University of Georgia, Bradley C. Courtenay, head of the Department of Adult Education, and Edward G. Simpson, Jr., Director of the Georgia Center for Continuing Education, supported our efforts by funding the symposium. Their personal commitment to this event and to the development of this book was invaluable and most gratifying.

We are also grateful to the W. K. Kellogg Foundation for the financial support of the symposium and for their visions for the future of our field. Cyril O. Houle attended the symposium on behalf of the Kellogg Foundation. He deserves special recognition for the work he has done in illuminating the field of continuing professional education and in providing the inspiration for our symposium.

During the symposium, there were three individuals from The University of Georgia who provided critical feedback to authors, helping them to further develop and refine their papers. We are grateful for this critical input from Alphonse Buccino, Dean, College of Education; Archie B. Carroll, professor, College of Business Administration; and Ellen R. Jordan, professor, College of Law. Additionally, we thank Eugene Younts, Vice President for Services at The University of Georgia, for his presence and support during the symposium.

In organizing the symposium, we especially thank Sherry Shepard-Conner for staying abreast of the ever-changing arrangements and coordinating the symposium; Roger Comley and Beverly Bourgeois for creating the outstanding special events for our authors; Pat Pinckard for the hours she spent attending to the many details, logistics, and typing involved with the symposium; Sherri Lee for continuing these responsibilities with the book; the telecommunications staff who taped the symposium; and the many others who gave their time and energy to this undertaking.

In producing this book, we are grateful to Rob Williams, Associate Director for the Division of Communication Services of the Georgia Center for Continuing Education at The University of Georgia, for his assistance and vision in developing this volume. We also acknowledge the efforts of Editorial Services of the Georgia Center (John Shores, managing editor; Nancy Flanagan, typist for the entire manuscript; Michael Hendrick and Thomas McConnell, final copy editors and proofreaders) and the Graphics Department of the Georgia Center (Susan Driver, manager; Ehsan Choudhury, typesetter; Michelle Davis, type production; Vickie Sharp, artist; Thomas Anderson, proofreader; Lori Barrett, layout and cover design). We are especially grateful to Judith Chandler, who served as editor for the manuscript.

Finally, we offer our deepest appreciation to Diane E. Tallman, who provided the connection between the conceptual and the technical aspects of the symposium and the book. She participated fully in helping to shape the symposium and made sure that all those involved in this complex activity were kept fully informed of what was needed from them and how it meshed with all the other project components.

Ronald M. Cervero
John F. Azzaretto

Athens, Georgia
December, 1989

The Authors

Yolande C. Adelson is Associate Dean, Human Resources, UCLA Extension, and is responsible for instructor and staff resource management. Her prior appointments at UCLA Extension were Director, Office of Instructional Affairs; and Director, Department of Human Development. Adelson is a Yale Law School graduate, former arbitrator and mediator, and member of the state bars of Virginia and Michigan. Her labor arbitration awards have been published by the Bureau of National Affairs (BNA) and Commercial Clearing House, Inc. (CCH). She has extensive experience in private law practice, city government, education, and private industry. She developed and administers UCLA Extension's Instructor Development Program, which won the 1985-86 National University Continuing Education Association-American College Testing (NUCEA-ACT) Program Award for Innovation in Administration.

John F. (Jack) Azzaretto was Assistant Administrator, Governmental Training Division at The University of Georgia while working on this book. Additionally, Azzaretto directed the Kellogg-funded Continuing Professional Education Project which established the Georgia Council for the Improvement of Continuing Education for the Professions. He was an adjunct faculty member in the Department of Political Science, and has published chapters in the textbook *Effective Supervisory Practices: Better Results Through Teamwork*. He has most recently completed a book chapter in *Competitive Strategies for Continuing Education* (C. Baden, ed). Currently, Azzaretto is Extension Professor and Director of the Institute of Public Service at the University of Connecticut.

Ronald M. Cervero is an Associate Professor in the Department of Adult Education at The University of Georgia. He has written several book chapters, numerous articles, and has edited a book, *Problems and Prospects* *in Continuing Professional Education* (1985, with C.L. Scanlan), in the area of continuing professional education. His newest book, *Effective Continuing Education for Professionals,* was awarded the 1989 Cyril O. Houle World Literature Award in Adult Education. Cervero has previously served as the Assistant Executive Director of the Illinois Council on Continuing Medical Education.

Luvern L. Cunningham is Novice G. Fawcett Professor of Educational Administration, Senior Professor at the Mershon Center, and Director of the Commission on Interprofessional Education and Practice at The Ohio State University. A former teacher, principal, and school superintendent in Nebraska, Cunningham has had a lifelong interest in the problems of youth. As former Dean of the College of Education at Ohio State, and Professor of Education at the University of Chicago and the University of Minnesota, he has been a central figure in shaping public education policy, having written widely on the governance of education, desegregation, and leadership in the public schools and interprofessional education. He has served on many national committees, including the American Association of School Administrators Commission on Children, and has advanced degrees from the University of Nebraska and the University of Oregon.

Christopher J. Dede is Professor of Educational Foundations at the University of Houston-Clear Lake, where he teaches courses in futures research, computer science, and education. He has been a Visiting Scientist in artificial intelligence at MIT and at NASA, studying advanced technologies for knowledge transfer. Dede is the Founding President of the Education Section of the World Future Society and works extensively with professional associations, corporations, public agencies, and educational institutions on preparing for uncertain futures. He also travels for the U.S. Information Agency and, over the past four years, has conducted workshops on American education in nine countries.

Arden D. Grotelueschen is currently President of Grotelueschen Associates, a firm that specializes in providing technical support services for organizations providing continuing professional education and training services. During the past 20 years, he has held faculty or administrative positions at three major educational institutions--University of Nebraska, Teachers College at Columbia University, and the University of Illinois at Urbana-Champaign. His recent publications have focused on topics of participation in continuing professional education, professionals' assessment of self-study learning, program evaluation methodology, and assessing the structure of professional knowledge.

Robert A. Hofstader is Manager of the Education and Development Division at Exxon Central Services and is responsible for Management Education, Technical Education, Computer Education, Staff Development, and Safety Education for Exxon. During his career as a chemist, he has made several contributions to the fields of analytical chemistry and environmental engineering. He was an industrial consultant and technical contributor to a National Science Foundation-sponsored project at the University of California-Berkeley which resulted in the publication of an eight volume series on Modern Chemical Technology. Hofstader was appointed as a member of the Governor's Advisory Board on Vocational and Technical Education for New Jersey and has served on the Advisory Board for Analytical Chemistry and Advances in Chemistry with the American Chemical Society. Hofstader has published in areas ranging from analytical chemistry and environmental science to education and co-authored a book, *Analysis of Petroleum for Trace Metals.*

Alan B. Knox is Professor of Continuing Education at the University of Wisconsin-Madison. Previously, he was a faculty member at Syracuse University, where he completed four degrees, and the University of Nebraska and Teachers College, Columbia. Additionally, Knox was a professor at the University of Illinois at Urbana-Champaign and also served as Associate Vice Chancellor for Academic Affairs and Director, Continuing Education and Public Service. He has served as president of the American Association for Adult and Continuing Education (AAACE) and chairs the Commission on Leadership of the National University Continuing Education Association (NUCEA). He was Editor-in-Chief for the *New Directions for Continuing Education* series published by Jossey-Bass from 1979-1984 and has authored over one hundred publications on various aspects of educational programs for adults. His current research interests are comparative adult education, continuing education leadership, and helping adults learn.

Robert T. McLaughlin is a Professor and Chair of the Department of Business, Leadership and Community Development at Goddard College. He teaches small business development and non-profit management. He previously served as Research Associate for the Commission on Interprofessional Education and Practice at The Ohio State University, where he conducted research regarding interprofessional education. Previously, he was an adult educator, planner, and development officer at higher educational institutions serving low-income minority students. His principal interest is in the use of educational resources to facilitate community self-development. McLaughlin's dissertation concerned a case study of a strategy of education for local development known as business retention and expansion.

Paul David Munger is President of Strategic Education Services, a consulting firm that provides management and marketing expertise to organizations involved in higher learning. Clients include associations, corporations, and universities. Previously, he was Director of the Commission on Future Academic Leadership, a project funded by the W.K. Kellogg Foundation through the National University and Continuing Education Association (NUCEA). Munger was also Assistant Provost for Academic Development at American University and served in the School of Continuing Studies at Indiana University.

Philip M. Nowlen is Dean of the University of Virginia's Division of Continuing Education. Nowlen also directs the J. Paul Getty Trust's Museum Management Institute. Previously, he had been Executive Director of the University of Chicago's Continuing Education programs. Nowlen has twice chaired the editorial board of *Continuum,* the journal of the National University Continuing Education Association (NUCEA) and edited a special issue. He co-directed a NUCEA-University of Chicago survey of university professional association continuing education relationships. He and Donna Queeney co-authored a statement of continuing professional education principles and issues which was adopted by NUCEA as the position of the association. Nowlen is the author of several chapters, and his book, *A New Approach to Continuing Education for Business and the Professions: The Performance Model,* was published by Macmillan in 1987.

Donna S. Queeney is Director, Division of Planning Studies, and Associate Professor of Education Policy Studies at The Pennsylvania State University. She is a frequent writer and speaker on higher education's role in continuing professional education, business/professional association/higher education collaboration, and needs assessment. She has served on the boards of several professional associations, most recently the American Nurses' Association and the American Institute of Architects. Additionally, Queeney provides guidance and designs research studies and strategic planning initiatives for Penn State's Commonwealth Educational System and serves as editor of *The Journal of Continuing Higher Education*. She is a member of the National University Continuing Education Association's board of directors and executive committee.

Wayne D. Smutz is Associate Director, Division of Planning Studies, and Head of the Division's Office of Continuing Professional Education at The Pennsylvania State University. The office, a research and development unit, works collaboratively with professional associations to develop innovative approaches to continuing education. Its projects include helping professionals better understand their learning needs through self assessment, providing educational materials via alternative delivery systems, and examining the impact of mandatory continuing education requirements. Smutz is Chair of the National University Continuing Education Association's Division of Continuing Education for the Professions and Assistant Editor of *The Journal of Continuing Higher Education*. His publications focus on higher education's role in continuing professional education and university/professional association collaboration.

Diane E. Tallman is Kellogg Project Associate at the Georgia Center for Continuing Education on The University of Georgia campus. She works in the Continuing Professional Education Office and has been instrumental in guiding the development of the Georgia Council for the Improvement of Continuing Education for the Professions and serves as Editor of *Crossing Lines*, a newsletter devoted to advancing the profession of continuing education for the professions. She has previously worked as graduate assistant in the Department of Adult Education of The University of Georgia and as an adult basic education teacher of the Southeastern Indiana Vocational School. Tallman recently completed her doctoral degree in Adult Education at The University of Georgia. Her research examined competition and collaboration among providers of continuing professional education.

Renewing and Redirecting Continuing Professional Education

Ronald M. Cervero
John F. Azzaretto
Diane E. Tallman

Systems of Continuing Professional Education Today

A central feature of American society in the 20th century has been the professionalization of its workforce. One recent estimate is that nearly 25% of the American workforce claims membership in a profession (Cervero, 1988). This increase in professionalism has occurred as a result of the further development of the established professions, as well as the appearance of new professions. The growth and development of pre-service programs, particularly within universities, accounts for much of this increase in professionalization. These programs have provided the necessary basic training to prepare individuals to begin their professional practice. Although few people are completely satisfied with current systems of pre-service preparation, most would agree that the essential elements for entry-level practice are provided in these programs.

But what happens to these individuals once they go into practice? Are there continuing education systems that are as well-organized as these pre-service educational systems? While pre-service education is the foundation of practice, the educational system must be responsive throughout one's professional lifetime to help insure ongoing practitioner competence. Until about 25 years ago, no systematic thought was given to the importance of these issues. The leaders of most professions, as well as the general public, believed that three to five years of pre-service training was sufficient for a lifetime of work. However, since the publication in 1962 of a conceptual scheme for the lifelong education of physicians (Dryer, 1962), this belief has been seriously challenged in all the professions. Evidence

1

indicates that most professions now embrace the importance of lifelong professional education (Meyer, 1975; Stone, 1986; Vernon, 1983) as an important means to maintain the competence of its members.

In representing an appreciable body of thought, Houle (1980) believes that systems of continuing education will eventually be built to rival the pre-service preparation programs now in existence. Already schemes have been proposed by several professions, notably medicine (Storey, 1988) and engineering (MIT, 1984), by which their continuing education systems could be organized and coordinated. However, "Only in the officer corps of the armed services -- where a continuing assessment of performance has been fully accepted -- has anything approaching a systematic career-long pattern of study been worked out" (Mawby, 1985, p. 5).

In the past 25 years, most professions have taken the first awkward steps in translating the need for continuing education into systems in the "real world." Although this increasing attention to continuing professional education is certainly a positive development, its widespread shortcomings are now prominently on display. Houle (1980) does not overstate the problems of continuing professional education today when he presents this typical scenario: "Faculty members who can be persuaded to do so give lectures on subjects of their own choosing to audiences they do not know, who have assembled only because they want to put in enough hours of classroom attendance so that they can meet a relicensure requirement" (p. 266). Furthermore, these programs are expected to secure the competent performance of professionals whose practices are marked by complexity, uncertainty, and conflicting values.

Systems of Continuing Professional Education for the Future

Proposition One: Early Stages

This book was developed on the basis of two major propositions. The first proposition is that existing systems of continuing professional education are in an early stage of development. As such, these systems are: 1) devoted to updating professionals about the newest developments, 2) transmitted in a didactic fashion, 3) provided by a pluralistic group of organizations, 4) not organized according to some overall plan, and 5) almost entirely unconnected to previous levels of professional education. In short, current systems are often elementary, sporadic, and reactive. Educators respond to the learning needs of professionals in a haphazard manner, without integrating the education into an overall scheme of lifelong learning. Nor do educators move out of their own professional domains to learn about professional education in other fields.

Proposition Two: Growth and Development

The second proposition of this book is that there needs to be tremendous growth and development in these current systems during the coming decades. By way of analogy, continuing education is in the same state of development as pre-service education was at the beginning of this century. At that time, systems of professional education were also in their infancy. Medical education serves as a useful example on this point. In his classic study of medical education, Flexner (1910) found that of the 155 medical schools in this country, only 16 expected their incoming students to have had any previous college work. Contrasted with the complex and sophisticated system of medical education that exists today, it is obvious that intense growth and maturation has occurred.

These two propositions -- what the field is and what it needs to be -- form the foundation for this book. The purpose of this book is to develop a series of possible futures for continuing education in the professions by critically examining what is and by imagining what could be. We have invited a group of individuals who have been intensely involved in this critical examination to share their current thoughts on possible futures for continuing education. As noted earlier, a number of leaders in the field foresee the growth of elaborate and extensive systems of continuing professional education in the next quarter century. The chapters in this book further conceptualize and provide alternate courses of action for the development of these future systems. We hope that as these papers become a matter of public record, they help to shape the agenda for future discussion and action on the development of systems of continuing education for the professions.

Organization of the Book

The 10 chapters that comprise this book are originally prepared manuscripts. Collectively, they describe ways to renew and redirect systems of continuing professional education for the future. Each chapter represents different components of a CPE system for lifelong learning. Authors have two distinct charges as part of their analysis. The first is to examine the current state of affairs related to their topic, with specific attention given to the strengths and limitations of present systems of continuing professional education. The second charge is to construct and describe the most desirable future for continuing professional education with respect to their topics. Authors, then, from their own unique and varied perspectives, examine present operating systems of CPE and articulate a vision of the ways in which we must renew and redirect the field.

Chapters are divided into two parts: *The Context of Continuing Professional Education* and *The Process of Continuing Professional Educa-*

tion. The thought-provoking writing encompasses the richness and diversity of the field as the authors identify the many challenges that need to be addressed as CPE moves toward being recognized as a separate professional field of practice. Taken together, we hope the topical discussions illuminate current problems that exist within CPE. Also, we hope to identify possible future systems of continuing professional education and, in so doing, provide creative energy and ideas for moving our field forward.

Part One: The Context of Continuing Professional Education

Future systems cannot be understood apart from the context in which they exist and are shaped. The chapters in Part One describe the context or arena of continuing professional education action. The chapter contributions in this part are authored by Philip M. Nowlen, John F. Azzaretto, Arden D. Grotelueschen, Robert A. Hofstader and P. David Munger, and Luvern L. Cunningham and Robert T. McLaughlin. Each shares a common concern for the contextual factors associated with the field of CPE practice. They demonstrate how the loosely structured, multiple systems of CPE which currently exist limit our ability to see professional performance in a holistic context of life and work.

Philip Nowlen sets the stage by describing new expectations and new roles required of those who practice CPE. He asserts that the contexts of the professions have changed and multiplied, thus challenging educators to adopt a holistic and lifelong approach to the design of learning activities. Two aspects emerge as vitally important in shaping future systems of CPE. First, Nowlen views the professional as being embedded simultaneously in multiple cultures: work, family, friends, professional associations, civic affairs, and church, for example. Each culture's hold on the professional varies in intensity and changes during his or her lifetime. Therefore, educators must become aware that an individual's performance may be affected by one or more of these different cultures. And, secondly, educators will be challenged to design holistic learning systems that simultaneously account for: 1) the narrow professional knowledge/skills base, 2) the evolving and multiplying context of practice, 3) the interactive environment of adulthood, and 4) the social nature of professional performance.

In the next chapter, Azzaretto builds on the societal implications of professional performance and accountability. Having acquired enormous power by virtue of their specialized service and influence over government's regulatory function, the professions in contemporary society are under increased public scrutiny. He believes continuing professional education has the capacity to strengthen and revitalize the role of the professions in society. The challenge to educators is to cultivate a renewed sense of calling and commitment among professionals.

Additionally, CPE can be an effective mechanism in protecting the public interest by promoting greater professional responsiveness to societal needs and expanding educational activities to the consumers of professional services. Azzaretto proposes that future systems of continuing professional education should promote sound, value-based professional practice. Continuing educators of professionals must take the lead in creating an environment that encourages ongoing professional reflection, experience-based learning, and development of the whole person. In so doing, he believes that educators of professionals will be able to strengthen the link between practitioner competence and social responsibility.

Azzaretto's discussion of accountability, power, and social responsibility highlights the tremendous stakes in CPE. Nowlen's second chapter suggests a reframing of the old question: Who should provide what and for whom? He suggests that a different set of questions may emerge by distinguishing between learning and teaching, needs and wants, individuals and organizations, competence and performance, and occupational and human development. The dynamic interplay of these forces yields even more relevant questions that have impact upon the structure and financing of universities, professional associations, and employer organizations. Educators can make a difference by designing learning experiences centered on professional performance rather than on the simple economics of demand and marketability.

Nowlen describes a case study of an educational response to the problem of greater teacher proficiency. A request for a continuing education program should be considered to be the beginning of a diagnostic process. He urges us to consider the differences in performance that exist and the particular assumptions that have been made about a requested program's capability before designing and delivering it. With this perspective, continuing educators will avoid the temptation of "the quick fix" and build toward longer lasting relationships with other CPE providers.

Nowlen believes that the individual is the ultimate provider of his or her learning and that organizations benefit from the enhanced performance of professionals that can result from participation in CPE. This view has significant implications for financing continuing professional education in the future. In his chapter, Grotelueschen pointedly asks: Whose responsibility is it to formulate and implement human resource policy which benefits the individual (and society) in a continuous manner throughout the lifespan?

From a societal perspective, the professions may be one of our most important national assets. Grotelueschen maintains that a national human resource development policy is required to nurture these professional resources which are essential to our society's well-being, particularly in the context of increased complexity and technological change. His penetrating analysis of participation incentives and revenue alternatives provides the framework for a national human resource development policy. Who would benefit from such a policy? Grotelueschen maintains that beneficiaries would include the professional practitioner, the employing organization, the client or patient being served, the professions at large, and the general public.

Further development of the contextual theme as it relates to CPE in the workplace is the subject of the next chapter by Hofstader and Munger. They assert that, more than at any other time in history, today's corporate leadership is probably more concerned with its ability to respond to change. Therefore, corporate leadership is highly concerned with maintaining a highly skilled and informed workforce. Hofstader and Munger discuss how employers are currently responding to this challenge and suggest future strategies for American business to remain competitive in a global economy. They contend that because work, teaching, and study support each other, corporations must actively encourage their intermixing to insure the maintenance and continuing development of a creative and effective workforce.

Today's world, they point out, requires corporations to use education more wisely--to concentrate on education as a strategic means of accomplishing corporate goals. What, then, should be the future corporate strategy for continuing education? Hofstader and Munger believe that education and training must be viewed by corporate leadership as tools for implementing the organizational mission and for meeting business objectives. The role of continuing educators, thus, is to identify areas and circumstances in which educational activities are linked strategically and proactively to the mission, goals, directions, and issues of the corporation. How can this goal be accomplished? "Perhaps," they conclude, "a new institution unencumbered of the traditions and missions of universities and more broadly focused than professional societies and other vendors could most effectively marshal the resources to meet our pressing national need for continuing education in the workplace."

While Hofstader and Munger focus their discussion of CPE in the workplace of the scientific, technical, and engineering community, the human service professions are the subject of the final chapter in Part One. Cunningham and McLaughlin develop the theme of interprofessional collaboration as a response to the uncoordinated, highly specialized human service delivery systems that currently exist. They contend that there is a growing awareness of the need for specialized human service providers and community leadership to communicate and collaborate, rather then act unilaterally as members of discrete expert and social systems. Human service professionals are less and less equipped to address complex concerns through monoprofessional approaches. Educators must therefore respond to this challenge. Cunningham and McLaughlin assert that providers of continuing professional education should assume a leadership role, fostering interprofessional collaboration. "Through sustained dialogue among professionals from diverse fields, we may develop a shared appreciation of the systemic, ethical, practical and educational challenges facing the human services professions."

Cunningham and McLaughlin's response to society's critical need for educational strategies which provide for interprofessional collaboration is to boldly recommend a national infrastructure for interprofessional continuing education. Modeled after the nation's Cooperative Extension Service, the authors contend that an interprofessional extension service has the potential to improve the quality of local care and positively influence decision-making processes. Human service professions working collaboratively could be a powerful force to improve the quality of patient/client care and would encourage a delivery system of continuing education that promotes interprofessional interaction.

Part Two: The Process of Continuing Professional Education

In this section, Christopher J. Dede, Ronald M. Cervero, Wayne D. Smutz and Donna S. Queeney, and Yolande Chambers Adelson take a searching look into the processes of continuing professional education. They converge around the idea that the lifelong learning growth and development of professionals in the future must be more of a systematic process to meet today's most urgent and challenging problems. The competitiveness and lack of integration that exist within the multiplicity of providers put enormous pressure on our current service delivery system. The dual demands of more discriminating consumers of educational services and a society which requires accountability among professionals force us to reconceptualize the present processes of continuing professional education. Chapters included in this section contribute to our understanding of how continuing professional education should be renewed and redirected to meet these changing needs.

Dede begins this section by calling into question our current educational paradigm. The emerging concepts in artificial intelligence and cognitive science, Dede claims, will improve the ability of continuing professional education to cope with rapidly expanding knowledge. Dede indicates that "the conceptualization of information technologies as symbolic manipulation is leading to research on how data and information can be converted to knowledge and wisdom."

The technological advances he discusses create the potential for a massive shift in professional roles to a "knowledge-added" economy. This shift will have profound implications both for the skills professionals need to keep abreast of their fields and for the methods continuing professional educators use to communicate this knowledge. Similar to Grotelueschen's view, Dede sees massive investments in continuing professional education as vital to the emergence of economic development policies which would promote a knowledge-added workplace. Moreover, the learning experiences professionals receive would increasingly be oriented to knowledge transfer rather than the assimilation of information. Dede concludes by examining the ways in which these developments would necessitate major changes in current instructional practices and also in the methodology for continuing professional education practice.

In a related approach, Cervero examines the role of the professional as a learner. In this process, professionals construct an understanding of current situations of practice using a repertoire of practical knowledge that has been acquired primarily through experience in prior "real-life" situations. Not surprisingly, Cervero believes that this model has implications for what is to be learned in continuing education programs in order to develop professional artistry.

Cervero and Dede agree: Professional creativity will become even more important in the future as the standardized aspects of problem solving skills are absorbed by intelligent machines. And Cervero argues that current models and approaches to continuing professional education do not accurately reflect the artistry and/or creativity inherent in professional practice. In future educational systems, guiding principles will emphasize what the *learner* does in determining what is learned, rather than what the *instructor* does. Cervero proposes that the CPE system of the future focus on experiential methods, such as case studies or direct coaching, thus allowing learners to uncover or develop their practical knowledge and the processes by which they use it.

Similarily, the chapter by Smutz and Queeney addresses self-managed professional development throughout an individual's life span. In order to create a comprehensive learning system, we must, they believe, prepare the individual, provide learning resources, and build an organizational infrastructure through cooperation and collaboration. These steps are necessary to enhance the performance of individual professionals throughout their careers.

Smutz and Queeney suggest that effectiveness in continuing professional education be addressed by focusing on both individual learning needs and attending to long-term, instead of only short-term, growth. Like Cervero, they emphasize the necessity of integrating learning into the practice context in a timely and efficient manner. They also believe that current systems of continuing professional education require a reconceptualization of the roles and the goals of professionals as learners. Viewing continuing professional education as self-managed professional development gives the individual ultimate control over his or her long-term learning and growth. At the same time, this view draws attention to long-term integrated development, not short-term remediation, which results, as Nowlen put it, from the "update" and "competence" frameworks that for so long have guided continuing professional education.

The final chapter by Adelson challenges continuing professional educators to consider two issues: whether they have given too much attention to technical competencies and too little to professional behavior, and whether "American educators in particular have failed to exercise their special obligation and responsibility to relate ethical values to the meaning and purpose of learning."

Joining Azzaretto, Cunningham and McLaughlin, Adelson calls for a renewed emphasis on ethics education for professionals. However, more is needed than current highly cognitive approaches, which some--whether mistakenly or not--see as passionless, reasoned responses to ethical conflicts which are ripping segments of our society apart. Ethics, she claims, needs to be understood in terms of addressing behavior that cannot be enforced and must, therefore, be entrusted to self-regulation. Continuing professional educators must approach ethics education based on the multidimensional aspects of the person--mind, emotion, spirit, and will. From this perspective, the impact of the ethically relevant curriculum will contribute to problem solving and decision making by professionals when values are in conflict.

In the summary chapter, Alan Knox discusses emerging themes in CPE shared by educators in many professional specialties. These themes take the form of imperatives for the field as we "learn our way into the future." Knox points out that there are important similarities and differences among the various professional fields regarding continuing education. In order to improve continuing professional education and move the field forward, we must become aware of the experiences within these different professional fields. Books, such as this one, help in learning from the experiences of others and provide opportunities to facilitate successful programs.

Knox organizes his chapter around five subjects that are critical to CPE theory and practice and which have repeatedly emerged in the preceding chapters. These subjects are participants, society, benefits, collaboration, and leadership. He frames each topic by posing questions related to it and suggesting useful sources of answers. Knox proposes that one use of his review of these themes is to develop a curriculum for continuing professional education coordinators. He believes such a development would be one of the best means of strengthening the field.

We hope the chapters that comprise this book can be used as a point of departure in analyzing current practices and needed reforms in continuing professional education. The two guiding propositions of the book--what the field is today and what it needs to be in the future--are powerful and risky challenges to address. Our goal will have been met if we have assisted the reader to reflect on future systems of continuing professional education and view education for the professions as a separate and unique field of practice.

References

Bruce, J. D., Siebert, W. M., Smullin, L. D., & Fano, R. M. (1982). *Lifelong cooperative education.* Cambridge, MA: Massachusetts Institute of Technology.

Cervero, R. M. (1988). *Effective continuing education for professionals.* San Francisco: Jossey-Bass.

Dryer, B. V. (1962). Lifetime learning for physicians: Principles, practices, proposals. *Journal of Medical Education, 37* (6, Part 2, entire issue).

Flexner, A. (1910). *Medical education in the United States and Canada.* New York: Carnegie Foundation for the Advancement of Teaching.

Houle, C. O. (1980). *Continuing learning in the professions.* San Francisco: Jossey-Bass.

Mawby, R. C. (1985). Lifelong learning and the professional. In W. K. Kellogg Foundation, *1985 Annual Report* (pp. 2-5). Battle Creek, MI: W. K. Kellogg Foundation.

Meyer, T. C. (1975). Toward a continuum in medical education. *Bulletin of the New York Academy of Medicine, 51,* 719-726.

Stone, E. W. (1986). The growth of continuing education. *Library Trends, 34* (3), 489-513.

Storey, P. B. (1988). Fragmentation of continuing medical education: A restatement of the problem and a proposed solution. *The Journal of Continuing Education in the Health Professions, 8,* 123-132.

Vernon, D. H. (1983). Education for proficiency: The continuum. *Journal of Legal Education, 33* (4), 559-569.

Part 1

The Context of Continuing Professional Education

New Expectations, New Roles: A Holistic Approach to Continuing Education for the Professions

Philip M. Nowlen

A Historical Perspective

Apprenticeship once seemed an indispensable preparation for career-long occupational competence but was succeeded by the professional school. Similarly, the professional school seemed to have an unending monopoly on qualifying persons for lifelong professional practice; but, during the 1950s, the professional school's monopoly was narrowed to the role of preparing persons to enter professional life. By the late 1950s, sustaining professionals throughout their careers was expected of a new player on the scene--continuing education.

Knowledge was expanding at an increasing pace, most often within the professional school itself. New nurses, architects, and engineers had knowledge and skills that seasoned professionals lacked. The mission of continuing education was to provide practicing professionals with levels of knowledge and skills comparable to those of persons graduating from professional schools. Closing this knowledge/skills gap called for continuing education simply to extend the updated curriculum of the professional school to professionals in practice. Continuing professional education was the phrase used correctly to describe both the client and the content's connection with the professional school.

In the 1950s, professionals were highly esteemed by the public. Most physicians and lawyers were in solo practice. Nutritionists worked in hospitals and schools, not in consumer associations and supermarkets.

15

There was only a handful of engineering and nursing specialties. Major associations counted the majority of professionals as members. Only a few teachers were members of unions. There was malpractice, but little malpractice litigation, and no huge fees for malpractice insurance. There were no for-profit hospital chains or correctional facilities. Lawyers did not advertise. Pharmacists did not need to speak Spanish.

Professional school curricula were matrices reflecting a few knowledge/skill specialties and two or three generic settings of practice. In Figure 1, which follows, medicine provides a case in point.

Figure 1: Updating Individual Professionals

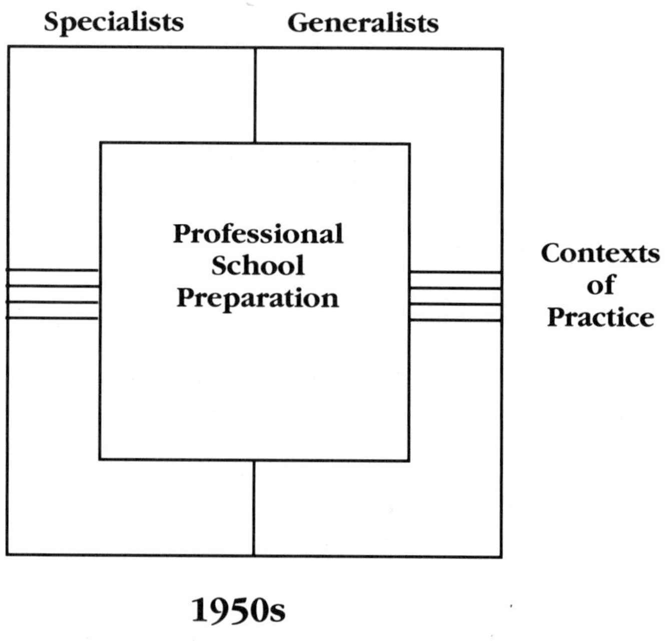

Specialists   Generalists

Professional School Preparation

Contexts of Practice

1950s

For physicians in an era of relatively few practice settings and specialties, the first generation response of continuing education for the professions was both simple and adequate. For 1940s graduates, such as pediatricians in community practice, the role of continuing medical education in the 1950s was to update professionals with the knowledge and skills that had been added to the field since they left their medical schools. The degree of need was directly related to the development of new knowledge, procedures, techniques, pharmaceuticals, and the like. There was substantial progress on all fronts and a few breakthroughs, such as the Salk vaccine, that virtually ended certain diseases. No one knew it then, but for many professions like medicine, the times resembled the early twentieth century more closely than they would resemble the 1980s.

The Profession at the Present

Just about everything has changed. The professions are not as esteemed. Newspapers headline major lapses by certified public accountants ("CPA's Called To Account") and physicians convicted of malpractice ("Incompetent Physicians--A Growing National Illness").

Some professions have undergone transformations. Among dentists, preventive care has replaced filling cavities and treating diseased gums. Among librarians, books represent but one of many learning resources. The contexts of practice have both changed and multiplied. A majority in many professions do not belong to the principal association that traditionally represented the profession. New professions have multiplied and are subject to dramatically increased legislation and litigiousness.

Practice Settings in the Health Professions

Consider the practice settings of the health professions by way of illustration. Hospitals have changed radically. Some in-house radiology units have become separate corporations. Hospitals may contract for lab work with independent, off-premises enterprises. HMO and "managed care" provisions of some insurance policies have the effect of reducing hospital-based physicians' decisions to admit patients. Government and private insurers' policies have greatly reduced physicians' freedom to individualize patients' length-of-stay. AIDS has complicated contacts with patients. Now, there are for-profit hospitals and chains of hospitals. More and more hospital-based physicians are salaried. In some hospitals, nurses have expanded responsibilities in patient management. Elsewhere, cost (or profit) is fueling the move to "layer in" a new patient care position somewhere underneath that of the licensed practical nurse and above that of the custodian. The number of allied health professions represented in hospital settings has risen, and partly as a result so has the task of coordination of care. Shifts in public attitudes toward the professions and the increase of malpractice litigation have added an adversarial tone to hospital-patient encounters. Substance abuse and thefts from hospital pharmacies make hospital care both more troubled and more expensive.

New practice settings include the following: health maintenance organizations, extended care facilities, sophisticated out-patient facilities (some of which are hospital related), women's clinics, clinics offering specialized care or treating a special disease, and residential mental health settings for adolescents or the chemically dependent. One familiar setting, the physician's office, has become a new setting for many procedures formerly performed only in hospitals.

On the other hand, some practice contexts have disappeared or declined. Solo practice has gone the way of house calls. Public support for mental health facilities has declined; and with this decline, mental health centers and sheltered care facilities have reduced their services or disappeared. Figure 2 captures these variables that make the 1980s a far more complex environment than the 1950s. This calls not only for updates in professional-school-based knowledge and skills (continuing professional education), but also for education derived from pluralistic sources (continuing education for the professions) found useful in assuring the competence required by what professionals actually do for a living.

Figure 2: Addressing Individual Competence

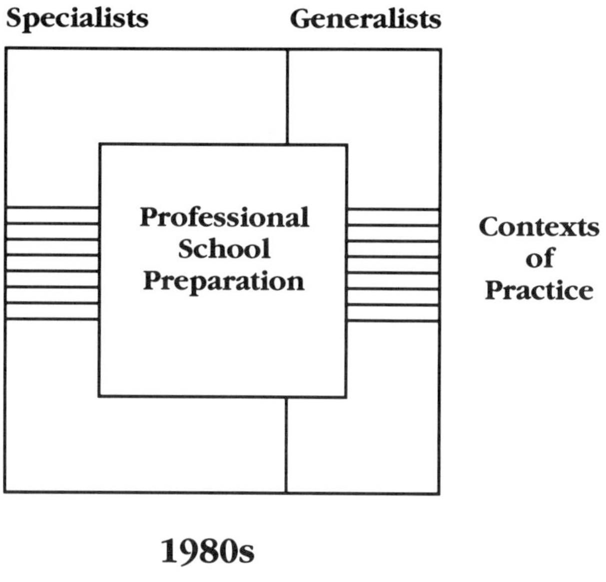

Specialists　　　　**Generalists**

**Professional
School
Preparation**

**Contexts
of
Practice**

1980s

The medical school graduate from the fifties still has a need to understand what has happened in his or her branch of medicine. However, closing this gap, as continuing education did in a simple linear fashion for the physicians in practice in that decade, no longer assures competence. Today there are medical specialties and subspecialties, conceptual frames of reference, bodies of knowledge, and packages of skills, as well as allied health professions and supportive technologies, that did not exist in the fifties. And from new protocols to constraints on hospital length-of-stay, it is all happening in a bewildering array of new contexts of

practice. Coordination of care is now among the most important characteristics of quality of care. For physicians in this new environment, knowing
what they do not know may be more important than making the possibly
futile effort to be completely up-to-date.

The Competence Model

Being up to date is, after all, only one aspect of the relationship
of knowledge and skill to competence. Continuing education updates
rarely address competence-related aptitudes and strengths, such as interpersonal skills and motivation, or the events and personal weaknesses that
impair competence. Many efforts in the professional environment have
begun, however, to focus on competence. Associations, employers, state
regulatory agencies, the courts, and higher education have all taken a
serious interest in the development of standards, evaluation of performance, certification and recertification, licensure and relicensure, planning
and implementing long-term continuing education relationships, and the
re-evaluation of professional school curricula.

These efforts attempt in most cases to identify the competence
actually required by professional practice. The starting point is identification of the basic functions performed. This process is sometimes called *job
functions analysis, role delineation,* or a *practice audit.* The chief
functions of a particular professional are observed, clustered in fields or
dimensions of activity, given relative priority, and assessed for demands
on time. The dimensions of practice include categories such as direct
patient services, organization and administration of services, and professional activities. Each dimension contains descriptors of individual acts or
sequences of activity.

The emerging profile of a practice is validated by similar professionals working in similar contexts. Panels of academics, professionals in
practice, and patients distinguish competencies significant to successful
performance in the dimensions identified. Academic panelists identify
requisite diagnostic knowledge. Frequently, patient panelists identify
interpersonal skills required to motivate patients to enagage in appropriate behavior. Lists of competencies which can be validated begin to
emerge.

A practice audit or job functions analysis of this sort becomes the
basis of an assessment center approach to a professional's educational
needs. Practice dimensions and their descriptors are simulated in physi-
cian-patient interactions, gamed in exercises addressing a cross section of
cases, and tested in written questions.

Role delineations, practice audits, and job functions analyses begin to answer broader questions. Do apparent differences in the settings of practice require significantly different kinds of competence? Do the successive plateaus of career paths pose challenges that might be generalizable across the professions? Why do some professionals flounder in one organizational culture and flourish in another, while other professionals thrive across culturally varied practice settings?

The competence model, particularly in its practice audit form, represents the second generation of continuing education for the professions--a creative response to increasingly complex challenges faced by professionals. As usual, by reaching this level of achievement, continuing educators are able to see its shortcomings.

The most serious flaw in the competence approach is its underlying assumption that performance is an individual affair. To be sure, some of the key influences on performances are found in the professional's possession of requisite competencies. Some competence approaches even address critical higher order skills of mind, motivation for excellence, the maturity to manage personal affairs well, and the grit to overcome setbacks.

Nevertheless, a wide array of other influences on performance exists outside the individual professional. These influences include the quality of the relationship individuals have to one another in the organizational setting--the society of peers, subordinates, superiors, and the structures in which they are found. As experienced by the client or patient, performance is very much an ensemble matter. For example, in the hospital a patient experiences well or poorly coordinated service by admissions and patient transportation staff, physicians, nurses, switchboard operators, chaplains, laboratory technicians, security personnel, custodians, and volunteers. Other influences upon individual performance stem from the quality of the relationship between the professional and society, the prevailing environment that enhances or restricts professional decision making.

More importantly, contemporary psychology advises against making too sharp a distinction between the individual and society. "Individual" human development is really a succession of cultures in which the so-called individual is deeply embedded for a time, only to withdraw in favor of deep identification with a new environment. An individual's identity is, in part, shaped and communicated by these successive cultures, as well as by the individual's skill in distinguishing the self, releasing the ties, and moving on. The professional is embedded simultaneously in multiple cultures: work, family, friends, professional association, civic affairs, church, and the like. Each culture's "hold" on the professional may vary. The professional may be on the way to much deeper identification with work, while the hold of family is weakened. Deeper embedment in one culture may not cause withdrawal from another, but the many cultures in which professionals find (or lose) themselves are certainly not perfectly sealed compartments from which no events or moods escape to influence other areas.

Beyond the Competence Model

These are the major insights that carry continuing education beyond the competence model: that professional performance, while an individual matter, is also an ensemble phenomenon; that reality will not support much of a distinction between "individual" and "social"; and how things go in any one of the cultures that holds an adult is likely to influence adult functioning in the other holding cultures. These insights move the field beyond the individual competence/contexts of practice model of Figure 2 to a holistic model represented in Figure 3.

Figure 3: Enhancing Team Performance

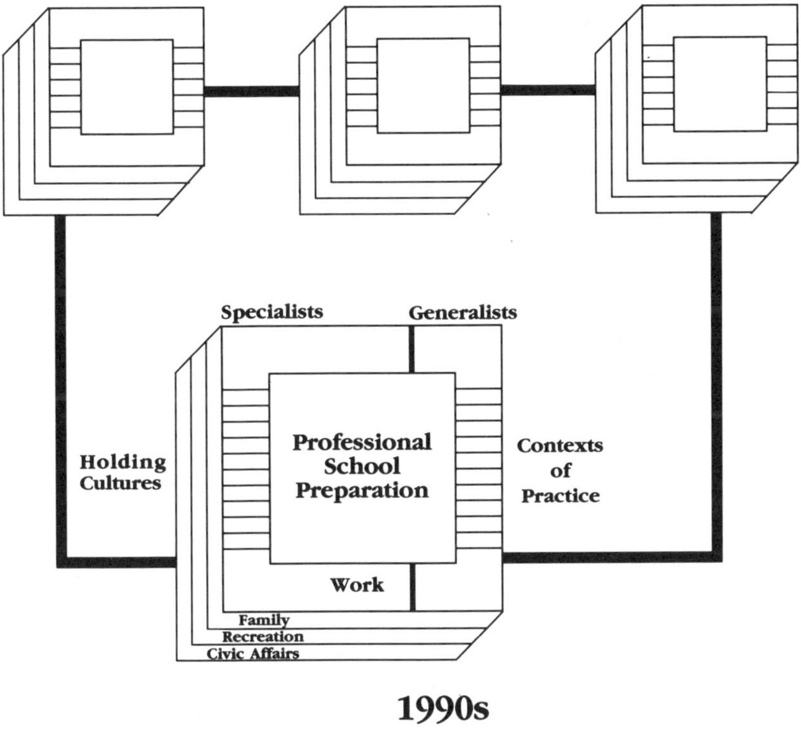

1990s

Four major dimensions of individual professional performance present themselves: 1) the narrow professional knowledge/skills base, 2) the evolving and multiplying context of practice, 3) the interactive environments of adulthood, and 4) the social nature of professional performance.

These dimensions suggest what is expected of continuing education. Continuing professional education updates are still expected. Although general practice is shrinking, some combination of generalist and specialist knowledge and skill updates will always be required. Competence related, job-functions-based continuing education is expected. Traditional categories of professional knowledge and skills do not automatically confer the special competencies required to perform in new or changing contexts of practice or in the new roles often thrust on professionals in mid-career. Continuing education will be expected to contribute to human development, not simply as an end in itself, but also as one more way to enhance professional performance. All the formative cultures of adult life influence the performance of the adult in any one of them. Continuing education will be expected to address the learning needs of inter-specialist and even inter-professional practices. Continuing education may be expected to address needs related to the interchange between professional and client. Professional performance is an interactive phenomenon involving more than one professional and often involving several professional specialties and allied occupations, as well as the patient or client.

These expectations imply new roles for continuing education for the professions. These new roles are additional--and not replacement--roles. No institution or association serving the professions through updates or competence-based programs needs to withdraw from or reduce its current portfolio of programs. The holistic and ensemble views of professional performance mean that university-based continuing educators need to marshal academic resources wider than those of the professional schools in order to respond. This also means a greater potential for linking continuing education with university research. The holistic and ensemble views invite continuing educators to address the structures that shape professional practices by developing programs for leaders of professional organizations. These programs, which may compare ways to design and manage the culture practice contexts, may address such topics as the formal and informal organization of work, mechanisms for judging and rewarding varied levels of performance, and the quality of informal learning such as mentoring.

The holistic and ensemble views of performance call for new alliances between professional association leaders, university-based continuing educators, and the helping professions. These new alliances might take the form of improved and wider ranging self-assessment centers where mid-career professionals take stock of their progress in all four dimensions of performance. Professional association leaders and the employers of professionals will want to integrate holistic concerns when they consider what range of learning and development experiences will be allowable for purposes of relicensure or recertification.

Expectations in the Future

The update approach, continuing professional education's first generation model, serves engineers, hospital administrators, lawyers, physicians, social workers, nurses, accountants, corrections personnel, teachers, librarians, and the allied health professions through their individual knowledge bases. Separate approaches are required with each profession. The expectations of the holistic or performance approach make it possible for continuing educators to address common concerns across professional lines.

Finally, the holistic view of professional performance enables continuing educators to help individual professionals everywhere make better judgments among their continuing education opportunities because they can review all the major influences on their performance. The client's or patient's view of performance as an ensemble affair may even bring working teams of professionals to begin defining multi-year learning agendas based on carefully assessed collective need. The growing demand for a holistic approach to professional performance and the consequent new roles for continuing education are exhilarating challenges to renew and redirect the field.

Note: This chapter provides a summary of the ideas presented in a recent book by Nowlen. For a fuller discussion of the holistic view of professional performance, see: Nowlen, P. M. (1988). *A new approach to continuing education for business and the professions.* New York: Macmillan, NUCEA, American Council on Education.

Chapter 2

Power, Responsibility, and Accountability in Continuing Professional Education

John F. Azzaretto

Professionals are often characterized by their intellectual autonomy and by their highly specialized knowledge which confines them to practice within specific boundaries. What emerges from this view is an ideology of professionalism in our society that is inward looking, directed to the attributes and the environment of the professional power structure, and not outward looking, addressing public needs or demands. Professionals in this system are accountable to the public for only their perceived expertise (Lieberman, 1970).

Definitions and approaches to continuing professional education (CPE) have been shaped by this ideology and the enormous power wielded by professional groups. Moreover, the position of power and control exerted by professionals over their own CPE is enhanced through the regulatory function of government. Yet, at the same time that power is increasingly being asserted by professional groups, the public perception of professional responsibility, accountability, and service has been called into question.

What was once the ideal of professional service is beleagured by such pressures as the following:

Professional contentiousness (with similar groups) over practice boundaries;

A public willing to contest professional authority;

Resentment of professional power and wealth;

Public scandal involving professional incompetence;

Uneven distribution of services;

Complex moral quandaries which professional training does not address;

Heightened consumer awareness and activism;

Legislatively mandated CPE; and

Deregulation and increased competition among professionals.

As a result of these and other pressures, the professional in contemporary society is under increasing scrutiny. The inexorable movement by professionals has been toward a purely technical-rational epistemology of professional practice (Schon, 1983). This dominant framework for professional practice is devoid of any value or moral underpinning, making the expert at once a hope and a danger to society. On the one hand, there is the benefit of precision and sophistication of special knowledge and skills. On the other, a myopic and antiseptic view of complex social problems is produced. Professional competence is seen as only the application of scientific knowledge to instrumental problems of practice. Because of this limited view, the public's perception of professional inadequacies has brought the legitimacy of the professions into serious doubt (Cervero, 1988).

Continuing professional education has the capacity to strengthen and revitalize the role of professionals in society. This goal can be achieved by cultivating a renewed sense of calling and commitment among professionals. But it can also be achieved by fully developing the capacities of professionals and the consumers of their services.

By improving the delivery of continuing professional education, by emphasizing collaboration among professions, and by offering integrated and holistic approaches to life span education, continuing professional educators can help shape the future of the professions in our society. This chapter will address these issues through the following questions:

1. Do the ideology and politics of professional power influence CPE in ways that work against promoting professional responsiveness to societal needs?

2. What is the role of government in regulating professions and utilizing CPE as a mechanism to protect the public interest?

3.	How can CPE of the future attempt to insure that professionals serve the public rather than their own self-interests?

The Ideals of Service and Professional Calling

Traditionally, when a professional had earned the right to practice in a specialty area, his or her client could count on the fact that the professional was technically competent following rigorous preparation and training, morally accountable for this expertise, and ready in some measure to place it at the service of human need. To be sure, the professional accepted pay for his or her work but did so recognizing that professional services must be rendered based on need rather than ability to pay. The professional joined knowledge and competence with moral substance, the power of knowledge with some measure of philanthropy (May, 1980, p. 205).

The professions in America have long been regarded as the sacred repositories of idealism and service. There was a time when many professionals held a sense of duty, a love of their work, and a commitment to humanity that had nothing to do with pecuniary rewards. However, after a period of rapid growth in knowledge, power, wealth, and institutional influence, the professions' original guiding concept of public service is eroding. Virginia Olesen (1979) identifies several typical examples of this eroded ideal:

1.	Patients, transformed to the new role of "consumer" and unhappy with health care costs, demand that medicine come under regulatory scrutiny.

2.	Physicians and nurses, ever edgy about the overlap of their professional dominions, become more so with proliferation of new groups such as physicians assistants, networks for nurses, and new group forms of practice for physicians.

3.	Lawyers, initially swept up in the era's rising adversary proceedings and malpractice suits against various professional groups, most notably physicians, increasingly find themselves the targets of such suits.

4.	Those who are dispossessed, whether by virtue of sex, ethnicity, religion or physical handicap, view professional roles and practice as elitist bastions to be breached by their numbers in the interests of redressing old inequities and assuring new services (pp. 199-200).

The traditional notion that professionals "do good" to individuals and society helps to differentiate these vocations from other work. This view gives the individual an earned right to respect and status based on his or her expertise, the sacrifices the individual makes, and the individual's commitment to society's need for a specialized service. For example, American teachers are not attracted to their profession by high salaries, prestigious career prospects, or high status in the local community. Generally, teachers enter teaching because they enjoy young people and because they believe the service they render to be an important societal function (Lortie, 1975). In fact, a recent study on the professionalization of teaching conducted by Benveniste (1987) indicated that a vast majority of teachers felt that 1) teaching was most important to the long-term interests of society and 2) teaching was characterized by a high degree of idealism and devotion (pp. 42-43).

Some professions institutionalize this commitment by asking their members to devote time to meritorious causes. The American Bar Association model code of professional responsibility includes a statement that lawyers have a responsibility for "pro bono" work. Even if this idealized vision of a calling is not always implemented or is even practical, it still highlights the potential importance of this sense of responsibility in many professions, particularly in the helping professions, such as health care, teaching, and social work (Benveniste, 1987, p. 43).

The concept of public service and calling affects the orientation of professionals to the organizational work situation as well. In his classic study, Alvin Gouldner (1957) described cosmopolitan and local orientations in the work setting. Cosmopolitans in organizations share their loyalty between the employing organization and their commitment to their professional role. These experts are never committed to a single organization, even if they spend their entire working life in one. Their first commitment is to their professional values--values that should also be important to the organization. This loyalty is in contrast to that of locals, who are committed solely to the organization but may have less of a professional role to contribute.

Professionals in organizational settings are motivated differently; thus, they need to be managed differently (Benveniste, 1987). In the absence of extrinsic rewards, strong intrinsic rewards concerning the significance of one's work matter more. If health care and social workers are committed to alleviating suffering and contributing to the general well-being of the community, it is imperative for managers to give them a sense of efficacy, a sense that their commitment is not unnoticed or unappreciated.

Likewise, the services of the lawyer, the physician, and others in the helping professions should extend beyond those parochial boundaries that ordinary life establishes. They should extend to the stranger and the needy. As May (1980) states, "A profession is corrupt if it defects from this catholicity of spirit and mission, if it becomes captive to the interests of a particular family or class" (p. 226).

A profession's obligation to public service involves the just and equitable distribution of professional services to the whole community. It also involves the development of the full range of specialized services. The two tasks are distinct, but related. When particular populations are unserved or underserved, a profession often fails as well to develop the full range of its resources. Until recently, some areas of the law (women's rights, rights of the economically disadvantaged, children's rights) remained relatively uncharted terrain, because these groups were under served. Conversely, when a profession develops its resources lopsidedly, it fails to meet the needs of special populations. Medical researchers have lavished attention on cancer and heart disease at the expense of AIDS and arthritis research. The underdevelopment of a specific area of professional expertise in this case leaves special populations largely underserved--homosexuals and the elderly. The link between the uneven development of a profession and populations left unserved demonstrates the symbiotic relationship of professionals to clients. Clearly, clients need professionals to address their needs; but professionals, just as surely, need a full range of clients if the professions and all their articulated services are to mature fully.

The result of this symbiotic relationship is troubling for professions because it raises perplexing questions such as the following: Why are we putting so much of our resources into medicine while our health care systems are not improving? Why are we putting so much into education when our children seem to be learning less? Why are we putting so much more into mental health systems and yet seem to have more mental illness? Or the even more troubling questions: Do we get more sickness from more medicine? Do we get more injustice and crime from more lawyers and police? Do we get more ignorance with more teachers and schools (McKnight, 1977, p. 112)?

The crux of this argument is that it is politically impossible to maintain a service economy if the public perceives that the service system hurts more than it helps, that professional services can become more hinderance than help. What is more, professionals themselves are frustrated because they are unable to understand why their care and service does not reform society, much less help individuals to function. What is the future for the professional's dilemma of serving society's unmet needs or serving one's own economic interests? Some experts (McKnight, 1977; Young, 1987) maintain that the politics of modernized professional power has institutionalized the service business and that this power will need to be offset by heightened consumer activism. The assumption is that balance will be achieved as citizens become powerful consumers and are able to know whether the service system's outputs help or hurt them.

Others argue that the responsibility to deliver services to the whole community rests on the society at large and not on the professional per se (Larson, 1977; May, 1980). This argument has the virtue of addressing the problem at a structural level. People should not depend upon charity for basic services. Obviously, society must respond because neither a single professional nor a profession at large can meet all the needs of the public without forms of communal support and assistance. The next part of this chapter will address the various definitions of professions and the powers that they hold in our society.

Power, Politics, and the Professional Community

"Professionalism" in the United States generally refers to the provision of expert, high quality service to consumers. Underlying this definition of professionalism is the assumption that professionals provide a service for clients which indeed distinguishes theirs from other occupations.

Historically, a profession was seen as a calling requiring specialized knowledge, often long and intensive preparation, and high standards of achievement and conduct for the primary purpose of rendering a public service. Members of professions who fit this description were trained in institutions of higher education and organized into institutionalized groups which positively influenced the conduct and commitment of their members. Freidson (1986), however, suggests a broader definition of a profession:

> It refers to more than dignity, prestige, or status and the possession of formal knowledge, implying a process of social control of professional behavior as well as institutions by which that process is carried out....In one circumstance of use it implies exalted motives and moral probity, but in another it implies crass motives and deceptiveness. (pp. 26-27)

The demands by various groups in society for professional standards of practice can be seen through the increased variety of highly specialized services. By establishing minimal standards for, among other things, their members' education and training, professional associations promote these specialized standards that are highly valued by a modern society.

Much has been written over the past few decades in an effort to define the term "profession." Most of the early work done by sociologists used an attribute model--that is, a "laundry list" of characteristics, which, when satisfied, transformed an occupation into a profession. Essential to any list which defined "profession" was the notion of established competence through standardized, rigorous training, principled standards of practice, and unselfish service to society.

No specific turning point marks the passing of this naive view of professionalism. May (1980), among others, laments the passing of this public service orientation:

> Traditionally, when the professional hung out his shingle and declared himself ready to take clients, he professed or avowed a technical competence based on a tradition of learning; and further, he declared himself to be morally accountable for this expertise, and ready in some measure to place it at the service of human need. The professional, to be sure, accepted pay for his work, but presumably he did not, in the fashion of other knowledge merchants--the magician or the wizard--use his knowledge primarily to acquire personal power, or to exhibit virtuosity. He joined knowledge and competence with moral substance, the power of knowledge with some measure of philanthropy. So goes the ideal. (p. 205)

Today, many people, including practicing professionals, assume that professionalism, although manifesting some abuses, does serve the public interest. Nevertheless, a growing number of citizens well understand that economic forces drive professionals' activities, just as they drive many activities in society. In fact, professional groups use the structure of government, especially through political lobbying and occupational licensure, to restrict entry, protect their turf, and enhance their marketplace value. For example, professional groups know that by reducing the supply of available practitioners, they can charge higher prices for services and consequently receive higher incomes.

Young (1987) makes the following rather biting observation of professional groups using artificial barriers to enhance their market value:

> This side of professionalism suggests something very different from the conventional view of a group dedicated to public service; it smacks of elitism, exploitation, and monopoly. Many citizens

therefore view the professions as elitist groups responsible to no one but themselves and argue that, while professionals eschew economic gain in theory, they realize it in practice. This attitude is best reflected in George Bernard Shaw's famous dictum that "all professions are a conspiracy against the laity." (p. 4)

Economist George Stigler (1971) espouses a theory of regulatory behavior also at odds with the traditional public interest view of professionals. His model suggests that professional groups use the coercive power of government for their own economic advantage. In effect, they capture the regulatory apparatus and use it to restrain competition and raise income. Young (1987) asserts that an important implication of Stigler's theory is that regulation is enacted primarily because of political activity on the part of professional groups, not because the public demands it.

Heightened citizen awareness of monopolistic professional practices and consumer advocacy groups' uses of the legislative lobby may offset some of the political power of professional associations. For example, many states now have sunset provisions that require state regulatory boards to justify their existence or go out of business. Also, public (consumer) representation on licensing boards, though limited, has become a way of improving the accountability of those boards.

However, despite a trend of growing consumer advocacy, professions are still occupations with special power and prestige. Their positions are enhanced through the political influence they exert in the public policy arena of state regulatory legislation. In fact, consumers rarely engage in campaigns to license occupations. Crucial licensing decisions that can affect vast numbers of people are often made with little or no input from the public. Rather, it is generally the strongly felt self-interest of professional groups that affects each of the key decision points in the licensing process: when a state legislature is considering a law to license a given occupation, when an already licensed group is proposing rules and regulations that would determine standards for entry and professional practice, and when the legislature considers whether to continue or terminate a licensing board (Shimberg, 1982, p. 138).

The pervasive power of professions is lodged in several dimensions (Larson, 1977):

1. Cognitive--the dimension that is centered on the body of knowledge and techniques which professionals apply in their work and in obtaining the training necessary to master such knowledge and skills;

2. Normative--the dimension that covers the service orientation of professionals, and their distinctive ethics, which justify the privilege of self-regulation granted them by society; and

3. Evaluative--the dimension that distinguishes professions from other occupations and underscores the professions' claim to autonomy and prestige.

Taken together, these dimensions represent a unique community of interests (Goode, 1957) with an ideology that supports power and special privilege in our society. Professions are communities whose members share a relatively permanent affiliation, a sense of identity, personal commitment, shared values, specific interests, and general loyalties (p. 194).

Wilensky (1964) argues that these communities are concretely identified by typical organizations and institutional patterns: professional associations, professional schools, regulatory bodies, and self-administered disciplinary procedures and codes of ethics. It is not clear how much community would exist without these institutional supports; yet these supports are features that occupations which aspire to the privileges of professional status can imitate without possessing the cognitive and normative justifications of "real" professions (Larson, 1977, p. xi).

In his path-breaking analysis of the profession of medicine, Freidson (1970a) does much to clarify the nature of special privilege within the professional community and the potential this privilege has for producing an inherent ideology of professionalism. His examination of the "archetypal" profession leads him to argue that "a profession is distinct from other occupations in that it has been given the right to control its own work" (p. 78). Among other occupations, "Only the profession has the recognized right to declare outside evaluation illegitimate and intolerable" (pp. 71-72). This distinctive autonomy is, however, based not only on status and technical expertise, but also on political power. Professions ultimately depend upon the power position they have with government's legislative and regulatory functions. For it is in the governmental realm that occupational groups attempt to negotiate boundaries of practice, establish social control of performance and the conduct of their members, and determine who is included and excluded in this process. Once in a protected position, professions can develop with increasing independence; exert considerable influence in maintaining their autonomy, preserving their role in self-evaluation and self-control; and become almost immune to external regulation. As Larson (1977) states, "Their autonomy thus tends to insulate them: in part, professionals live within ideologies of their own creation, which they present to the outside as the most valid definitions of specific spheres of social reality" (p. xiii).

Knowledge itself does not give special power: Only exclusive knowledge gives power to its possessors. Thus, the professions claim exclusive knowledge and skill as a basis for their privileged place in society. It is the power of government which grants the profession the exclusive right to use or evaluate a certain body of knowledge and skill. Granted the exclusive right to use knowledge, the profession gains additional power (Freidson, 1973, p. 29). It is in this sense that the professions are intimately connected with formal political processes. Such connection has generally been implied through the process of professionalization (Jackson, 1970) and desire for both public recognition and formal political recognition in the form of exclusive registration, licensing, and the like.

Freidson (1973) maintains, however, that we should distinguish between the development of a profession and the maintenance and improvement of the profession's position in society. In the development of a profession, rigorous training and the quest to master a particular body of knowledge produce a sense of duty among members. Once established, professionals turn their attention to earning income within a largely value-free context, not really concerned with the moral or ethical consequences of their actions and certainly not ready to think about continuing their professional education. It is not coincidental that, even if established practitioners condescended to participate in continuing professional education, their participation would only be at the rational-technical level for an updating of skills (Nowlen, 1988). What is missing, then, is the continuation in the development of the professional as a whole person once the practice credential and license to practice are earned.

The maintenance and improvement of a profession's position, however, requires continuous political activity to preserve and assert an ideological imperialism (Freidson, 1970b) that seeks to justify inequality of status and closure of access in the occupational order. "No matter how disinterested its concern for knowledge, humanity, art, or whatever, the profession must become an interest group to at once advance its aims and to protect itself from those with competing aims" (Freidson, 1973, pp. 29-30).

How then, do the ideology and politics of professional power influence CPE in ways that work against promoting professional responsiveness to societal needs? Oftentimes, the professional group will assert power by determining the answers to the following questions: Is CPE needed? What is needed? How much is needed, and who is to deliver it to professionals? The ways in which professional groups respond to these questions have substantial implications for the role of CPE and the power, privilege, and money that are associated with providing it.

This rather critical and instrumental view of professionalism provides the basis for what Hughes (1958) calls "license and mandate"-- setting up the legal authority for the profession to recruit, train, examine, license, and review performance--and establishes the formal limits of its exclusive jurisdiction.

The next section will look at CPE as the connection between governmental regulations and educational practices.

Achieving Professional Accountability

Ours is a highly specialized, service-oriented society. Professionals operating in this environment are assumed to act with competence and responsibility. However, these assumptions do not always hold true. The public wants greater accountability from its professionals. Continuing professional education, through its part in governmental regulation and established educational standards, can play a significant role in developing future systems of professional accountability.

Government Regulation and Intervention

The critical claim that professions hold monopolistic powers and the lament that modern day professionals have become more interested in income than in calling cannot be discerned in the everyday activities of practitioners. The average professional, either in an organizational setting or with self-employed status, is more likely to complain of the stressful trials of everyday worklife, including clients who grant little respect and are suspicious--or even indignant--about the professional's expertise and service and supervisors and employers who may serve as obstacles to committed and effective work. Individual practitioners do not create the credential system; neither do they establish the content and scope of professional training and education for continued competency nor establish the standards that define the substance of what is acceptable professional work.

However, the public interest must be protected from charlatans and the unscrupulous and abusive behavior of incompetent professionals. Our society is built on a legal and ethical system that demands accountability. Individual professional behavior and conduct is thus reviewed in the aggregate, and accountability results when there is the identification and implementation of recognized standards of competence against which behavior and professional performance are measured and evaluated. The roles of government in regulating professions and educational systems in credentialing and training play a crucial role in defining and determining professional accountability.

Understanding the extent and types of occupational regulation prevalent in the United States requires distinguishing among three levels of government intervention (Young, 1987, p. 5). The first and simplest form of regulation is registration, which usually requires little more of individuals than listing their names on official rosters. Any person willing to list his or her name has the right to engage in the given activity. It is the least restrictive form of state regulation; and, typically, in this form of regulation, exams are not given and enforcement of the registration requirement is minimal.

The next level of regulation is certification. Certification generally refers to a credential issued by a non-government agency or association which recognizes an individual's achievements of predetermined competence and standards. States do adopt "statutory certification," which limits use of particular titles to persons meeting predetermined requirements (The National Clearinghouse, 1986). Often, the requirements include graduation from an approved training program, a certain amount of work experience, and passage of qualifying exams.

But non-governmental organizations, such as professional associations and colleges and universities, may also develop certification programs for occupational groups. Financial analysts, for example, have created the designation "Chartered Financial Analyst" (CFA) and have imposed rigorous entrance requirements to obtain it. Over 8,000 charters have been granted by the Institute of Chartered Financial Analysts, a private organization, since its formation in 1959 (Young, 1987, p. 19).

Likewise, colleges and universities may develop a standardized, nonacademic credit curriculum around an occupational category, such as service and hospitality for employees of the tourist related industry. This process can be effected or developed independently or in cooperation with the occupational group (Azzaretto, 1987) and is used by occupational groups to differentiate highly skilled practitioners from the less skilled. These voluntary certification programs do not prohibit anyone from engaging in a particular occupation, but they do provide a way for the public to identify individuals who have passed certain tests and met other requirements.

The third form of government regulation is licensure, which requires that individuals obtain a license from the state to engage in a given trade or profession. [For a historical analysis of occupational regulation, see Hogan (1983) and Young (1987).] As a form of governmental regulation, mandatory licensing's principal justification is "the public interest." Licensing advocates maintain that certain occupational groups are so closely associated with public health and safety that without a form of regulation the public would have no protection against incompetent practitioners who might do serious harm. Moreover, advocates insist that licensure is a legitimate exercise of the state's police powers because the public is ill-equipped to judge whether an individual offering services as a doctor, dentist, or pharmacist is sufficiently well trained in his or her specialty. Thus, regulatory boards are established to investigate the qualifications of would-be practitioners (Shimberg, 1982).

As licensing has evolved, the agencies designated to administer the basic legislation and to be responsible for determining the qualifications of applicants have assumed the additional responsibility of policing the field to prevent unauthorized persons from practicing. These agencies have frequently been given the authority by law to suspend or revoke the license of any practitioner who fails to uphold accepted standards or engages in unethical practices. In the exercise of this last function, the licensing agencies have assumed a quasi-judicial role (Shimberg, 1972, p. 7).

Proponents of licensure agree that its purpose is to establish standards of practice, insure quality service, protect the public interest, and maintain a minimum level of ethical practice through the enforcement of codes of ethical conduct. In recent years, there has been a growing awareness of licensure's concomitant responsibility to promote maintaining competence through continuing professional education.

Critics of licensure (Gross, 1984; Young, 1987) argue that it restricts entry into the professions, decreases competition and innovation, and results in higher costs to consumers. Furthermore, while licensing and entry level training requirements may promote a minimum level of competency initially, critics would say that licensing boards have done little to insure that practitioners maintain competency and have not aggressively stripped incompetent and fradulent practitioners of their licenses.

Emergent Trends

Several emergent trends are likely to play a critical role in revolutionizing professional accountability through regulatory licensing. A discussion of these trends follows.

An important priority for state legislators and regulators is finding and dealing with incompetent practitioners. Legislators are providing increased funding for strengthening enforcement activities against licensed practitioners. Separate from the regulatory bodies, state consumer protection agencies are taking a much more active role in protecting the public against fraud, professional improprieties, and charlatans.

One of the most perplexing licensing decisions to face legislators in the future is deciding when an occupation should be regulated by the state. Recently, many states have developed informal criteria, called *sunrise programs,* for deciding when to regulate an occupation. By 1984, six states had adopted sunrise programs (The National Clearinghouse, 1986, p. 5). These programs include such factors as what potential there is for public harm from unregulated practice, whether specialized skills or training are required, whether effective public protection exists through non-regulatory means, and what the overall cost-effectiveness and economic impact of the proposed regulation are.

Sunset legislation is another response to the perceived need for more public accountability of regulatory bodies. Such legislation requires that regulatory laws, agencies, or programs be terminated at a specific date unless recreated by the state legislature. The hope is that legislators will be forced to evaluate the results of regulations. Though well-intentioned, sunset provisions to date have not been used because of the time consuming effort of the review process by legislators and pressure from the professional associations not to deregulate.

The rise of consumerism in the 1970s and 1980s has resulted in greater public participation on licensing boards. For example in most states, licensing boards, traditionally comprised exclusively of members of the regulated professions, now have one or more consumer members in recognition of the fact that self-regulation may not produce the best public policy. In addition to the composition of licensing boards, the composition of state legislatures--once the exclusive domain of professionals, especially lawyers--is changing. Consumer advocates, small business owners, women and other minorities, and retirees are special interest groups whose members are entering politics in increasing numbers and are shifting the balance of power away from the traditional organized elites.

Licensing laws have traditionally specified an exclusive scope of practice within which it is illegal for anyone without a license to perform any of the activities covered by the law. Established professions have guarded their turf jealously, especially when related service providers attempt to infringe on an area of their practice. However, the excessive protectionism of established professions, the concern over escalating costs, and the legal claims of discrimination and lack of accessibility of service have caused a re-examination of the use of professional auxiliaries. For example, the Washington, DC, City Council enacted the Health Care Facility and Licensure Act of 1983 (National Clearinghouse, 1986a) to prohibit class discrimination against five groups of health care providers--podiatrists, psychologists, nurse practitioners, nurse anesthetists, and nurse midwives--in the granting of clinical privileges. Increased use of paraprofessionals and professional auxiliaries by the public will result in the increased democratization of professional services.

Perhaps the greatest ally of regulators in achieving professional accountability in the future is to establish educational standards that assure minimum competencies. The next section will examine current educational standards for professionals, and then address the potential use of standards for CPE.

Current Educational Standards for Professionals

Licensing provisions and scope of practice laws assume an articulated and specialized body of knowledge. Nearly 4,000 years ago, laws were written establishing regulatory mechanisms to protect the public by means of examination, education, and experience requirements. With today's rapid growth in technology and knowledge, a particularly vexing problem for regulators in years to come will be the maintenance of professional competency.

The formalization of professional education in the early part of this century was based on much more than the desire to raise the professions' prestige and restrict the supply of practitioners. The institutionalization and reorganization of professional education was an attempt to create a more reliable system of training and preparation for occupations serving critical societal needs (Freidson, 1986, p. 74). Characteristics of this early period of instability in professional education included the following:

Unsystematic body of knowledge required in a particular professional area;

Lack of a uniform curriculum which defined the body of knowledge;

Lack of predictability and assurance of minimum practitioner competence;

Irregular length and terms for successful completion;

Lack of agreed upon standards of professional practice;

Lack of agreed upon credentials for practice;

Little or no integration with the group already engaged with the practice of the profession;

Insufficiently developed standards of quality teaching; and

Lack of agreed upon qualifications for instructors.

The institutionalization of colleges and universities and the maturation of professional fields of practice remedied many of these flaws. For instance, growth in the movement of accreditation bodies assured that an institution conformed to minimum standards before including it on an official list of approved institutions. Thus, having been evaluated, officially accredited programs were known to fall within certain qualitative boundaries and to have implemented minimum standards. Consumers and employers possess knowledge of the preparation, training, and practice credentials of graduates of accredited institutions. Taken together, the formal practice credential awarded by the institution of higher education and the license to practice granted by the state create a monopolistic and exclusive marketplace position for the members of a particular professional group. Higher education today, working in concert with professional associations and regulatory bodies, is the sole provider of a practice credential, a degree that is relatively predictable in terms of completion of a known curriculum with minimum standards of knowledge, skills, and abilities.

Our present system of continuing education for the professions is similar, however, to the flawed system of professional preparatory education experienced at the turn of the century. Maintenance of professional competency is crucial and yet very difficult to measure. Periodic re-examination as a condition of relicensure is a topic of strong debate and opposition within professions and, to a lesser degree, by state regulators.

Currently, continuing education is the most widely accepted tool in the effort to insure public protection. Yet continuing professional educators find themselves in an archaic position characterized by: 1) a multiplicity of educational providers, each claiming its legitimate right to assist the practitioner in remaining competent; 2) various degrees of unmet needs among professions and professionals; 3) lack of educational standards that define quality of teaching and quality of educational programs; 4) wide divergence among professional groups as to what their members need to know in order to maintain their competence; 5) dissension as to who should pay for continuing professional education; and 6) issues regarding who should decide on the level of participation, what should count as continuing education, and what should be the frequency of professional participation. Given this set of circumstances, what role can government play in regulating professions and utilizing CPE as a mechanism to protect the public interest?

In an effort to promote the continued competency and accountability of professionals, state regulatory agencies and private certifying agencies have experimented with a variety of methods. Examples include self-assessment inventories, periodic re-examinations, chart audits, peer reviews, practice audits, and computerized simulations. There is no widely accepted method to assure continued competency among professional groups; however, the movement from voluntary to mandatory continuing education (MCE) is gaining in popularity.

Since the late 1960s, many states have passed legislation requiring licensed professionals to participate in CPE on a periodic basis in order to be relicensed. There remains a question whether continuing education should be mandated and whether it is, in fact, an effective corrective measure to incompetent practice. The move from voluntary to MCE was stimulated by the belief that all professionals were not equally conscientious in keeping up with their fields. Louis Phillips (1987), an expert on MCE who has systematically tracked MCE among 14 occupations in all 50 states, writes:

> The implementation of MCE represents a long term commitment of minimum amounts of CE participation that remain in force for the duration of each professional's license. It requires essentially every licensee to initiate some form of educational activity on a regular basis with freedom to select those activities the licensee feels most appropriate to his current status. The ultimate responsibility as to whether this long term pattern of educational participation improves the licensee's performance is the responsibility of the individual. No form of relicensure will ever subvert that ultimate responsibility. (p. 2)

Others indicate that to mandate a system so loosely conceived as CPE is an invitation to abuse. Gross (1983) maintains that if professionals ever do take courses which relate to their practice, then a resulting effect on performance would assume that professionals know what they need to learn, that they participate in a way to learn something, and that they are then able to apply that learning to their practice. Also, after reviewing the research, Shimberg (1982) concludes that there are no demonstrated relationships between participation in CPE and either job performance or measures of medical care outcomes.

Two conclusions seem obvious. First, there seems reason to believe that those most in need of CPE may be the least likely to participate; they are labeled by Phillips (1987) as "laggards." And, second, there is inconclusive evidence that MCE can be linked positively to improved performance. Thus, MCE does not necessarily provide us with a solution to public accountability for marginal to incompetent professionals or provide consumers with protection against providers who fail to keep up to date.

Given this scenario of power, responsibility, and accountability, what lies ahead for CPE? How can CPE of the future attempt to insure that professionals serve the public rather than their own self-interests?

CPE: The Link Between Professional Service, Accountability, and Competence

The future of continuing professional education lies with determining methods to link practitioner competence with public service and accountability. This link has been a deeply rooted tradition in professional training and continuing education for professionals. What has occurred is a shift in emphasis in professional and continuing education. Educators of professionals at one time saw their mission to be teaching participants proficiency in the requisite knowledge and skills of the latter's practice, tempered with a sense of responsibility--for, after all, a profession was seen as a calling. Greater trust resulted because professionals exhibited ethical service and were accountable and responsive to societal needs.

This philosophy of education has eroded over time, having been displaced by very different norms: the development of the frontiers of new knowledge, highly specialized career training with periodic updates of the practitioner's knowledge and skills, and the power and politics of protection and self-interest. The shift in educational emphasis has not been a conscious effort by educators, and certainly the consequences have not been all bad. However, educators of professionals must assert a leadership role in redirecting the educational process back to emphasizing responsible and responsive public service.

CPE of the future should link practitioner competence with service and accountability in the following ways: (1) providing practitioners with an understanding of the value dimensions and ethical context of their work; (2) developing professionals who are competent, technically expert, yet sufficiently educated to understand the human purposes of their special skills from preservice throughout their careers; and, (3) advancing specialized knowledge and expertise, while simultaneously promoting techniques of cooperation, interdependence, and interprofessional collaboration to solve society's complex problems.

Educating for Ethical Practice

Educators of the professions should recognize the importance of moral education by encouraging a genuine concern for societal problems and the ethical consequences of professional action. The development of critical inquiry in professionals is itself a social act. It makes a person publicly accountable and responsible for his or her judgments and decisions. Such inquiry is indispensible to a professional life that has more to offer than technical services for private gain.

Harvard President Derek Bok (1987) had this to say about the university's role in reestablishing a commitment to moral development and ethics:

> Thus, even if presidents are overburdened and professors happen to prepare themselves in specialized disciplines, universities have an obligation to try to help their students understand how to lead ethical, reflective, fulfilling lives. One can appreciate the difficulty of the task and understand if progress is slow and halting. What is harder to forgive is a refusal to recognize the problem or to acknowledge a responsibility to work at it conscientiously. Advanced knowledge and specialized skills are important in many ways. Yet they are not the only ends of education. (p. B4)

Educators of professionals should not only nurture their students as critics and citizens, but also cultivate them as teachers. The professional needs to be more than a dispenser of technical services. He or she must accept the role of an instructor with clients and patients. The degree to which the professional accepts the service recipient as a partner or collaborator--both working in concert to solve problems--will promulgate a reversal of the public skepticism toward professional services. For example, the physician or psychiatrist must function as a teacher, enlisting patients to pursue more actively their own physical and mental health maintenance. Nurturing this expert-client relationship so that it is more balanced and equitable will enhance professional credibility. Thus, CPE should cultivate in professionals the fundamental qualities of the teacher: a capacity for critical inquiry, a direct grasp of one's subject, and a desire to share it with one's audience.

Developing Professionals Through Lifelong Education

Educators of professionals must go beyond fundamental teaching to gain a mastery of more difficult forms of activity, to incorporate new knowledge into continuing practice, and to work in increasingly sophisticated ways to collaborate with other professionals in discharging their common social responsibilities (Mawby, 1985, p. 3). Educators and professionals alike are becoming aware that preprofessional education must be planned with continuing education in mind. As Queeney (1984) writes, "Students receiving their entry-level education should be imbued with the notion of continuing professional education as an essential component of their professional life, and one for which they, as individual practitioners, must assume responsibility" (p. 13). In this sense, the professional's need to learn is unending; and professionals must continue to learn if they and the professions they represent are to maintain quality in their service to society.

Learning itself takes on a new meaning in continuing professional education. It becomes a self-sustained process of experiencing, reflecting, forming new concepts, and testing one's judgment and abilities in action (Mentkowski, 1988, p. 114). It demands a learning strategy that is integrative and a "reflection-in-action" orientation as described so eloquently by Schon (1983, 1987). Responsive and responsible CPE in the future should equip the professional to develop linkages between thought and action and knowledge and behavior within a framework of values.

Kolb (1988) extends this learning strategy to that of wholeness. His research indicates that advanced professional development presents to mid-life professionals integrative challenges that are markedly different from the specialized demands of their early careers. Young professionals spend most of their time polishing their expert skills in a work environment that is competitive and oriented toward rewarding the individual. Mid-career and advanced professionals, however, face new tasks requiring new skills--especially integrative skills necessary to seek balance among career, family, personal well-being, and a desire to contribute to society. The developmental challenge of educators of professionals is to equip them more effectively to speak publicly for their profession, to mentor and lead younger professionals, to strike a comfortable career/personal balance, and to serve society. Knowledge alone does not guarantee effective professional performance. Educators cannot ignore their responsibility to educate for personal growth as well as for specialized knowledge. As Kolb states:

> A career planning process that begins with a holistic assessment of one's current life situation, past experience and accomplishments, and future dreams and aspirations is a good starting place for a program of advanced professional studies. Advanced professionals are a diverse and unique lot. They all differ in the specifics of their life experiences and personal styles. If there is a common successful response, it is the integration of one's strengths and weaknesses into a centered process of executive action. To

develop this individualized, integrated executive action style would be the goal of a life/career planning process with three components: holistic self-assessment, setting personal learning goals, and personal development planning. (pp. 86-87)

Interprofessional Collaboration

CPE of the future must also provide the framework and opportunity for shared expertise across professional lines. Indeed, the educational challenge of the future will be to still provide specialized knowledge, but also provide professionals with the ability to relate to one another's different areas of expertise. Complex social issues do not occur in isolation and usually affect a variety of interests and professional concerns. Thus, future systems of education should stress interdisciplinary approaches to problems and teams of shared expertise. Such collaboration among CPE providers and practitioners will further refine the professions themselves and make them more capable of solving society's problems.

CPE is neutral ground and may be the only arena for interprofessional collaboration. Once together in the neutrality of a learning environment, professionals realize they have much in common. Capron (1988) writes, "The sharing may consist not simply of representing the interests of one's profession, in representing the needs of one's clients, or in advocating a particular technical vantage point, but of leading us collectively, not only in the professions but in the broader society, to a new understanding of commitment to seeking the common good" (p. 7).

The Role of Government

What is the role of government in this future scenario? If systems of continuing professional education fail to meet these challenges, government's regulatory function will increase in intensity and oversight in order to protect the public interest. Licensing boards would continue to invoke mandatory participation in some form of CPE to set standards and to raise the minimum level of practitioner competence. However, should this result come to pass and there still be the public perception that professionals perform poorly and lack accountability, then CPE will be severely discredited. A more legitimate role for government would be to educate consumers and to assure that their voice in public policy debates is at least equal to that of professional associations.

Future systems of continuing professional education should promote sound, value-based professional practice. And continuing educators of professionals must take the lead in creating an environment that encourages ongoing professional reflection, experience-based learning, and development of the whole person. By taking the steps necessary to accomplish this goal, educators of professionals will have strengthened the link between practitioner competence and social responsibility. Even more importantly, they will have helped restore the tradition of instilling in professionals a sense of idealism, service to society, and calling.

References

Azzaretto, J. F. (1987). Competitive strategies in continuing professional education. In C. Baden (Ed.), *Competitive strategies in continuing education* (pp. 45-58). San Francisco: Jossey-Bass.

Benveniste, G. (1987). *Professionalizing the organization.* San Francisco: Jossey-Bass.

Bok, D. (1988, April 27). Report to the Harvard University Board of Overseers. *The Chronicle of Higher Education,* p. B4.

Capron, A. M. (1987). Collaboration in action: Innovative problem solving. In R. T. McLaughlin (Ed.), *Proceedings of the First National Leadership Symposium on Interprofessional Education and Practice.* Columbus: Ohio State University Press, pp. 6-7.

Cervero, R. M. (1988)'. Book review of Schon, D.: Educating the reflective practitioner--Toward a new design for teaching and learning in the professions. *Adult Education Quarterly, 38* (3), 182-184.

Friedson, E. (1970a). *Profession of medicine.* New York: Dodd and Meade.

Friedson, E. (1970b). *Professional dominance.* New York: Atherton.

Friedson, E. (Ed.). (1973). *The professions and their prospects.* Beverly Hills: Sage Publications.

Friedson, E. (1986). *Professional powers: A study of the institutionalization of formal knowledge.* Chicago: The University of Chicago Press.

Goode, W. J. (1957). Community within a community: The professions. *American Sociological Review, 22* (2), 194-200.

Gouldner, E. M. (1957). Cosmopolitans and locals: Toward an analysis of latent social roles. *Administrative Science Quarterly, 2* (3), 281-306.

Gross, S. J. (1983). The professional as regulator and self-regulator. In M. R. Stern (Ed.), *Power and conflict in continuing professional education* (pp. 172-193). Belmont, CA: Wadsworth.

Gross, S. J. (1984). *Of foxes and hen houses: Licensing and the health professions.* Westport, CT: Quorum Books.

Hogan, D. B. (1983). The effectiveness of licensing: History, evidence and recommendations. *Law and Human Behavior, 7* (2/3), 117-138.

Hughes, E. C. (1958). *Men and their work.* New York: Free Press.

Jackson, J. A. (Ed.). (1970). *Professions and professionalization.* Cambridge: Cambridge University Press.

Kolb, D. A. (1988). Integrity, advanced professional development, and learning. In S. Srivastva and Associates (Eds.), *Executive integrity: The search for high values in organizational life* (pp. 68-88). San Francisco: Jossey-Bass.

Larson, M. S. (1977). *The rise of professionalism: A sociological analysis.* Berkeley, CA: University of California Press.

Lieberman, J. K. (1970). *Tyranny of the experts.* New York: Walker and Company.

Lortie, D. C. (1975). *Schoolteacher: A sociological study.* Chicago: University of Chicago Press.

Mawby, R. G. (1985). *Lifelong learning and the professional.* Battle Creek, MI: W. K. Kellogg Foundation Annual Report.

May, W. F. (1980). Professional ethics: Setting, terrain, and teacher. In D. Callahan and S. Bok (Eds.), *Ethics teaching in higher education* (pp. 205-241). New York: Plenum Press.

McKnight, J. (1977). The professional service business. *Social Policy, 8* (3), 110-116.

Mentkowski, M. (1988). Paths to integrity: Educating for personal growth and professional performance. In S. Srivastva and Associates (Eds.), *Executive integrity: The search for high human values in organizational life* (pp. 89-121). San Francisco: Jossey-Bass.

The National Clearinghouse on Licensure, Enforcement, and Regulation. (1986a). *State credentialing of the behavioral science professions: Counselors, psychologists, and social workers.* Lexington, KY: The Council of State Governments.

The National Clearinghouse on Licensure, Enforcement, and Regulation. (1986b). *State credentialing of the behavioral science professions: Counselors, psychologists, and social workers.* Lexington, KY: The Council of State Governments.

Nowlen, P. M. (1988). *A new approach to continuing education for business and the professions.* New York: NUCEA, American Council on Education, and Macmillan.

Olesen, V. (1979). Employing competence-based education for the reform of professional practice. In G. Grant and Associates (Eds.), *On competence* (pp. 199-224). San Francisco: Jossey-Bass.

Phillips, L. E. (1987). Is mandatory continuing professional education working? *Mobius, 7* (1), 57-64.

Queeney, D. S. (1984). The role of the university in continuing professional education. *Educational Record, 65* (3), 13-17.

Schon, D. A. (1983). *The reflective practitioner.* New York: Basic Books.

Schon, D. A. (1987). *Educating the reflective practitioner.* San Francisco: Jossey-Bass.

Shimberg, B. (1982). *Occupational licensing: A public perspective.* Princeton: Educational Testing Service.

Shimberg, B., Esser, B. F., & Kruger, D. H. (1972). *Occupational licensing and public policy.* Princeton: Educational Testing Service.

Stigler, G. J. (1971). The theory of economic regulation. *Bell Journal of Economics and Management Science, 2* (1), 3-21.

Wilensky, H. (1964). The professionalization of everyone. *American Journal of Sociology, 70* (2), 137-158.

Young, S. D. (1987). *The rule of experts: Occupational licensing in America.* Washington, DC: Cato Institute.

Chapter 3

New Questions for Continuing Professional Education

Philip M. Nowlen

Periods in continuing education's history can be distinguished by the reign of powerful, if not always right-headed, questions such as, "Who should provide what for whom?" This question, now a decade old, triggered the lively but fruitless Alford - Stern "Power and Conflict" books (Alford, 1980; Stern, 1983). These books represented--as well as rein-forced-- arguments over provider primacy and turf. If we put the question again but in a way that is centered on learner performance, we move well beyond these issues by reason of the sheer complexity of professional performance, thus redirecting and renewing the field.

Essential Distinctions

What should be provided in order to sustain or enhance perform-ance?" "Who should provide it?" "How do we decide?" These are questions that necessitate explicit distinctions between the following: learning and teaching, needs and wants, individuals and organizations, compe-tence and performance, descriptive and prescriptive ways of thinking, contexts of practice and professional identities, and occupational life and human development. Forces at play in continuing education for the professions (a phrase I prefer so as to include any learning related to performance) discourage those in the field from spending much time with these distinctions. These forces include the structure and finance of universities, professional associations, and employer-organizations. It is easier to provide a program someone wants than to design a learning experience that will make a difference. It is cheaper to pull a program off the shelf than to study the professional performance it is expected to serve. Salary and social mobility, idealism and mythology, trendiness, as well as a zest for knowledge, influence what is wanted. Major programs involving thousands of professionals and millions of dollars are still contemplated without attention to the distinctions essential if performance is to be influenced.

A Virginia Proposal

A recent proposal in Virginia is a case in point. The governor-appointed Commission on Excellence in Education recommended that by July 1, 1993, every teacher should have, or be working toward, a graduate degree in the arts and sciences (Governor's, 1986). The Virginia Legislature will consider the master's degree recommendation during its next session. The announced goal is improvement of Virginia's public schools. The Commission neither stipulates a set of teacher proficiencies as means to the end nor expresses the intended benefit in either teacher performance or student achievement terms. Proponents assume that teachers currently holding master's degrees in the disciplines are more effective than teachers with master's degrees in education. (Are there not ineffective liberal arts and sciences trained teachers, and what is to be done with them?) Proponents do not require research testing these hypotheses or identifying the variables that distinguish successful from unsuccessful teaching. Nor do proponents ask teachers' judgments about these questions.

Ten years ago the question continuing educators might have rushed to answer was: "Who should provide the proposed master's degree?" Today, it is more likely that those in the field would pose: "What difference in teacher performance is wanted?" and "Is the program you propose the best way to achieve what is wanted?"

The Commission intends to improve Virginia public schools -- a highly complex system of teachers, students, families, facilities, regions, and cultures --through the actions of any accredited institution of higher education prescribing and providing discipline-based knowledge through any master's track in the liberal arts and sciences to all teachers. While the Commission's language provides some latitude, "a graduate degree appropriate to her or his teaching area" (Governor's, 1986, p.14), it takes no account of differing contexts of practice (e.g., a Spanish class for gifted students, an English class for children whose native language is not English, or a math class for children with learning disabilities). The Commission makes no distinctions with respect to the differing strengths of Virginia's universities. When these factors are considered, together with the Commission's insistence upon an undergraduate degree in arts and sciences disciplines for new teacher certification, one might legitimately infer that the Commission has been disadvantaged by one of this century's larger myths --"one size fits all"--when it comes to K-12 teaching.

All Virginia teachers achieving the prescribed master's degree will receive a pay increase, the one definitive outcome projected for the new program. Those who remember the late 60's and early 70's studies of nursing preparation effectiveness will recall that the only consistently distinctive results attributable to three, four, and five-year programs were differential starting salaries. And so it goes.

Studies of Teacher Effectiveness

University research on K-12 teaching includes a number of descriptive models of teacher effectiveness. Several national foundations have for decades evaluated the impact of educational interventions purporting to improve teacher effectiveness. Some divisions of continuing education understand what is required in designing learning experiences intended to make a difference in the way professionals perform. Many corporations have expressed interest in assisting public education, and their human resources development directors have appropriate expertise to accomplish this task. Neither was wisdom from these sources sought by the Commission nor did university researchers and continuing educators, foundation personnel, and corporate human resource directors seek to testify. More importantly, what would continuing educators have testified? What follows might be considered a case study in the form of testimony. The testimony provides a measure of the field's movement in the last decade.

Testimony from Continuing Educators: A Case Study

The Virginia Commission hopes to influence teacher performance. How will the Commission know whether it has succeeded? Is there a set of critical variables toward which teachers should move? In what ways will the new, improved teacher differ from the present teacher? Why propose the master's degree in a discipline of the liberal arts and sciences as the single vehicle for moving all teachers toward the goal? Can we answer these questions with the certainty demanded by the level of expenditures required to finance the proposal and to command the human investment of the approximately 40,000 Virginia teachers who lack graduate degrees in liberal arts and sciences? If we cannot and if our faith in the efficacy of the discipline-based master's degree as the single path to improved teacher performance is misplaced, what is the cost of failure in time and human capital wasted?

Permit us to suggest a process that addresses the crucial questions. First, what is the model toward which we should teach (i.e., the ideal represented by measurable standards of achievement and the knowledge, skill, and traits required to sustain those standards)? Second, at what distance do we find teachers from the model? And, third, what are the most promising ways to facilitate teacher excellence?

Step One: Consensual Validation of Models of Excellence

What are the profiles the research literature provides? Which are prescriptive and which descriptive? Are there significant characteristics commonly appearing in these models?

Who are the consensual teachers of excellence within a reasonable cross section of years of experience, schools and school divisions, disciplines, and contexts (honors tracks, special and gifted student populations, high drop-out situations)? What are the characteristics that distinguish these high performance teachers and their teaching.

Do those teachers validated as teachers of excellence share the characteristics that predominate in the research literature on teacher excellence? Are there consistent and measurable differences in student achievement under the direction of such teachers, as opposed to student achievement under those who are not considered models? Do the consensual teachers share any significant characteristics that distinguish them from those not nominated with respect to college and graduate studies, unusually effective mentors, and/or supportive fellow teachers? Have they enjoyed pre-professional or continuing education experiences that they judged crucial to their success?

What are the variables, if any, occurring significantly among those not nominated (e.g., an undergraduate degree in education; affective difficulties in relating to their current teaching contexts; experiences which might depress performance, such as a messy divorce process, death in the family, or personal illness)? Are there any variables occurring significantly among those not nominated who have strong liberal arts and sciences backgrounds?

This process might establish that the crucial variable separating superior from marginal teachers is completion of graduate studies in the liberal arts and sciences. If so, the Commission will have performed a great service by substantiating through research its accurate intuition. The process will have the added advantage of providing teachers with very strong motivation to participate in the proposed discipline-based graduate studies.

On the other hand, if a strong liberal arts and sciences background is but one of several variables key to superior teacher performance, the Commission and the Commonwealth will know that a pluralistic approach is required.

Step Two: Development of Guided and Self-Assessment Experiences

Searching the literature and researching issues such as those described above defines in general terms the gap between ineffective or merely adequate teachers and superior teachers. The process objectively identifies the discrepancy in terms of discipline-based knowledge and teaching techniques and can even usefully isolate crucial qualities, such as positive regard for students. The process inventories, again in general terms, the barriers, inhibitors, and depressors of teacher performance. Those who possess the qualities and background typical of superior teaching may nonetheless have disabling impediments of mind or body, often the result of circumstances quite apart from the school setting but seriously intrusive on the classroom just the same. In other cases, their performance may fall short because of the intrusion of less gifted superiors or fumbling bureaucracies.

This information must be translated into individual teacher self-knowledge and professional and organizational insight. Teachers are not better or worse than other professionals in this respect. They are not often in one another's classrooms. Many do not know what they do not know. Others come to believe they are not gifted. Some suffer from lack of feedback; others from unskilled feedback.

The model(s) toward which the Commission would have teachers move must be proposed to teachers. The consensual validation reached and described in Step One must be communicated to teachers in ways that encourage reflection and criticism, the prerequisites for teachers to come to own the model(s) (i.e., by reworking the data in their own frames of reference, seasoning it with personal experience). Only when this is done will teachers be eager to give themselves to an assessment process, to a consequent personal development agenda, and to the programs which serve that agenda. Effective adult learning rests heavily upon adult investment in the objectives of learning.

The Commission also endorses the principle of assessment centers for those who are principals or want to become principals. The Commission proposes periodic assessment programs for principals to define their need for growth and suggests that this assessment become a regular step in the recertification process (Governor's, 1986, p. 13). We suggest that guided assessment and self-assessment exercises (i.e., assessment "centers") would serve teacher development in the same way.

Assessment centers are not merely facilities. They are highly mobile storehouses of capably administered and reliable instruments, simulations, interviews, observation techniques, special assignments, and advisory services. Providing a mix of guided and self-assessment processes, they are diagnostic and developmental in nature. They are meant to lead individual teachers to grounded personal insights comparing their performance with that of the validated model(s). Assessment center techniques help professionals to confirm strengths, identify weaknesses, and come to see such barriers as may exist between competence and performance, capacity, and execution. Assessment center advisors can help teachers distinguish between reversible or temporary distractions and deeper disorders that may be rooted in their individual development.

If this were all assessment centers did, teachers might be more devastated than helped. Assessment can empower people, however. Assessment center staff can counsel teachers toward a wide variety of options in gaining performance-related strengths and addressing the barriers that prevent them from performing as effectively as possible. Teacher "A" might well conclude that graduate studies in the liberal arts and sciences are required. Teacher "B" might judge that so long as serious family issues were unresolved, she would not have the concentration or energy for her teaching and might seek marriage counseling. Teacher "C" might decide to pursue formal studies, supplemented by a collaborative mentoring relationship arranged by the assessment center. Teacher "D" might reach a prudent decision to enter administration or to leave the field. Teacher "E" might defer a final decision until physicians had completed thorough medical examinations.

We urge that the Commission recommend legislative support of personal development agendas inspired by validated models of excellence and formed under capable guidance at approved assessment centers. Some agendas will, doubtless, involve graduate studies in the liberal arts and science. Other agendas will seek enhanced skills in rapid detection of reading difficulties or greater knowledge of adolescent development. Still other agendas will pursue counseling as a means of overcoming a personal barrier to effective teaching.

Simple processes that insure anonymity (sending an unsigned copy of completed self-assessment instruments to state teacher-development staff, for example) would assist in identifying teachers' aggregate distance from models of excellence. This procedure would permit a variety of institutions outside public education to anticipate the demand for their resources or services, (e.g., degree programs, graduate courses, special conferences, mentoring matches, family therapy, substance abuse counseling, and the like).

Superintendents and principals could review the generalized data to see if the prevailing culture had been sufficiently supportive to enable teachers to express and pursue their counseling needs or to test the need for other responses. Examination of the aggregate data will usually lead to thoughtful decisions about organizational needs (change management, orchestration of culture in complex organizations, and so forth).

Step Three: Marshaling the Responses

Teachers themselves, institutions of higher education and their state coordinating council, the state department of education and its teacher-development staff, members of appropriate helping professions, corporate human resources development leaders, and relevant professional associations will have been involved in Steps One and Two. They have much to contribute to validating models of excellence and to organizing and conducting assessment centers. They also represent diverse but significant strengths in entering long-range teaching and learning relationships with K-12 public school teachers.

We use language such as "entering long-range teaching and learning relationships" rather than "providing programs" to distinguish continuing education's response in 1988 from the "Power and Conflict" (Alford, 1980; Stern, 1983) discussions of a decade ago. Today's response differs in several respects. First, today's providers must be involved in the process of model validation and teacher assessment. Second, providers today must learn much in order to design responses sensitive to the nuances of individual teacher agendas and will learn even more in the process of designing their responses. Third, today's providers must be involved in design and conduct of follow-up assessment centers that measure and reinforce teacher progress. Fourth, providers' contemporary responses must be coordinated for the sake of coherence, access and choice, and cost. Fifth, for maximum benefit to teachers' schools and divisions, current providers must be positioned to scan aggregate teacher assessments for organization related learning and development needs.

Today's providers must remain open to the widest possible number of appropriate ways to help teachers learn. Teacher organizations or school divisions can facilitate mentoring relationships. Family counselors can help teachers reach beyond issues that drain their energy and distract their attention. Corporations can help school divisions test whether the prevailing organizational culture facilitates or inhibits teacher development and can suggest strategies for sustaining some or changing others. School divisions or service agencies can address the child-care needs of single-parent teachers who cannot otherwise engage in professional development activities. Universities can individualize master's degree tracks and, in cooperation with principals and teachers, provide frameworks within which actual classroom situations become learning laboratories for teachers. The very complexity of the responses required reduces the relevance of "provider turf" and "primacy" issues.

In any event, continuing education has come to understand that the real "provider" with power over both agenda and outcomes is the adult learner--in this case, the teacher. All learning is self-directed, and at any given moment an adult is likely to be pursuing several learning agendas, some more explicitly than others. The teacher's conviction about the validity of the model(s) of excellence, the teacher's willingness to undertake probing (though confidential) assessment, the teacher's capacity to construct a personal development agenda for acquiring knowledge and skills and for reducing impediments, and the teacher's skill in directing several learning and development strategies at the same time will determine whether the cause of excellence in education has been advanced.

We therefore recommend that assessment include evaluation of teachers' self-directed learning skills and that opportunities for enhancing such skills be made available. We further recommend that assessment centers act as referral agencies, presenting teachers with a range of possible learning and development strategies and alternative ways to pursue them, including classroom learning, interactive telecommunication, paired mentoring, independent study, and counseling resources.

Concluding Reflections

This testimony represents a redirected and renewed continuing education field in the ways described below.

The Medical Model

First, in renewing and redirecting continuing education for the professions, the medical model deserves attention. The patient is but one of several persons important in reaching a diagnosis. As patient-reported symptoms are subjected to extensive diagnostic procedures, patient and physician arrive at joint decisions about a course of action. Education, like medicine, is an intervention. When a professional or an organization employing professionals requests a specific educational intervention, such as the master's degree for teachers discussed above, the typical assumption is that the intervention will make a desirable and even specific difference in their work. The continuing educator must know what those desirable differences are and what assumptions have been made about the requested program's capability for delivering them. A request for a continuing education program should be considered only the opening of a diagnostic process. In such a way, continuing educators will avoid the temptation of a quick sale or the quick fix and build toward longer lasting learning relationships.

Exemplars of Performance

Second, continuing educators need to identify exemplars of outstanding professional performance and to validate this identification among the exemplar professionals' peers. (As a principle, the field should start with successful performers.) The competencies (knowledge, skills, qualities, motivation, absence of impediment) related to such professionals' job functions will be important. Of equal or even greater importance will be identification of variables that distinguish superior performing professionals from those who are merely adequate and from those who are inadequate. Assessment of individuals as compared with the exemplars then takes place with continuing education assisting the professional to move toward the exemplar's level of performance.

Effective Organizations of Professionals

Third, there are organizations of professionals that are consensually judged to perform better than others. It is important to discover what critical variables distinguish these highly effective organizations from those which are inadequate or merely adequate. For example, what are the structures, policies, motivational systems, and mentoring relationships of highly successful group practices? How does one distinguish such organizations from others that are merely adequate? Assessment of organizations of professionals compared to the model of successful organizations must take place because the performance of individuals is so heavily influenced by the qualities of organizations to which they belong and by their "fit" with the culture of those organizations.

The Importance of the Individual

Fourth, the individual is the ultimate provider of learning. The individual sets learning agendas throughout life, often pursuing several learning paths at the same time. The individual brings to learning experiences frames of reference outside of which knowledge may be temporarily present but for which little assimilation will take place unless the individual finds a home for the knowledge in a new frame of reference. An individual's learning can make a difference to an organization or context of practice only through individually developed skills of application, motivation, or negotiation. Continuing educators will want to increase an individual's knowledge and skills in setting personal learning agendas. Continuing educators will want to check whether learners share conceptual frameworks essential for the assimilation of new knowledge. Continuing educators will also want to address implementation issues and related skills when new knowledge is expected to make a difference to an organization or practice setting.

Development of a Comprehensive Plan

Finally, development of a comprehensive plan for continuing education interventions for professional groups in similar contexts of practice involves pluralistic responses of considerable complexity. With respect to teacher development, for example, the responses include regional assessment centers for teachers and administrators; organizational assessment processes for schools and school divisions; individual learning sequences of a wide variety from noncredit to degree programs in disciplines related to what is taught, to the process of teaching itself, and to understanding learners; identification and reinforcement of promising mentoring relationships; and development opportunities related to physical and mental well-being.

I cannot imagine a single continuing education provider capable of this range of responses, although it might be in the best interest of teachers to have a single agency coordinate this range of responses by multiple providers of various kinds. A far greater degree of inter-provider collaboration than now exists is probably in the future of a renewed and redirected effort on behalf of the professions.

References

Alford, H. J. (Ed.). (1979). *Power and conflict in continuing education* Belmont, CA: Wadsworth.

Governor's Commission on Excellence in Education. (1986). *Excellence in education: A plan for Virginia's future.* Richmond, VA: Commonwealth of Virginia, Governor's Office.

Stern, M. R. (Ed.). (1983). *Power and conflict in continuing professional education.* Belmont, CA: Wadsworth.

Chapter 4

Investing in Professional Development: A Need for National Policy

Arden D. Grotelueschen

In the 1880s, my Grandpa Grotelueschen followed the Platte River west to east-central Nebraska to settle on a 160 acre tract of land. Here he fulfilled his dreams of raising a family and developing the land for livestock and crops. He was successful, in large part, because he was strong, determined, and resourceful. He and Grandma were fortunate to have several sons who helped with the *manpower* needs of the farm.

One son, my father, stayed on the family farm and developed it further, contouring the land, developing spillways to prevent erosion, and rotating crops. Although my father and mother were also resourceful in that they had a large family, Dad increasingly relied on *machine power* to do the farming. As sons and daughters grew up, there was no need for them to stay on the farm to help. Instead, they migrated from the farm to town or distant cities. When my father died, only my older brother stayed on the farm; Mom and I moved to town. I was eight years old.

Little did I know at the time, or even for years thereafter, that I was entering an era in which *muscle power* would play an increasingly insignificant role in my life. I was on my way to cultivating the potential of my mind -- developing *mind power.* Although some might question whether I ever attained this goal, the pursuit of mind power continues with our children as they explore opportunities for enhancing the power of their minds.

Labor and Societal Economic Progress

The progression I see in the evolution of labor in my own family over several generations is a microcosm of the major labor developments in our society. When agriculture was a dominant aspect of our economy, most workers could contribute, even if they had little knowledge or skill. This situation was also true with the mechanization of industry which followed. While this gradual substitution of machine power for muscle power required some changes and the acquisition of new knowledge and skills, certainly little formalized education was necessary to prepare people for the changing character of working life. This fact was reflected in the major concerns of governmental labor supply policy which were focused on the under-utilization of available qualified labor needed to produce material goods. This quantitative focus paid only lip service to the qualitative nature of the labor supply.

In our contemporary lives, however, the quality of the labor supply has become a major issue; human resources have become a fundamental concern of the education and business communities in our country. In recent years, a number of high level commissioned studies have documented serious shortcomings of our educational products. For example, in old and new industries alike, employers are finding that older workers are educationally unqualified to work in modernized technical work settings; change has outstripped their educational preparedness. Tragically, younger workers are also often found to be inadequately prepared to perform even the most basic tasks which build upon our new trinity of basic skills: reading, writing, and computing. Purely and simply put, our human resources are inadequately developed to support the contemporary needs for mind power and knowledge developed through educational preparation and achievement.

The problem becomes even more serious when one considers the diminishing total number of young adults available to enter the labor market. In order to maintain sufficient quantity in our labor force, our society must, for the near term, rely upon the ongoing trends of delayed-entry of women into the workforce, persons immigrating to this country, and the re-entry of retired persons.

The Need for a Comprehensive National Approach

There is a need both for more workers and for better qualified workers. But whose responsibility is it to formulate and implement human resource policy which benefits the individual (and society) in a continuous manner throughout the life span?

The United States differs fundamentally from other major industrial democracies in its approach to this basic question. Other nations, such as Germany and Japan, assume as their national responsibility the provision of assistance to workers who, through no fault of their own, need additional training to maintain or enhance their knowledge and skills to remain effective participants in the workforce. In the United States, however, this responsibility remains largely with individuals, local or state governments, or the private sector. With the exception of the armed forces and related areas of national defense, as well as in areas where vested interest groups have exerted political pressure to achieve their own objectives, there is no national policy which recognizes the need to invest in human resource development in order to strengthen the employability and productivity of its workforce.

What is needed in this country is a national policy directed toward the development of human resources and benefiting all levels of human resource development. This need has been recently and poignantly stated by Briggs (1987):

> In an environment of rapid shifts in employment patterns, it is necessary to recognize that both job and occupational changes will occur frequently over one's working life. Indeed, a typical worker entering the labor force in the mid-1980s can be expected to change jobs six or seven times and to change occupations three times over his or her working life. In this context of flux, there is a need to have in place a human resource system that can provide job retraining, up-to-date labor market information, ample opportunities for educational upgrading, and relocation assistance to promote the readjustment process for those who cannot easily, if at all, make these transitions. The system should not just help the working poor. It should also be designed to assist all income groups who become vulnerable to unemployment. (p. 1228)

Human Resources and Economic Growth

Assuming the value of a comprehensive national approach to human resource development, the question that arises is: How much do human resources contribute to economic growth and well-being, and on which sectors of the human resource pool should such a policy be focused?

Early theories of economic growth relied heavily on the production of goods and services with little regard for the contribution of human resources to the production process. However, actual studies relating human resource development with productivity and economic growth by Denison (1985) and Carnevale (1983) indicate that approximately 75% of the growth of the U.S. economy since 1929 can be attributed to the development of human resources through on-the-job training, education, formal training, and improved health. Thus, while economists have concentrated on physical capital as the major contributing factor for long-term economic growth, the major contributor appears to be human resource development efforts. It is not surprising, then, that a nation's most important resource is its people. What is surprising is that this growth in human resources potential occurred without a national policy. Maybe this "accidental" growth is a good argument to continue to "muddle along." Most informed authorities would argue that current and future educational, economic, and demographic factors call for a greater involvement at all levels of government in the formulation and implementation of human resource policy.

The Case for the Development of Professional Human Resources

As has been noted, where the development of human resources has been recognized in the past, the focus has been largely upon either the working poor or persons displaced through changes in industrial production technology, markets, and needs. In stark contrast are professionals. Professionals do not change occupations, but their occupations do change over time. This fact, the unique prospects and problems it creates, and the resulting implications for human resource development are the focus of this paper.

Why, one might ask, should one be concerned with the development of professionals? Professionals, after all, are already highly developed and specialized human resources. But in an economy and society which is increasingly specialized and service oriented, the fact that a group is specialized does not insulate it from the impact of change. In fact, as can be seen in the immense growth of continuing professional education, these professionals are greatly affected by such change. Given this effect, professionals similarly should not be excluded from consideration in the formulation of a national level human resource policy. Because in our specialized society we rely heavily on professionals to assist the public in a growing array of elements of daily life, investing in the ongoing development of these professional resources is central to maintaining the quality of everyday life.

Professionals are privileged members of society. They receive relatively high levels of status, income, and power. They typically occupy positions of leadership and provide services upon which individuals and society depend. Paradoxically, professionals are often neglected in public policy matters because of this privileged status. They are more likely to be ignored because they are assumed to be self-sufficient and not in need of any assistance.

From a societal perspective, however, one cannot ignore the fact that our professionals are a national resource, one which is respected worldwide. For example, who did the Soviets turn to for expert medical assistance after the Chernobyl incident? An American medical doctor. Who did France and England turn to for expert advice in the design of machinery to dig the English Chunnel? American engineers. And so on. To lose this competitive edge (and there is evidence based on educational achievement differences between American youth and other nations' youth that our future's competitive edge is all but lost) would be to lose one of our country's last primary resources.

So long as our professional resource base continues to maintain itself, our society may continue to reap the rewards. However, resources need to be understood and tended as part of our investment for the future. From a societal perspective, our professional resources may well be one of our most important national assets. The nurturing and continued development of these resources is essential to our society's well-being, particularly in the context of increased complexity and technological change.

Understanding how to formulate a human resource policy which adequately takes into account the development of the professional sector is fundamental to successful investment in our country's future. As with many astute investments, it is often difficult to understand the value or the strategies involved. Investment in professional human resources is no different. The remainder of this paper will present a number of questions and issues which together provide background for discussing professional human resource development as well as related policy formulation and implementation.

Continuing Professional Education and Its Effectiveness

There are, of course, a number of approaches to enhancing the quality of our professional human resources. From the educational perspective, for purposes of the present discussion, continuing professional education will be advocated as the primary means of enhancement. Not only does this position reflect a special interest in education, but in view of the central role of new knowledge and skills in enhancing professional human resources, education is arguably the most fundamental approach.

Although the effectiveness of continuing professional education is frequently debated, the conclusion to be drawn is that it can be effective. Just as there are no effectiveness service guarantees in professional medical service, professional accounting service, professional legal service, and even in professional ministerial service, there are no guarantees in continuing professional education. Effectiveness is attainable, however, depending on the quality of the service, the needs of the person(s) receiving the service, and the criteria used to assess service effectiveness.

Documentation of Effectiveness

In continuing professional education, if effectiveness is not documented, it is typically because (a) the basic elements of continuing professional education (systematic instruction, professional content, and an appropriate learning environment) are not present; (b) there is a deficiency between learner needs and presented content; or (c) the criteria used to assess and/or to measure effectiveness are deficient or nonexistent. Each of these elements is a necessary, if not a sufficient, condition for ascertaining effectiveness.

It is often assumed that what is offered as "educational" is in fact educational and that participants have a need to learn what is being taught. These assumptions should be challenged from time to time for specific continuing professional education activities. Where they cannot be verified, the existence of an educational program should not be assumed.

The debate over criteria used to assess effectiveness generates most of the heated discussion. Criteria for effectiveness range from rating satisfaction with a program, judging elements of instructional quality, testing a professional's change in knowledge and attitude, observing changes in professional practice performance, and recording improvements in the recipients of professional service.

It is the view of this writer that the most valid and practical criteria are those that judge instructional quality and assess changes in knowledge and attitude. Satisfaction with a program, although helpful in practical terms, is a concept so maligned that it has little validity. Professional performance and client or patient outcomes, on the other hand, are impractical to measure because they require considerable effort and cost to ascertain.

And, I will assert that they are also not really valid -- an assertion that many readers would no doubt like to challenge. This claim is based on the belief, which is not without evidence, that much of practice performance and subsequent impact on client or patient outcomes is dictated by "everyday-practice theories" (psychological, sociological, and financial considerations that are influenced by personal and contextual considerations in practice settings) and not solely by knowledge attained from participation in a continuing professional education activity. Therefore, the effectiveness of continuing professional education should be based primarily upon the quality of instruction and learning that occurs. And attending to the improvement of the quality of current instructional practice will probably be more effective than diverting attention to new models of instruction and learning.

Two Comprehensive Analyses

The role of skeptics has an admirable place in the history of knowledge, and from within that tradition I suggest that continuing professional education stands in good stead. However, to dispel the skeptic's contention that continuing professional education has not been shown to be effective, I will briefly review two comprehensive analyses that have recently been completed.

In the health professions. The first of these is a review of the effectiveness of continuing professional education as reflected in the literature of the health professions (Nona, Kenny, & Johnson, 1988). This review analyzed all studies of effectiveness published since 1970. Studies which solely used participant satisfaction were excluded from the analysis on the grounds that they have become generally suspect in the research community. Of the remaining 142 identified studies, a majority (53 percent) focused on continuing medical education, one-fifth (20 percent) involved continuing nursing education, and smaller numbers (12 percent, 8 percent, and 6 percent) involved allied health, pharmacy, and dentistry continuing education, respectively.

In these studies, the criteria used to ascertain effectiveness were the following: 6 percent of the studies focused on changes in attitude, 32 percent studied changes in knowledge, 55 percent studied changes in performance, and 4 percent studied changes in patient outcomes. The results indicated that 72 percent of the studies reported some degree of educational effectiveness as a result of continuing professional education. Twenty percent reported mixed results and 7 percent reported no evidence of effectiveness. The conclusion reached by the authors of this review is that continuing professional education can be effective. This is particularly the case where continuing professional education is properly designed and meets professionals' needs and interests.

An empirical study in progress. The second study is an empirical study currently in progress (Grotelueschen Associates, Inc., 1988). The purpose of this study was to ascertain the effectiveness of mandatory continuing professional education on the professional knowledge of licensed accountants engaged in public practice in the state of New York.

Initial findings of an assessment of 633 representative public-practice accountants indicate that the ability to use professional knowledge is (a) positively associated with participation in continuing accountancy education; (b) positively associated with size of accountancy firm; and (c) negatively associated with years in active accountancy practice, only if the practitioner is primarily engaged in general practice. The knowledge-use ability of specialists in practice did not decline with increased years in active accountancy practice.

These two studies point to findings in which, I feel, we can believe. They reflect a basic optimism about the contribution that continuing professional education can make to strengthening our society's professional human resources. These studies also provide evidence to support participation in continuing professional education as a means for helping reassure the public about professional quality.

I would now like to turn to a discussion of the beneficiaries of strengthened professional human resources and policy considerations which must be addressed to make progress in this area.

Benefits and Beneficiaries

The question of who gets the benefits and who pays the cost is central to the resolution of almost all public policy problems and issues. An understanding of the major benefits of investing in human professional resources and an identification of the major beneficiaries of such benefits is basic to developing a policy to promote and foster continuing professional education.

As has been argued, a professional practitioner, over the course of his or her professional practice career, represents enduring human capital. However, as I have also argued, a professional must keep pace with changes in professional practice in order to continue to provide the best possible professional service to his or her clients or patients. Within this context, continuing professional educational may be viewed as necessary maintenance of the investment of resources which each professional practitioner represents.

If the fundamental benefit of continuing professional education is an educated and up-to-date professional, who benefits? Beneficiaries basically include the professional practitioner, the employing organization or institution, the client or patient being served, the professions at large, and the general public.

The professional practitioner benefits by assuring that he or she is in a position to provide professional services which are based upon the most recent advances in his or her profession. This translates directly into professional marketability, job security, and the development of a loyal practice base. The employing organization or institution benefits from an increased likelihood that services received will reflect the best of contemporary professional practice. The professions themselves will benefit from increased consumer confidence through the demonstration of commitment to continuing education and the public good. The general public will benefit from assurances of a stable professional service base.

Often benefits and costs go to different people. But it is feasible to consider, in the case of continuing professional education, that those who benefit should pay. More about costs will be presented next.

Costs

The costs associated with continuing professional education reflect another area of concern which needs to be addressed as policy issues are explored. A major consideration in this area is obtaining an overall picture of just what the total costs are when offering a program and participating in a program. Although accurate information on costs will undoubtedly be difficult to obtain, a reasonably clear picture of direct and indirect costs is important in understanding possible alternatives for financing continuing professional education.

When computing the cost of *providing* a continuing professional education program, consideration should be given to the full range of program development and delivery expenses. Every effort should be made to avoid hidden subsidization which would mask actual costs incurred. Similarly, the costs of *participating* in continuing professional education should be better understood. Fees and material costs are relatively easy to document. In addition, travel and lodging costs are other areas of expense often associated with participation in continuing professional education. These costs are also relatively easy to document. The time spent in learning and the foregone earnings costs incurred while away from practice, however, are more difficult to assess and are rarely documented.

Once costs are identified, one must address the question of who should be expected to cover these costs. It is often argued that consumers of products or services ultimately pay for the costs associated with capital improvements, whether they be in the areas of physical or human capital. The "assessment" typically appears as a pass-through cost which, in the case of professional services, results in increased fees for these services. In order to insure that the consumer is not unduly burdened with such costs, it is important to look closely at the question of who should pay for continuing professional education.

From the provider's perspective, continuing professional education programs have been expected to pay for themselves. That is, the providing organization is expected to be able to cover the costs of providing continuing education by fees collected from those attending. This conceptualization suggests that the costs of continuing education should be borne by the participants and assessed through the vehicle of the registration fee. However, because full cost accounting is not generally practiced, it is important to look beyond participant fees for supplemental sources of revenues.

Supplemental Revenue Sources

Supplemental revenue sources for continuing professional education include tax subsidies by states, membership subsidies by professional associations, or educational allowances by employing institutions. Or, in the case of health professions, such as medicine and pharmacy, considerable subsidies are available from the pharmaceutical industry. And how might the federal level equitably contribute toward its responsibilities for maintaining a vital national resource? Some ideas are presented below.

A National Policy Directive

To this point I have argued in favor of a national policy of enhancing the investment in professional human resources through continuing professional education. It is my proposal, then, that participation in continuing professional education should be systematically fostered as a national policy priority, in order to insure the maintenance and enhancement of our society's professional human resources. With this view in mind, incentives for inducing participation in continuing professional education are explored, along with alternative sources of revenue to support implementation of these suggested incentive systems.

Participation Incentives

In support of this national policy directive, several approaches to designing incentives to participate in continuing professional education are offered. It is emphasized that these policy ideas, for the most part, preserve the concept of freedom of choice for individual professionals, while also fostering a diversity of options. It is also realized that policy formulation and implementation are guided by political and social factors. So, the ideas that follow would have to be translated into feasible and realizable policies derived from political and legislative action.

Capitation to professional schools. Continuing professional education is undertaken to some degree by most professional schools in the country. The extent of any given professional school's involvement in this area of service is dependent upon the inclinations of faculty, the philosophy and leadership of the administration, and various other policies, including the professional school's position on compensation of faculty for being involved in continuing professional education activities and the school's position concerning the relationship of service to promotion and tenure.

In view of the dramatic variance which exists among the professional schools, both with and among professions, it is recommended that a federal capitation grant system be implemented, depending on a national human resource need, whereby a professional school would receive a federal grant in accord with its involvement in and success in providing continuing professional education activities to its attendant professional community. This system would not only assist professionals, but also give some needed clout to a continuing professional education focus in professional schools.

Tax incentives for individuals. Another approach would be to recognize a professional's involvement in continuing professional education through a policy of preferential federal income tax treatment. Under this suggestion, professionals in targeted groups would be awarded a special tax-reducing incentive whereby they would receive tax credits for participating in a prespecified minimum amount of continuing professional education. This method would provide an indirect monetary incentive and create a positive incentive for participation within a voluntary system.

This approach would also carry a potential for a "snowball" effect. Once offered to a single profession or small group of professions, it might be expected that other professional groups would lobby in favor of a similar tax benefit to members of other professions. Such requests could be reviewed according to criteria related to the perceived need or urgency for continuing education participation in select professions.

Tax incentives for corporations. Similar to the approach to provide tax incentives for individuals, tax preferential treatment incentives could be offered to corporations which employ significant numbers of professionals and have experienced a significant downturn in the ability to complete, particularly with foreign competitors. Examples in recent years include professionals in the automotive, aerospace, and heavy equipment industries. These corporations could be offered tax incentives for providing in-service continuing professional education opportunities for professional employees. In this manner, opportunities for participation could be fostered in settings which are convenient for professional employees and which would be likely to take into consideration topics which were directly germane to professional performance in the work setting and the long-term interests of the company.

Federal reimbursement premiums. Closely related to the previous suggestion, a policy of offering a premium payment on federal reimbursement programs could be instituted. For example, medicare reimbursement payments might be higher for institutions with established and accredited continuing professional education programs for employees. The success of programs which provide payment to farmers for not planting crops might be enhanced if those farmers participated in Cooperative Extension Service programs designed to improve farming skills and practices.

Malpractice insurance premium rebates. A federal policy of preferential corporate earnings tax treatment might be developed for companies offering premium reductions for professional malpractice insurance for professionals who participate in a prespecified amount of continuing professional education.

Preferred loan opportunities. A government program could be established to give preferential loan rates to professionals who demonstrate that they have participated in a prespecified amount of continuing professional education activities each year. In this approach, the federal government might work directly with banks and other financial institutions which offer preferred loan rate programs. Preferential loan rates might be awarded based on the expectation that professionals who regularly keep up with their professions represent stronger human resources and therefore better investments. This approach might be viewed as a subtle way to increase participation without mandating it.

Federally mandated continuing professional education. A federal law could be enacted whereby whenever a two-thirds majority of the states mandate continuing professional education participation for a given profession, the minimum number of hours required by those several states shall become a federal requirement for all practitioners in that profession. It is anticipated that the social benefit from national policy can be attained by mandating a minimum level of participation of a specific kind for all. Beyond this level, it is assumed that the benefits would be mostly, or exclusively, private.

National standards for continuing professional education. Most of the previous recommendations are predicated on the assumption that the continuing professional education activities are of value. However, as alluded to earlier in this chapter, it would be a mistake to assume that everything which is labeled as being an educational activity in fact is one. For this reason, it is further recommended that a set of national educational standards be established and that all of the previous policy recommendations be restricted to participation in educational programs which are nationally recognized. Such an approach has precedent in the U.S. Department of Education's program of recognizing national accreditation agencies for determining eligibility for federal educational loan and grant programs.

The above examples are presented to show a variety of approaches that might be developed and implemented. It would be preferred to develop several approaches and to implement them on a trial basis. Upon their evaluation, those that yield desirable outcomes would be kept; the others would be discarded. To be sure, approaches that are developed must address a national interest and must be complementary to policies developed at other levels of human resource development.

Revenue Alternatives

As recognized earlier in this chapter, the costs associated with continuing professional education program development and delivery can become extensive. These costs, in addition to the costs implied by the several policy suggestions offered above, strongly suggest a need to explore alternative sources of revenue in support of a national professional human resource policy. Among suggestions for alternatives to program registration fees as a source of revenue are the following.

Professional service tax. It is suggested that a federal tax on professional services be implemented. Whether this tax would be a sales tax administered on selected services by states or whether it would be an income tax applied, for example, to corporations providing services, is a matter that would have to be investigated. Clearly, looking to the service sector as a revenue source is attractive because approximately 85% of all new jobs are in this sector. In addition to its growth, economists suggest that services also act as a buffer in a recession, because consumers who delay buying goods during a downturn in the economy often continue to purchase services. Because such a procedure would yield substantial revenues, only an indexed proportion of this tax would be allocated for investment in and development of professional human resources.

Employee benefits tax. Since most employee benefits are not taxable, a source for additional revenue would be a tax on the employee benefits of workers. Generally, industries with high wages have accrued high benefit levels. According to a recent U.S. Chamber of Commerce survey (1986), the average benefit paid to employees in 1986 was $10,283. This average was for all industries; the range was from $4,743 in the textile and apparel industries to $13,402 in the primary metals industries.

Because high salary or wage earners prefer additional benefit compensation to even higher--but taxable--wages, and lower-paid employees typically prefer cash income to additional benefit compensation, a benefit tax to support professional human resource development should be explored. Taxing benefits of employees above a prescribed income level would have the added effect of targeting high-salaried employees, many of whom are professionals. This would in effect tax professionals to pay for their own professional development.

Incidentally, the same U.S. Chamber of Commerce survey (1986) reports that among all categories of employee benefits, education benefits amounts to an average of only $41 per employee annually. The only category of benefit on which less money is spent is company-furnished meals.

In this and the preceding major section, I have offered some suggestions for providing incentives for participation and means for their support. Obviously, I have not explored all the possibilities, nor have I critically examined their feasibility. This is a task for experts in the policy arena. I take responsibility only for raising the issues and offering some exploratory suggestions. Nevertheless, by investing in the continuing development of professionals through whatever means, the government can and should expect a return on its investment.

Concluding Comment

It should be recognized that much of what is advocated in this paper represents a subtle extension of the traditional continuing education literature on participation. Building on the general concept of participation as a purposive activity (Grotelueschen, 1985), the concept of providing an incentive system is, as a fundamental base, an effort at the national level to increase participation. Participation in continuing professional education is viewed as having a significant value to practicing professionals; and since it has grown from a grass roots movement from within the several states, it is perhaps timely to begin to consider participation from the national policy level.

The thesis and supporting ideas presented in this paper are offered for consideration. While it is recognized that the concept of a national policy in the area of professional human resource development is probably not imminent, I do feel that the quality of professional service is a fundamental component of our everyday quality of life and that a coordinated national effort to foster its development would make an important and enduring contribution to the nation.

References

Briggs, V. M., Jr. (1987). Human resource development and the formulation of national economic policy. *Journal of Economic Issues, 21*(3), 1207-1240.

Carnevale, A. (1983). *Human capital: A high yield corporate asset.* Washington: American Society for Training Directors.

Denison, E. F. (1985). *Trends in American economic growth,* 1929-1982. Washington: The Brookings Institution.

Grotelueschen, A. D. (1985). Assessing professionals' reasons for participating in continuing education. In R. M. Cervero and C.L. Scanlan (Eds.), *Problems and prospects in continuing professional education* (pp. 33- 45). San Francisco: Jossey-Bass.

Grotelueschen Associates, Inc. (1988). *Participation in continuing accountancy education and the accountancy knowledge of public-practice accountants in New York State.* (Report No. 2). An Interim Report to the Mandatory Continuing Education Study Committee, State Board for Public Accountancy, New York State Education Department.

Nona, D. A., Kenny, W. R., & Johnson, D. K. (1988). The effectiveness of continuing education as reflected in the literature of the health professions. *American Journal of Pharmaceutical Education, 52, 111-117.*

U.S. Chamber of Commerce (1987). *Employee Benefits, 1986.* Washington, DC: U.S. Chamber of Commerce Publications Fulfillment.

Chapter 5

Education in the Workplace: An Integral Part of the Development of Professionals

Robert A. Hofstader
Paul David Munger

The essence of the problem is that the human resources that are being invested in making new knowledge readily accessible are disproportionately small compared to those invested in generating it. The net result is that new knowledge is not being absorbed into the culture as rapidly as it is being generated, and some of the value of that knowledge is lost by its not being readily accessible to the people who need it. (Bruce, Siebert, Smullin, & Fano, 1982, p. 9)

The Transformation of the Workplace

The American workplace is being transformed by two major trends. One is the proliferation of corporations, large and small. The other is the rapid expansion of technology and knowledge. Each trend fuels advances in the other, and these trends increasingly force us to take an interdisciplinary approach to work. More and more workers will find themselves knowledgeable and sophisticated members of work teams. The tight and thorough specialization made possible by these trends must be balanced by a broad awareness of other team members' skills and specialities and their applicability to the job at hand. Additionally, the growing trend for professionals in all fields to work in corporations, rather than in smaller partnerships or as independent practitioners, may give broader appeal to our subject now than a few years past.

Educating the work force has become increasingly important for American corporations. Knowledge of technology, markets, and administration has always been essential to business success. Today's corporate leadership is probably more concerned with its ability to respond to change--and thus is more concerned with maintaining a highly skilled and informed work force--than at any previous time in history.

It has been estimated that 90% of all scientific knowledge has been generated during the past 30 years. "This knowledge pool will double by the end of the century, making any set of skills and products obsolete in five to ten years" (Learning Technology Institute, 1985, p. 5). The constantly accelerating pace of change in technology and the corresponding growth of knowledge are, of course, quite evident to most business leaders. For corporations, remaining competitive requires investing in the career-long learning of their employees.

A Lifelong Commitment

To respond to this challenge, we must develop a lifelong commitment to formal and informal education on the part of professional and technical employees. They must actively participate in the learning process within their corporations, not only as students, but also as teachers. Because work, teaching, and study support each other, corporations must actively encourage their intermixing to insure the continuing development and maintenance of creative and effective workforces. Every worksite must include learning facilities for "updating, broadening, and deepening the knowledge and intellectual skills" of employees (Bruce et al., 1982, pp. 32-33). Education must become "an organic part of work" (Bruce et al., p. 60). The technical knowledge of employees must be compared to and assessed against their constantly changing duties and the training they already have received (Learning Technology Institute, 1985, p. 12).

Anthony Carnevale, chief economist for the American Society for Training and Development, points out that due to the growth of computer-assisted technologies, "Constant, job-specific retraining will be required to supply the engineers necessary for ever-changing production requirements. These incremental and less sensational formal and informal employee job training requirements are closely connected to the nation's economic adaptability" (Carnevale & Goldstein, undated, p. 9).

As economic and technological change accelerates, on-the-job training and retraining requirements grow at a similar rate. As the nations of the world become more competitive with each other, the importance of the adaptability of each nation's human economic resources becomes greater.

The quality of human resources will determine each country's competitive positioning. As technology penetrates not only the high-tech production field but also consumer and leisure products and services, Americans will need to become more technologically literate. "And so while we won't need more engineers, we will need to know more about engineering" (Carnevale & Goldstein, undated, p. 10).

To maintain a workforce that can compete worldwide, we must make the opportunity for lifelong learning available and convenient to the workforce, and companies must continuously reskill themselves and their employees (Learning Technology Institute, 1985, p. 6). Most high technology businesses today recognize that education and training are essential to keeping workers and management up-to-date.

Factors other than technology and its changes also are having significant impact. For example, as labor markets tighten, companies view training as the only way to get some of the skilled people they need. This is particularly true of scientific, technical, and highly skilled occupations (Olson, 1986, p. 35).

Another important factor has been the adoption of "new strategies and goals--responses to heightened global competition, deregulation, and other changes in the business environment" (Lusterman, 1985, p. 1). Training is one way to insure that such responses are known and practiced by the corporate employees.

Corporations also use training to respond to deficiencies in the work force. In particular, poor language and math skills among many young people coming into the workforce continue to concern many corporate employers (Lusterman, p. 23).

Recently, some corporations have begun to use education to help their workers adjust to the most severe change of all. More than 60 of the *Fortune 500* companies participate in programs "to retrain displaced workers--that is, employees whose jobs have been eliminated" (Lusterman, 1985, p. 23).

A Definition of "Corporate Continuing Education"

Before we go further, a definition of what we mean by "corporate continuing education" is in order. In this paper, we use the term to include all "structured activities organized by the corporation or its vendors to facilitate learning." We specifically exclude college-level degree course work. Such courses, we believe, are the base upon which corporate continuing education builds. In our terminology, corporate continuing education also is not "on-the-job" training, or informal mentoring, or that education which an individual, through her or his own initiative, achieves by independent study and reading.

We will focus on companies significantly involved with technology. We trust that there may be implications for other types of companies and organizations as well.

Economic Incentives for Corporate Continuing Education

Increasingly, corporations are able to point to specific returns on their investment in continuing education as justification for further expenditures. General Electric compared the costs of two approaches: hiring new employees and the technical renewal of current employees. Training 20 employees in digital circuit analysis and design in 1977 cost GE $76,000 in salaries, instructor fees, and course development. To have laid off these 20 people and hired replacements would have cost about $200,000. This is persuasive evidence of the cost-effectiveness of continuing education (Zukowski, 1983, p. 40). Moreover, while an examination of department sales at GE showed an increase of 41.3%, it was necessary to increase the engineering staff by only 23.7%. Although the increased productivity was not due entirely to the training program, there is indication of efficient use of engineering personnel, "and this is possible only because we now have the properly trained people for all of our engineering tasks" (Zukowski, p. 40).

Godkewitsch (1987) has suggested a formula for calculating the effect of training (an educational "intervention") when complete information regarding the training is available:

F = N[(E x M) - C], where
F = financial utility; N = number of people affected; E = effect of the intervention; M = monetary value of the effect; C = cost of the intervention per person. (p. 79)

However, calculating the return on investment in continuing education is difficult because obtaining precise measurement of effects and results is very problematic and because so many other variables affect the results of training (Hoover, undated)[1].

Taking another tack, Hoover acknowledges this problem, exercises common sense, assumes that education will increase productivity by at least a small margin, and then determines how much a company could afford to pay to achieve that increase:

For a typical high-tech firm, operating with the parameters given, we find that a firm could afford to invest much more than the canonical 2-4 percent to get a 10 percent productivity increase. Anecdotal experience that says that return on education can be very high, suggests that firms may find it advantageous to invest more than 2-4 percent. In an ideal situation, a firm would initiate or increase its education, track the effect and optimize its investment in education along with its other investments. (p. 2)

The Status of U. S. Corporate Continuing Education Today

All the major indicators--rates of employee participation in training, numbers of staff employed, involvement of non-professionals in training, use of outside resources--point to large scale growth in corporate training during the past five years (Lusterman, 1985, p. 6).

Corporate Training

Training has grown from 7 million to 10 million employees being trained yearly in 1977 to over 40 million as of 1984. One in eight Americans participates in a formal employer-sponsored training course each year. Employers spend $30 billion yearly on formal courses; they spend $180 billion on informal coaching and supervision (Craig & Evers, 1981, p. 112)[2]. This figure does not include trainees' salaries, expenses outside of formal training department budgets, or informal, on-the-job training (Geber, 1987, p. 39)[3]. In addition, employers provide at least 17.6 million formal courses each year (Carnevale, 1986, p. 20).

Nonetheless, executives generally recognize that formal instruction accounts for only a small portion of learning--"many place it at 10 or 20 percent"--and that on-the-job experience accounts for the remainder (Lusterman, 1985, p. 15). However, organized education is recognized as one of the significant ways an organization can respond to its environment. It is a part of the organizational and employee development process, which increasingly is viewed as key in developing a competitive edge in the marketplace.

The education and training efforts of major American corporations generally average 2 to 5 percent of their total income. High-tech companies and companies undergoing significant internal change tend to the higher side, while others at steadier states tend to the lower.

Carnevale's research (1986) has revealed some interesting parameters of corporate training:

Most training occurs in services (29% of all trainees); manufacturing (21.5%), especially durable goods (15.7%); public administration (13.2%); and finance, insurance, and real estate (11.6%).

Training is most intensive (the greatest percentage of employees receive training) in federal government, public administration in general, communications, state government, local government, mining, insurance and real estate, and public utilities (other than transportation and communications).

Most money is spent on training in services ($8.7 billion); manufacturing ($6.5 billion); durable goods ($4.7 billion); public administration ($3.9 billion); finance, insurance, and real estate ($3.5 billion); trade ($2.9 billion); and transportation and public utilities ($2.6 billion).

Most money is spent on the average employee in federal government ($897/employee); public administration ($645); communications ($603); state government ($591); mining ($566); local government ($566); public utilities (other than transportation and communications) ($549); finance, insurance, and real estate ($529); professional services (other than education) ($490); instruments manufacture ($484); and machinery manufacture ($430). (p. 20)

Within *Fortune 500* companies, more employees in all major job categories are now involved in formal training than were five years ago. The rise in participation has been highest for managers and supervisors, as well as for professionals and sales and marketing personnel. More than half of these top tier corporations have increased the size of their training staffs.

Large companies tend to spend heavily on training, in part because their expertise has risen to the point where they cannot easily find qualified workers trained elsewhere. High-tech companies devote much effort to training because it is the only way they can obtain skilled work in time to develop new products and services. Companies in service or service-intensive industries often train their workers thoroughly to insure that customers are treated well and that "their automated service and customer interaction systems work as planned" (Olson, 1986, p. 33).

Many large firms require that every manager spend at least 40 hours per year on some form of learning activity. A 1985 study of Fellows of the Academy of Management forecast that the average manager in the year 2000 will spend 82 hours per year on educational activities.

Most formal training in the workplace concentrates on the 25 to 44-year-old age group and on white collar managers, professionals, and clericals. Better educated workers receive proportionately more training than less educated workers: "Workers with four or more years of college were 18 percent of the labor force, but 35 percent of the trainees" (Carnevale, 1986, p. 20). The higher the skill level, the more education a worker is likely to receive. White-collar workers are only half of the work force, but they receive 75 percent of the training (Carnevale & Goldstein, undated, p. 35).

Within the *Fortune 500* companies, training departments use more than 55 percent of their budgets to develop executives, middle managers, and supervisors. Eighteen and one-half percent is devoted to technical training (Stephan, Mills, Pace, & Ralphs, 1988, p. 30).

Corporate training activities appear to focus on particular types of people as well. As Lusterman (1985) states:

> Female participation in training and development activities is reported to have increased considerably more than male participation--nonwhite much more than white. These differences, respondents say, are basically a reflection of greater representation of women and minorities in the employee population. (p. 22)

While there is almost no type of course which business does not offer to its employees, the largest single subject area is "business," which accounts for 40 percent of all courses. Engineering and related technical training is the second largest category, with 19 percent of all courses. Computers, data processing, and mechanical engineering are the largest categories in this group (Carnevale, 1986, p. 20).

In general, at least within the *Fortune 500* companies, training expenditures (Geber, 1987, p. 40) may be described as falling into the following categories and percentages:

	Percent
Training staff salaries	71
Facilities/overhead	7
Seminars/conferences	7
Hardware	5
Outside services	4
Custom materials	3
Off-the-shelf materials	3

Training departments are being asked to perform many duties. They have responsibility for providing traditional training and development; administering the training function; handling recruitment, development, and succession of potential managers; providing executive and management development; providing supervisory training; and supporting the business strategy with all forms of training and development activities. In addition, some training units appear to have special or more limited assignments to evaluate, consult, design, and develop curricula, or provide only sales training (Stephan et al., 1988, p. 31).

Providers of Corporate Education

By any measure, "employee training by employers is by far the largest delivery system [in the United States] for adult education" (Carnevale & Goldstein, undated, p. 36). More than half of all the courses (57 percent) are given in-house; over 64 percent of all engineering and related courses are given in-house (Carnevale & Goldstein, pp. 60-61).

Nonetheless, the reliance of corporations on outside assistance in providing education and training has given rise to a healthy service industry. The manufacturing industry is a big user of outside training, especially for technically-based activities related to machinery, chemicals, and electrical equipment.

There are more than 4,000 for-profit providers of education and training. Total training revenues for companies providing training to other corporations grew from $821 million in 1977 to over $2 billion in 1984; 1990 training company revenues are forecast to increase 2.25 times to $4.6 billion. More than half of all training provided by training companies is "off-the-shelf" standardized training programs; one quarter is custom designed; one quarter consists of seminars. Most training is provided (in descending order of predominance) in management/organizational development, supervisory skills, data processing, trade skills, sales/marketing/customer service, and interpersonal communications.

While there are no dominant firms--no IBMs--in this field yet, there is beginning to be a shakedown in the market. Forty suppliers received 43 percent of total contract training revenues; these companies averaged annual revenues of $22,000,000. Suppliers with more than $5,000,000 in annual revenues are the fastest growing segment of the training industry. They dominate the market in off-the-shelf programs and generic seminars. On the other hand, suppliers with under $1 million in annual revenues dominate custom-design work.

Corporate Education Outside the United States

A brief description of corporate continuing education efforts outside the United States is in order to offer a perspective on how other countries view and respond to the need for continuing education in the workplace.

European Corporate Education

In European business, government, and academic circles, there is an increased interest in continuing education. Not surprisingly, the primary motivation is the need to stay technologically competitive with the rest of the world. Two continuing education programs sponsored in the European community are: COMETT (Community in Education and Training for Technology), which funds joint industry-university programs; and DELTA (Development of European Learning through Technological Advance), which is a telecommunication network (Arnett & Tyson, 1986, p. 78).

In another European effort, PACE (the Program of Advanced and Continuing Education), businesses are working with academic institutions to develop advanced professional continuing education which will be delivered via satellite telecasts. Most of the instructors will be academics; however, top specialists in industry also may be invited to prepare courses. Principal "students" will be engineers, scientists, managers of firms seeking advanced training, and members of the academic community. The primary benefits of PACE to industry are expected to be direct access to top quality advanced training programs and the availability of these programs on firms' premises (Bieber, 1987, pp. 241-243).

In some European countries, continuing education receives important national attention. Both France and West Germany tax employers to finance nationwide continuing education (Bruce et al., 1982, p. 34). A West German law, modeled after the U.S. G.I. Bill, specifically encourages workers in professions which are becoming obsolete to enroll in programs which retrain them for developing industries. For example, public expenditures in the Federal Republic of Germany for training and education amounted to a total of DM 58 billion in 1976. Of this amount, DM 1.4 billion went to continuing education. Expenditure by the private sector of the economy for training and education is estimated at DM 10 to 15 billion for the same period. Continuing education is likely to account for half of this estimate (Golling, 1979, p. 148).

Within some industries in Europe, partnerships among professional organizations provide specialized and well-focused continuing education. Two leading examples are IRFIP in France and INSKO in Finland. Each conducts seminars for employees of paper and pulp companies. IRFIP is closely connected with the French Papermaking School and Research Institute in Grenoble, which holds 12 to 16 seminars a year, with about a dozen participants in each, dealing with specific phases of the industry. In 1985 it also conducted 60 in-house seminars for various firms. INSKO provides continuing education through seminars for engineers and architects for 9 or 10 industrial groups, one of which is the Association of Finnish Paper Engineers. In 1984 INSKO gave 72 seminars; 20 percent dealt directly with pulping and papermaking, and the others dealt with closely related fields (chemistry, plastics, printing, and so forth) (Gottsching, 1985).

Unhappy with the theoretical courses currently offered by academic institutions, more international companies are setting up their own business schools ("Multinational Management," 1987). At Siemens AG, a large engineering firm in West Germany, continuing education programs have to be developed for 21,000 engineers and scientists, 7,600 technicians, and also about 8,000 engineers working outside of Germany. The annual cost is DM 1,350 per technical employee. Some 3,000 regular employees of the company double as instructors. Four hundred instructors are engaged full time at company "schools." The instructors for continuing engineering education are selected primarily from experts within the given fields (Golling, 1979, p. 146).

Although the consensus appears to be that Great Britain lags behind the rest of Europe, Japan, and the United States in corporate continuing education (Bayley, 1986, p. 38; Eales, 1981, p. 40; "Report Envisages," 1987, p. 5; Sparrow & Pettigrew, 1987, p. 109; Suarez, 1986, p. 21), many British companies are giving much attention to this area (Arbose, 1987; Bayley, 1986, p. 39; Benson, Helme, & Lenton, 1987; Bruce, 1987; "I'm in Personnel," 1987, p. 59; Kenaghan, 1986; Moorby, 1982; Upton, 1987). The United Kingdom's Engineering Industry Training Board initiated an imaginative Fellowships in Manufacturing Management program. This program gave training in basic manufacturing and management techniques to graduate technologists with no manufacturing experience. They were then given an urgent problem that needed to be solved. The results were so impressive that more than half the Fellows were offered permanent positions with their project companies (Walker, 1984).

Japanese Corporate Education

The major difference between Japanese corporate continuing education and that in the United States is that the Japanese appear to be very proactive in their training. They devote much effort to anticipating changes in the future and preparing the workforce for new challenges, environments, and technologies. Japanese corporate leadership views education as essential to developing a workforce that is prepared to work productively in tomorrow's workplace--a workplace that may be dramatically different, technologically and also sociologically.

Certain other trends stand out as well. For many Japanese companies, including Nissan Motor Company and Japan Synthetic Rubber Company, the education of researchers and the development of future research leaders is an important undertaking. Most Japanese observers seem to agree that "training should be a managerial strategy" (Naito, Yamamoto, & Inoue, 1985) and that educational needs have to be related to a business strategy (Henmi, 1987).

Many Japanese firms, including Seibu Department Stores, Nanking Electric Railway Company, and several banks, are beginning to address their training programs to the special attributes and liabilities of the younger generation of workers. A number are focusing on the particular problem of motivation. The same concern influences a number of training programs addressed to older workers. Other Japanese corporate education programs train workers to handle multiple production processes and technologies and educate workers to perform well within several cultures.

Today's Japanese corporate executives are beginning to agree that the "function of job training specialists is not to give employees guidance in acquiring particular knowledge and skills but rather to foresee what knowledge and skills will be required in the future and to design the most economical and effective training system" (Naito et al., 1985, p. 49).

Strengths of U. S. Corporate Continuing Education

Today's larger high-tech firms--with their essential emphasis on R & D--are centers for the most active and innovative education and training programs, many of them directed toward constant training of their own scientists and engineers (Eurich, 1985, p. 11).

American corporate continuing education exhibits several important strengths:

1.	*Corporate Continuing Education Is Problem-Focused.*

Corporate training emphasizes skills and information that students can apply right away in their jobs (Wilcox, 1987,

p. 52). The client is the corporation (Wilcox, p. 52). Organizations that define training objectives in terms of results get better performance from their employees than those that do not (Bayley, 1986, p.41).

Decisions regarding training are made on the basis of marketplace needs (Eurich, 1985, p. 107). Companies directly control their own training and education programs and can adjust them for changing purposes and content. Corporate training can introduce and accommodate quickly new time frames and schedules (Eurich, p. 50).

2.   *Corporate Continuing Education Is Learner-Centered.*

Corporate education and training assume that all employees can learn to work more effectively. Consequently, if most employees do not master the material at first, it is taught again. Generally there is immediate discussion of performance during training to reinforce correct learning and eliminate misunderstandings (Wilcox, 1987, p. 54).

Since education is directed at effective learning and performance, it is not surprising that corporate continuing education places particular emphasis on the continuing evaluation of faculty and courses (Eurich, 1985, p. 120). Instructors who have first-hand experience and expertise in the subject matter are the most valued, and they are encouraged to put presentation skills ahead of research and academic publishing. Most corporations will train subject matter experts to teach, rather than train teachers in the subject matter (Wilcox, 1987, p. 55).

Teaching in corporations is generally well planned, with stated goals, controls, and measurement of performance. Course development usually adheres to professionally established procedures, starting with an assessment of need for the instruction. Under the best circumstances, instructional designers work closely with operational personnel who know what they want and who help to establish the course objectives. Courses are reviewed by subject matter experts and frequently tested before being offered. This assures that students will be able to meet the objectives of the course (Eurich, 1985, p. 54). The attempt to make learning useful and easy is probably the foremost attribute of all corporate training, no matter the level at which it occurs (Eurich, 1985, p. 121).

3. *Corporations Possess Expertise That Does Not Exist Elsewhere.*

Much of the development of new technology now takes place in industrial labs, rather than on university campuses. This is a relatively recent phenomenon, and our society currently lacks the mechanisms to transmit this new knowledge from industry to academe quickly (Gilda, 1987, p. 9). Consequently, corporations doing the inventive and creative work on the cutting edge of many disciplines can turn only to their own people for instructional resources when it comes time to train other employees.

Every time a new product is created, there must be training for its applied use. High-tech companies which depend on engineering and scientific research for their very survival must do extensive training to continue to exist. Basic scientific and technological training continues to expand as new knowledge is created because such training is essential to maintain a vigorous supply of the creative individuals "who will invent the future" (Eurich, 1985, p. 72).

Upgrading technical personnel is a process that cannot end. Advanced educational offerings must continue to expand if corporations at "the cutting edge" wish to remain profitable (Eurich, 1985, p. 73).

4. *Corporate Continuing Education Is Strong in the Application of Learning Technology.*

In addition to placing great emphasis on instructors' teaching skills (Wilcox, 1987, p. 52), corporate training facilities are often equipped with the latest audiovisual materials and computers. In an attempt to identify the most effective instructional methods and learning modes, "Methods are tried, adjusted and changed, so one finds a much broader range of teaching-learning techniques here than in conventional education" (Eurich, 1985, pp. 52-53). Trainers who are selected for company experience and subject matter expertise are increasingly exposed to teacher training courses and practice teaching sessions.

A number of corporate education centers actively conduct research on the learning process, motivated by concern for effectiveness and efficiency. "New insights into the educational process are coming from corporate classrooms" (Eurich, 1985, p. 55). "The corporate curriculum is making a major contribution to adult learning" (Eurich, 1985, p. 83).

Weaknesses of U. S. Corporate Continuing Education

Although corporations are performing impressive feats, corporate continuing education generally is not well managed. Corporate executives understand the need for education and training, but they do not apply to corporate education efforts the same sophisticated management and evaluation that characterizes most corporate decision-making. Present weaknesses of U. S. corporate continuing education include the following problems:

1.   *While Top Management Seems to Understand That Education is Important, There Are a Large Number of Companies That Do Not Support Training and Education to the Extent Necessary.*

Too often corporations allocate the "required 2-4 percent" but never strongly express a conviction that education helps achieve corporate goals. Managers and supervisors frequently let short-term goals deter employees from participating in training activities which are necessary to long-term growth. Too often, all initiative for attendance rests with individual employees. Rarely is there an evaluation of the impact of corporate training programs on the corporation's goals (Zukowsky, 1983, p. 39).

Given the lack of attention to training at the central decision-making level, training tends to be overlooked as a vital ingredient in corporate success. Consequently, it occasionally is underfunded, but more importantly, it is often under-utilized.

Among the prerequisites for good training is one essential: Training must be linked to operational performance.

Training staff need to understand what the business plans of the corporation are and how training will help accomplish corporate goals. Training must be accepted throughout the organization as a key management responsibility in support of operational objectives. Line managers must be responsible for making sure all their employees are fully trained (Bayley, 1986, p. 40).

2. *There Is Little or No Anticipation of Future Education Needs.*

Training is generally an *ad hoc* and reactive function of American corporations (Olson, 1986, p. 33). It is used to fix what is broken or to prevent immediate difficulties; rarely is it used to prepare for the long-range future.

With the great pressure on managers for productivity, they judge training in part by how quickly workers can learn a skill and get back to work (Lusterman, 1985, p. 11). Because of these concerns, training in the United States (especially when contrasted with that in Japan and Germany) has short-term goals and expects immediate outcomes.

Executives speak of human resources as their most valuable asset, yet omit the long-range renewal of those resources from high-level discussions of planning and implementation (Learning Technology Institute, 1985, p. 13). Even at IBM, often considered one of the world's best managed corporations, training and education were only recently included in the annual planning and commitment process for the achievement of corporate goals (Bowsher, 1987, p. 14).

Consequently, training budgeting tends to be short-sighted and not comprehensive. Department budgets generally are modified in incremental fashion, based on previous years, rather than judged against the corporation's goals and circumstances and the amount of training needed to meet them.

3. *There is Little Concern for Motivating Learning Within the Workplace.*

Devoting effort to formal study and learning is demanding, but it is even harder when the individual is attempting to cope with the pressures of employment and other matters (Bruce et al., 1982, p. 21). This situation could be changed if corporations would look at learning and formal study as normal and desirable parts of productive work, allocating the appropriate time necessary to accomplish these functions. "This practice would be the equivalent of budgeting preventive maintenance and scheduling downtime for equipment" (Bruce et al., 1982, p. 22).

However, many high-tech companies assume that workers or managers will identify their own needs for learning and will be anxious to take courses to improve their skills or level of knowledge. Yet, one study of RCA engineers found that high-achieving engineers were less likely than lower performers to rate continuing education courses as useful (Adams, 1984).

While learning must be the responsibility of each employee who must devote to it the necessary time and effort, industry must recognize and reward the effort required to keep up to date (Bruce et al., 1982, p. 21-22).

4.   *Education and Training Are Not Always Well-Connected to the Bottom Line: Productivity.*

A number of studies have focused on the issue of the return on training investment. The results are not encouraging. Most corporate education and training productivity studies are performed by the training departments themselves and appear to be designed primarily to promote the idea of training to management. They are not aimed at assessing the value of the experience (Olson, 1986, p. 33). Evaluation of the return on training investments does not take place either regularly or frequently (Stephan et al., 1988, p. 30).

However, in the final analysis, continuing education programs must face the same tests as every other corporately supported program: They must contribute to the "bottom line" (Janney, 1984, p. 302). Corporate leadership needs to learn to measure the success of corporate continuing education by its contribution to corporate goals.

5. *Training Is Not Fully Utilized as a Tool in Achieving Corporate Strategy.*

    Corporate leadership has not yet developed an understanding of the distinctions among the providers of education and training, the assessment of training needs, the implementation of training policy, and the use of education to achieve corporate goals. Little attention is paid, in particular, to the employment of education to create a workforce that is motivated, informed, and skilled enough to insure competitive production and service. Too often, training is viewed simply as the transmission of skills needed to complete today's tasks. Rarely are employees educated as to the challenges facing the corporation and encouraged to learn more in order to help create the corporation's future.

6. *United States Corporations Are Less Proactive in Their Approach to Training Than Are Some Corporations in Other Countries.*

    America has traditionally invested more in the maintenance of human capital than have its European counterparts. Some evidence does suggest, however, that resource investments are relatively greater in the Soviet Bloc, Japan, and other parts of Asia, especially in technical education and employee training (Carnevale & Goldstein, undated, p. 23).

A Direction for the Future

At least as early as the late nineteenth and early twentieth centuries, changing technology "required *reeducation* of workers that would keep the labor force as finely tuned and up-to-date as the machinery" (Eurich, 1985, p. 34). But the limits of the educational system and the expense of the machinery meant that "only individual industries could offer--or afford--this type of situation-specific instruction" (Eurich, 1985, p. 34).

The situation today is very similar. Especially in the high technology areas, only major corporations have the equipment and the expertise to train their knowledge workers effectively. Research and development, manufacturing, and service firms must continuously introduce new technology, tools, and techniques to increase productivity and competitiveness and to maintain or increase market share (and sometimes just to keep market share from declining more than it otherwise would). Employees must learn these new technologies, tools, and techniques to remain productive.

Finally, it is clear to many that tomorrow's employees will be knowledge workers employed by companies whose main business is focused on processing information and providing services. These people will have greater responsibility and greater latitude to make decisions. They also will require more support, especially training and education. Consequently, "company budgets will be extended to offer these employees continuous reeducation to ensure high performance" (Harris & Harris, 1982, pp. 14-15).

The intense competitive pressures of the workplace and the pace of technological advances lead to shorter development cycles with increased demands on engineers' time and energy. Education and training must therefore be specific, efficient, and economical.

Employers recognize the need to provide education and training to equip their employees to use these new technologies, tools, and techniques but often would prefer not to develop and deliver the education themselves. Moreover, small firms cannot afford the new means that increase efficiency in development and delivery of education and training. The most effective education and training utilize state-of-the-art laboratory and computing facilities. These facilities are so expensive that the only practical way to provide such facilities is within the host companies.

Indeed, the largest companies spend more proportionally on training than the smaller and seem to be spending at an increasing rate. Smaller companies seem to be spending on training at a decreasing rate (Geber, 1987, pp. 43-45). Smaller companies, if they can afford training at all, can offer few options. They are more likely to make cooperative arrangements with outside institutions and vendors when necessary and possible. Yet, while there are increasing numbers of small firms engaged in high-tech and related fields (Eurich, 1985, p. 51), existing vendors of education and training tend to serve niche markets and have little motivation to customize their offerings to meet the individual needs of specific corporations.

The amount of dollars and time spent on corporate education may well be sufficient. (Indeed, it seems likely that some corporations may be spending more on education than is required.). Unfortunately, what is spent is often not spent wisely.

Many corporate leaders are concerned with the high costs of internal training staffs and facilities. They are interested in "reducing or containing education and training costs even as they seek more from that function" (Lusterman, 1985, p. 8).

Increasingly, companies are using line managers and other non-training specialists to conduct training. Simultaneously, there is greater use of outside consultants and instructors for designing and conducting training programs. Increasing use is being made of programs run by universities and training organizations (Lusterman, 1985, pp. 8-9).

While there are several factors which serve to increase in-house training (including competitive pressures to link the training and development function to specific needs and strategic directions), cost pressures are likely to encourage corporations to look for external and less expensive sources of training for employees (Carnevale, 1986, p. 23).

These companies would benefit from collaborative course development. In areas such as the semi-conductor industry and space exploration, corporations are cooperating on research. Industry-wide involvement in and cooperation on curricular concerns could eliminate costly duplication of effort (DeSio, 1987, p. 12).

Strategies for Effectiveness

Today's world requires corporations to use education more wisely to concentrate on education as a strategic means of accomplishing their goals. How, then, do we build the strategies appropriate to our needs for more effective continuing corporate education?

Education: One Tool for the Corporate Mission

Management must view education as a tool for implementing the corporate mission and meeting its business objectives. Figure 1 of this chapter depicts how education, like technology, finance, systems, people, communication, environment, and development, is one of the major areas requiring balance to achieve organizational goals.

Education and training must be linked strategically and proactively to the organization's activities.

Management of the Education Process

Management determines the mission, goals, directions, issues, and priorities of the organization. Management also is responsible for determining the employee and organization development plans and policies which are part of the ways in which the organization intends to accomplish its mission, meet its goals, establish its directions, resolve its issues, and live within its priorities. In turn, the planning and implementation of training are part of these corporate plans and policies.

The group providing education to the corporation must respond effectively to these directions. It should identify areas and circumstances in which training can have an impact on the mission, goals, directions, and issues of the corporation. It then is responsible for the process by which the organization's needs for education and training are identified. It obtains or develops the programs to meet these needs and delivers them

Figure 1: Education: One Tool in Achieving the Corporate Mission

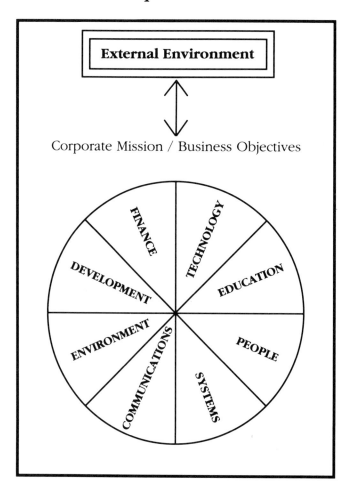

to the appropriate people in the organization. With management, it evaluates the impact of these programs in meeting the organization's needs and in contributing to productivity and profitability. The corporate education group should be able to identify and manage the corporation's "knowledge resources"--who knows what and how to "weed through" all the relevant information that is available.

The Training Development Process

We can describe the management of corporate continuing education as a series of steps. Figure 2 of this chapter illustrates how corporations can effectively link training to the development of the organization through the development of its people.

Step One: Management Determines Strategy, Goals
In the first step of the process, corporate management determines the strategy and goals for the organization.

Step Two: Knowledge, Skills Indentified
In the second step, management and employees working together determine the knowledge and skills needed to implement corporate strategy and achieve corporate goals. Many within and outside the corporation play a part in this needs analysis. This very key element is the major difference between those programs developed by academe and those developed by or for industry.

Step Three: Sources Identified and Programs Developed
Thirdly, the corporate education group inventories knowledge sources and encourages the development of programs to transmit knowledge and develop skills among appropriate people. This step requires monitoring, evaluating, and managing sources of knowledge that are relevant to the corporation's goals, personnel, and situation. It includes designing courses, workshops, and programs which will most effectively and efficiently meet those needs. While the education unit may possess unique expertise for developing and conducting educational programs in some areas, more often it will assist others in developing and presenting those offerings.

Step Four: Training, Education Implemented
Implementing training and education into employee career and organizational development processes is the responsibility of supervisors as part of the corporate development activity.

Step Five: Impact Determined
The impact of education and training on corporate strategy and goals must be determined. The corporate education group may need to manage this process. In any event, it certainly must be involved in monitoring the effectiveness of education and training activities and their contribution to productivity. Corporate management, of course, will

Figure 2: Effective Leading of Education to Organizational Development

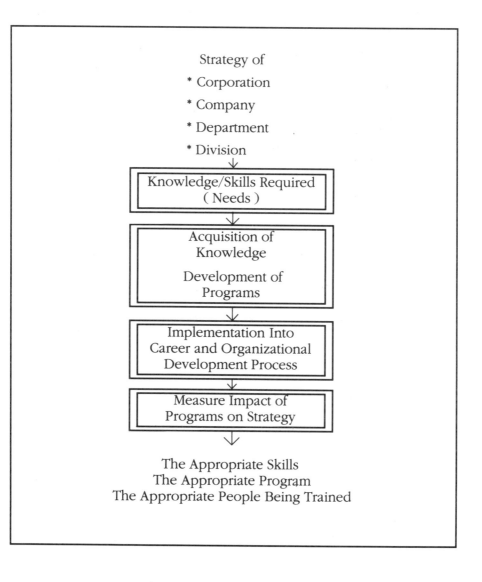

make the final determination of whether the return on investment in education and training is optimal.

Step Six: Programs Developed, Revised, Eliminated
Educational programs are developed, revised, or eliminated based on the evaluation of their effectiveness in meeting corporate goals and on changing corporate goals and strategy. Here the process starts over, but not from scratch. Each new education effort should be enhanced by the knowledge gained from previous efforts.

Building the Future

The continuing development of corporate education is extraordinarily significant for professionals' continued learning. As Eurich (1985) writes, while "corporate classrooms may offer training to some eight million adults, that is still less than one-tenth of the total work force" (p. 133). Workers in the remaining work force need training and do not have ready access to it. Even with all the institutions, educational corporations, and other providers, continuing education for workers remains spotty and uncoordinated. Thus it is ineffective in meeting our total national needs. In particular, the individual efforts of these providers are targeted at generating income by responding to immediate demands. They do not anticipate future developments and jobs.

A relatively few companies offer extensive programs. "Most engineers, however, are left to fend for themselves" (Bruce et al., 1982, pp. 26-27). Since education unquestionably provides competitive advantages, one of our concerns must be the availability of such education to all professionals, whether they are self-employed or employed in small companies.

Although our society is continually building great incentives for a system for continuing education, we still lack an effective system for making education available to working adults. Such a system must be continuous, effective, and accessible. Although economic and other incentives for such change are great, the inertia of our traditional educational organizations and corporations is perhaps greater. Such a situation does not bode well for either America's corporations or the country itself.

Alternatives To Be Addressed

Under these circumstances, we must address the following three alternatives.

1. *The Development of New Relationships Between Business and Universities*

Now is the opportunity for new partnerships. Perhaps these could be modeled after the research relationships that have been developed among universities and corporations which have resulted in the development of research institutes such as Stanford's SRI.

The establishment of centers for corporate/university instructional interaction would afford faculty more opportunity to work with their counterparts in industry. Collaboration on curriculum and course development should be encouraged. Faculty teaching in industry should have their efforts acknowledged as at least equivalent to on-campus teaching for purposes of promotion and tenure determination. Colleges and corporations should share developments in instructional technology to make best use of their resources.

Junior and senior faculty should be encouraged to work in industry, either to do research, serve as consultants, or engage in practical learning experiences. In some fields, such activity may well be the best way to keep faculty up-to-date. Industry, too, should actively encourage engineers and scientists to return regularly to college classrooms, especially as instructors.

Since much of the development of new technology and science now takes place in industrial labs, it is essential that industry develop better ways to communicate its discoveries to the universities. Without such communication, this new knowledge cannot be incorporated into the curriculum (Gildea, 1987, p. 9).

2. *The Development of Totally New Institutions To Meet Our Increasing Needs for Continuing Education*

Universities and engineering schools are ill-equipped and undercapitalized to provide the breadth of training or the facilities needed in most cases. New technology tends to move into university curricula unevenly and with unacceptably long delay. In many cases, universities and engineering schools do not give priority to providing the breadth or specificity needed by industry.

It may be that our universities simply cannot become responsive to corporate objectives without giving up some of the missions to which they are now dedicated. This may be found to be too high a price to pay. Corporations, on the other hand, do not see education as a major line of business and would benefit from outside resources if their needs for both proprietary and generic programs could be met. This finding is supported by MIT's study which concluded, "The depth and projected course of the engineering manpower 'crisis' demand substantially greater investments of human and material resources than at present, as well as the establishment of new cooperative institutions for the development and management of these resources" (Bruce et al., 1982, p. 9).

Professional societies, like universities, are undercapitalized to provide the continuing education needed by corporations and their professional employees. Unlike universities, they have not played a major role in meeting the corporations' needs for continual updating of employees. Rather they have focused on the needs of the professionals themselves. This emphasis is certainly appropriate given the societies' membership bases, but it undoubtedly will limit their ability to respond to the needs of corporations.

Perhaps a new institution unencumbered of the traditions and missions of universities and more broadly focused than professional societies and other vendors could most effectively marshal the resources to meet our pressing national need for continuing education in the workplace. In the past, corporations have provided financial, personnel, and material support for research-directed organizations which have focused university expertise on corporate needs. Institutions, such as the Stanford Research Institute and Battelle, have grown from these efforts and have made important contributions to corporations. A similar effort which would focus the expertise of continuing education in universities and elsewhere directly on the strategic educational requirements of industry could help to overcome the inertia and diversity of mission which prevent existing institutions from addressing corporate continuing education needs in a comprehensive fashion.

3.   *Continuation of Corporate Continuing Education Efforts*

Some United States corporations are doing an effective job of providing for their own continuing education needs. They already provide as much education and training as all of the nation's higher education institutions as a whole. In these cases, we must direct our attention to reducing the duplication of effort among them and developing thorough communication about new knowledge and technology.

The strongest possible future for the United States is one in which education is both continuously available to professionals and constantly keeping them up-to-date. Until we have more experience and more success in this critical endeavor, the best way to assure this future is to encourage development along all three lines.

Endnotes

[1]   Godkewitsch (1987, p. 79) also notes: "You can't get results from training without management reinforcement of the new skills . . . and you can't isolate the effects of the training . . . . Even if you could separate those . . . factors . . . chances are almost nil that the training/support package was the only variable affecting [the result]."

[2]   These estimates are for 1980. This seems to be accepted as the most realistic estimate (see Carnevale and Goldstein, page 35). However, as Carnevale points out, estimates of employees receiving training in 1980 range from 11.1 million to 100 million, and estimates of 1980 training expenditures from $5 billion to $100 billion. Carnevale also indicates that many factors bias reporting of training statistics downward. (Carnevale & Goldstein, undated, pp. 34-36.)

[3]   Geber (1987, p. 39) also confirms Carnevale's estimates: "We estimate that U.S. organizations with 50 or more employees expect to spend $32 billion on training in 1987, an 8.4 percent increase over last year's $29 billion."

References

Adams, J. (1984). Continuing education NY. The gulf between managers and employees. *Proceedings of the 1984 International Congress on Technology Exchange*, 346-347.

Arbose, J. (1987). What's behind the rebirth of Dunlop in Europe? The Japanese. *International Management, 42* (7-8), 65-68.

Arnett, B., & Tyson, L. (1986). Continuing education in Europe: Cooperation on the rise. *Training and Development Journal, 40* (11), 78.

Bayley, J. (1986). Adult training through college/company partnerships. *Personnel Management*, 38-41.

Benson, J., Helme, L., & Lenton, S. (1987). Nabisco's winning strategy. *Personnel Management, 19* (5), 36-39.

Bieber, J. (1987) PACE--A European programme of advanced continuing education. *Computer Networks & ISDN Systems, 13* (3), 241-243.

Bowsher, J. (1987). Quality and accountability: The foundations of collaboration. *In Challenges for Continuing Higher Education Leadership* (p. 14). Washington, DC: National University Continuing Education Association.

Bruce, J. D., Siebert, W. M., Smullin, L. D., & Fano, R. M. (1982). *Lifelong Cooperative Education.* Cambridge, MA: Massachusetts Institute of Technology.

Bruce, L. (1987). British Airways jolts staff with a cultural revolution. *International Management, 42* (3), 36-38.

Carnevale, A. P. (1986). The Learning Enterprise. *Training and Development Journal, 40* (1), 18-26.

Carnevale, A. P., & Goldstein, H. (Undated). *Employee Training: Its Changing Role and An Analysis of New Data.* ASTD Press: Washington, DC. ASTD National Issues Series.

Center for the Utilization of Federal Technology. (1985). 23-24.

Craig, R. L., & Evers, C. (1981). Employers as educators: The shadow education system. In G. Gold (Ed.), *Business and Higher Education: Toward New Alliances*, (pp. 95-146.) San Francisco: Jossey-Bass.

DeSio, R. (1987). The corporation and the campus: Developing new partnerships. *In Challenges for Continuing Higher Education Leadership: Corporate/Campus Collaboration* (p. 10). Washington: National University Continuing Education Association.

Eales, R. (1987). Getting British managers on the right track. *Multinational Business*, p. 40.

Eurich, N. P. (1985). *Corporate classrooms: The learning business.* Princeton: The Carnegie Foundation for the Advancement of Teaching.

Geber, B. (1987). Training budgets still healthy. *Training, 24* (10), 39-45.

Gildea, T. L. (1987). High-tech industries: Staying on the technological forefront through employee reeducation: Implications for academia. *In Challenges for Continuing Higher Education Leadership: Corporate/Campus Collaboration* (p. 9). Washington, D.C.: National University Continuing Education Association.

Godkewitsch, M. (1987). The dollars and sense of corporate training. *Training, 24* (5), 79-81.

Golling, E. (1979). Facts and figures on continuing education for Siemens AG engineers. NY: *Proceedings of the World Conference on Continuing Engineering Education.*

Gottsching, L. (1985). Continuing education and development in Europe outside Germany. *Papier, 39* (10a), 133-139.

Harris, P. R., & Harris, D. L. (1982). Human resources management, part 1: Charting a new course in new organization, a new society. *Personnel, 59* (5), 11-17.

Henmi, Y. (1987). How to grasp education needs. *Sangyo Kunren, 33* (8), 12-16.

Hoover, C. (1988). Unpublished manuscript.

Human factors, technology and productivity. *Proceedings and Summary of the Learning Technology Institute.* Washington, DC: Center for the Utilization of Federal Technology, National Technical Information Service.

I'm in personnel. (1987). *Personnel Management, 19* (3), 59.

Janney, H. L. (1984). Continuing engineering education at AT&T Technologies. Philadelphia, PA: *Proceedings of the 1984 Frontiers in Education Conference,* 302-304.

Kenaghan, F. (1986). Adult learning: Take a tip from Rothmans. *Personnel Management, 18* (10), 58-63.

Moorby, E. (1982). The case for company training programme. *Personnel Management, 14* (11), 28-31.

Multinational management strategies. (1987, autumn). *Multinational Business,* 53-61.

Naito, T., Yamamoto, M., & Inoue, R. (1985). Investigation of training in a changing era. *Sangyo Kunren, 31* (3), 46-52.

Olson, L. (1986). Training trends: The corporate view. *Training and Development Journal, 40* (9), 32-35.

Report envisages "apprenticeship" system for managers as part of new national framework. (1987). *Personnel Management, 19* (5), 5.

Sparrow, P. R., & Pettigrew, A. M. (1987). Britain's training problems: The search for a strategic human resource management approach. *Human Resource Management, 26,* 109.

Stephan, E., Mills, G. E., Pace, R. W., & Ralphs, L. (1988). HRD in the Fortune 500: A survey. *Training and Development Journal, 42* (1), 26-32.

Suarez, G. (1986). Front-end loading to the rescue? *Accountancy, 98,* 21.

Upton, R. (1987). Xerox copies the message on quality. *Personnel Management, 19* (4), 34-37.

Walker, M. (1984). Engineering tomorrow's managers. *Management Today,* 74-77.

Wilcox, J. (1987). A campus tour of corporate colleges. *Training and Development Journal, 41*(5), 52.

Zukowski, R. W. (1983). Managing technical career transitions. *Proceedings of the IEEE Careers Conference*, New York, NY, 38-40.

Chapter 6

The Role of Continuing Professional Education in Addressing Interprofessional Problems

Luvern L. Cunningham
Robert T. McLaughlin

Snyder (1987) has written of the growing need in our society for interprofessional collaboration:

> Cumulative complexity and change have produced conditions and trends that call into question the adequacy of monoprofessional practice in a growing number of cases and for a growing number of patients/clients. Among the more important dimensions of complexity are: pervasive specialization and the challenge it presents to the orchestration of knowledge and skills in behalf of cases whose contours do not fit the boundaries of specialties; the number of causal factors and the many patterns of relationship among them that may be involved in diagnosing particular cases; the ramifications of alternative treatments--how far these extend in what directions and how ascertainable this is; and the fragmented system of policy making that affects health care and human services. (p. 94).

The need for interprofessional collaboration between human service professionals is increasing, in part because problems facing professional practitioners, educators, and decision makers are generally more complicated than ever before. Three historical developments have led to the growing intricacy of problems which human service professionals confront. These developments concern the increased diagnostic and treatment capabilities of professionals, the decreased ability of family and community to meet the individual's needs, and the emergence of ethical dilemmas for which professional standards have not been developed.

Increased Diagnostic and Treatment Capabilities

The intricacy of professional problems has increased partly because of dramatic improvements in professional knowledge, expertise, and technological capabilities. Our scientific understanding of clinical problems has increased exponentially . We now know how to assess and respond to a tremendous range of previously insoluble or intractable problems. Thus, to some extent, ever more complicated clinical problems reflect positively on our heightened professional capabilities.

Improvements in professional capabilities make possible more effective methods for addressing human needs. However, there are also attendant costs, one of the most significant being a steadily growing requirement that practitioners receive continuing professional education. The escalating need for such education throughout one's practice career places further demands on the practitioner's limited time and resources.

Another cost of professional care is the increasing frequency with which practitioners face stressful uncertainty regarding the selection of the most appropriate method in a given clinical situation. Such uncertainty is not insignificant given that practitioners now work in a litigious environment. Faced with the growing threat of liability for negative care outcomes, practitioners are often apt to apply multiple diagnostic and treatment procedures simultaneously to a greater extent than they feel is strictly necessary from a purely technical perspective.

While refinements in professional understanding have enhanced our *perception* of the complicated nature of various human concerns, it is also true that many of these concerns have become objectively more complex, regardless of how well their intricacy is perceived. Perhaps the greatest single reason for the mounting untidiness of problems facing professionals is the growing inability of family and community to meet basic human needs. Human service professionals are being asked to provide an ever broader range of services, as the capacity of family and community to do so diminishes. In other words, the relative failure of family and community support systems is generating more challenging problems for professionals. This development is a direct result of modernization.

Modernization: The Declining Role of Family and Community in Meeting Human Needs

Societal change compounds the uncertainties which human service professionals face. As Snyder (1987) states:

Values may become obsolete and replacements may be slow to emerge. New patterns of conduct lead to strange problems that do not fit neatly into practitioners' preparation. Conflicts of values increase as circumstances become more volatile. Scientific advances add to the repertoire of problem solving but also require new choices for which there are no reliable precedents. (p. 94)

With increasing modernization, our society has undergone change in the patterns of human interdependence. It appears that we are at the threshold of another change, a period of transition, which is characterized by confusion and debate regarding the role and responsibilities of human service professionals. An understanding of the modernization process can help make this transition less jarring and help us see the exciting opportunities which such problematic change offers.

In the traditional society of early colonial times, one relied on the significant others in one's extended family and community. As our society began to modernize, individuals came to depend less upon significant others and increasingly upon those with whom one shared an ethnic or other subcultural affiliation. As social and commercial interaction between communities grew and as individuals and families began to move more frequently from one community to another, there arose a need for new ways of insuring that others would be helpful in times of trouble. When the family and community one left behind could not support the individual in an adopted, new community, individuals began to look for others who shared at least the same cultural, ethnic, and linguistic traditions.

Our society entered a new phase of modernization as the inefficiencies and conflict inherent in ethnic patterns of interdependence became apparent. Those denied access to social resources because of membership in less powerful ethnic groups came to view ethnically based resource allocation as unjust. To reduce the inequities of ethnically based resource allocation, there emerged patterns of organization and interdependence founded on rational rules and policies. This phase constituted an important social revolution. For the first time in our nation's history, neither family, clan, nor even ethnicity or religious faith would provide the primary basis for assuring that one could depend upon others for one's well-being.

As organizations and occupations grew more and more specialized, individuals had to develop new mechanisms for insuring that they could trust one another. The more highly specialized a person's skills and knowledge became, the more arcane such expertise appeared to others and, therefore, the more difficult it became for others to assess the quality of the specialist's services to them. Professions began to become important in American life at this time, largely because they provided assurances that experts were service-oriented and, therefore, trustworthy.

Until recently, human service professionals have generally enjoyed high esteem. Their expertise and commitment have been equal to the task of addressing the needs for which they have been given responsibility. However, a new phase began in the United States by the 1940s, one characterized by global patterns of human interdependence. The United States and other industrialized nations began to catalyze processes of modernization in other less developed countries. Perhaps chiefly for economic reasons, the former concertedly began to encourage the latter to develop industrialized methods of production, to train workers for increasingly specialized labor markets, and to eschew traditional folkways for more urban customs.

Within two decades of the beginning of this phase of global interdependence, social scientists began to speak of the "global village." Awareness grew during this time that all persons, indeed all forms of life on the planet, are interdependent. Such ecological awareness was quickly followed by the realization that all persons are increasingly influenced by global economic forces. At this time, many also became concerned that certain forms of military conflict (i.e., nuclear, biological, and chemical) could destroy all humanity.

Today we sense increasingly that the specialization we fostered to serve us more productively has now wrought such ferment that it confounds us. Just as we have recognized that there are limits to growth, so we consider today that there may be limits to the effectiveness of uncoordinated specialized decision processes and service delivery systems. In other words, there is growing awareness of the need for specialized service providers, leaders, and other social change agents to communicate and collaborate with one another, rather than act unilaterally as isolated individuals and members of discrete expert and social systems. Experience has taught us that actions based on specialized knowledge occasionally lead to unanticipated consequences, some of them unpleasant. Given the extraordinary turmoil of modern life, the task of achieving an integrated perspective has never been more necessary or more difficult.

Of particular significance to continuing professional education is the notion that human service professionals are less and less equipped to address complex concerns through monoprofessional approaches. In earlier times, the practitioner could depend upon the client's family, community, or clan to provide support to complement a professional's services. Today, because of the diminishing role of family, community, and clan in individuals' lives, professionals must rely on practitioners in other fields to insure that clients with even moderately complex concerns receive the range of diverse services needed to augment and render their efforts more effective. The implication for practice is that it is important for human service professionals to acknowledge an ethical responsibility to address complicated needs collaboratively.

Unprecedented Ethical Challenges to the Professions

The professions share several major areas of concern which are best addressed collaboratively. According to Dunn and Janata (1987), these include the following:

1) *The analysis and response to ethical issues.* Among the issues that require the expertise of a number of professions are decisions about death and life, genetic screening and counseling, confidentiality, informed consent, enforced treatment, and professional accountability.

2) *The understanding of changing societal values as they confront professional practice.* Societal changes that offer new challenges for interprofessional comprehension and cooperation include changing family life-styles, professional-consumer relationships, allocation of resources, social accountability of the professions, right to human services, and governmental control (p. 100).

Obstacles to Collaboration

There are two sorts of obstacles to collaborating interprofessionally to address human concerns comprehensively. The first type of obstacle involves resistance to restructuring the manner in which professional care is provided. Experience in interprofessional collaboration, though limited, suggests that the technical problems of restructuring service delivery are indeed surmountable. The second sort of obstacle must be addressed before restructuring can occur. This obstacle consists of the greater value which professionals and others tend to place on individualism and personal success, rather than upon collective well-being.

Although human service professionals are generally committed to providing compassionate, high quality care to their clients, professionals also often subscribe to the socially approved value of maximizing one's income and status. Fortunately, in the majority of situations, professionals gain greater return and prestige by delivering care effectively and compassionately. Thus, the contradiction between commitment to service and a desire for personal success is not usually obvious. It even appears that the opportunity for personal gain serves as an effective incentive for delivering better care. However, in some situations professionals are forced to choose between providing the most effective and compassionate service and delivering care for greater personal gain.

Perplexing and rapid changes are placing great stresses upon this value tension within the professions. What, for example, is the most ethical way of limiting health care costs? In responding to this issue, do we assume that health care providers have the right to maximize their incomes? Should individuals be held more financially accountable for illnesses which their life-styles have caused? And, in what ways and to what extent should a practitioner be held liable for care that was not as good as it might have been? Underlying these ethical issues is a recurring question: What is the nature of the responsibility which professionals and other individuals should exercise toward one another? In other words, what kind of interdependence should we seek?

The Need for Interprofessional Collaboration

Through sustained dialogue among professionals from diverse fields, we may develop a shared appreciation of the systemic ethical, practical, and educational challenges facing the human service professions. Interprofessional collaboration, therefore, may be helpful in 1) making comprehensive assessments of and providing coordinated responses to increasingly intricate human problems, 2) filling the gap in support to individuals caused by the reduced capacity of families and communities to meet individual needs, and 3) developing professional ethical guidelines responsive to contemporary societal concerns.

Providers of continuing professional education can play a significant role in fostering interprofessional collaboration for these purposes. Continuing professional education has become an important determinant of the quality of care delivered by human service professionals. Therefore, continuing professional education which provides experience in interprofessional collaboration is able to have a substantial impact on practice.

We now offer an operational definition of interprofessional collaboration, describe briefly some examples of models for providing interprofessional continuing education, and conclude by proposing that we consider ways of establishing a national infrastructure for offering interprofessional continuing education to professionals across the country.

Interprofessional Continuing Education

Since 1973, the Commission on Interprofessional Education and Practice at The Ohio State University has been engaged in encouraging interprofessional collaboration in professional education, practice, policy, and continuing education. The Commission brings together practitioners and academicians from the fields of allied health, education, law, medicine, nursing, psychology, social work, and theology. To understand better the nature and potential value of interprofessional collaboration, it was decided that interviews with the Commission's professional staff might prove useful, since these staff persons have had considerable experience in and have reflected on interprofessional endeavors.

A series of personal field interviews was conducted in March, 1988, with the Commission's professional staff members to develop a clearer understanding of the nature of interprofessional collaboration and to identify what distinguishes it from other forms of interaction between helping professionals (McLaughlin, 1988).

A Definition of Interprofessional Collaboration

The Commission staff agreed that *interprofessional collaboration* is, as one interviewee said, "a situation in which all the participating professionals come together as full and equal partners in the effort to address a human problem comprehensively." Several elements of this definition were identified.

First, interprofessional collaboration is an *active process*, requiring that professionals are participating, rather than simply attending, the social processes through which collaboration takes place. Given the high degree of professional and institutional specialization in American society noted earlier, the tendency is to provide human services mono- rather than inter-professionally. For true collaboration to emerge, professionals must participate actively, investing sufficient energy to produce new, synthesized professional perspectives.

Second, in interprofessional collaboration, *professionals work together*, rather than as unaffiliated human service providers. Working together consists of sustained communication and cooperation.

Third, interprofessional collaboration involves professionals participating as *full partners*. Professionals need to act and be treated as full partners, interacting as whole persons rather than as anonymous repositories of specialized professional knowledge.

Fourth, interprofessional collaboration involves *equal partnership*. Typically, interprofessional interaction is characterized by hierarchical relations in which professionals have differential status, prestige, and authority to make decisions regarding client assessment, care, and follow-up. In collaborative interaction, professionals respect the contributions each can make to the other's efforts and to an understanding of the client's needs. Equal partnership involves equal participation in decisions, whether the decisions concern professional education, policy making, or clinical care.

Fifth, interprofessional collaboration involves the effort to address a human concern. *Effort* is understood as the active and inherently uncertain nature of the collaborative process. The outcomes of collaboration are uncertain because, while all enter collaboration agreeing to the broad goal of improving client or societal well-being, the participants still must set the objectives by which to meet this basic goal.

Sixth, the notion of collaboration as the attempt to address concerns suggests that before striving to resolve a client or societal concern, collaboration seeks first to achieve an *integrated comprehension* of that concern. Much of the time spent in interprofessional collaboration consists of dialogue aimed at developing a shared understanding of the nature of the concern to which participants will direct their collective professional energies. To comprehend a client's needs, however, the client also needs to be regarded as a full and equal partner in the assessment and resolution of his or her own concerns.

Seventh, the notion of interprofessional collaboration as endeavoring to address a human concern reminds us that the professional's role is to respond to *significant human needs*. Through interprofessional collaboration, professionals create an environment conducive to recognizing their shared responsibility for individual and societal well-being.

Whether one views collaboration as intrinsically rewarding depends very much upon one's fundamental disposition toward competition and other societal values. Does this mean that those who adhere to the values of competition will not collaborate? "No," one staff member responded, "not if you understand that competition is a developmental stage toward collaboration." A person who believes in the appropriateness of competition may "experience a crisis where you realize competition just won't work, where you realize you need more information, where you realize someone else can supply that information, or where you feel the problem is too tough for you to be able to maintain a competitive edge in dealing with it."

The Nature of Interprofessional Interaction

Interprofessional interaction ranges from referral and sequential care to teams which operate explicitly to address matters interprofessionally. The more collaborative the form of interprofessional collaboration, the less commonly it is found. Interprofessional collaboration may be differentiated into three broad processes: information exchange, perspective exchange, or perspective transformation. The least collaborative form of *information exchange* involves professionals acquiring fairly specific information from one another regarding the client's situation and needs. A somewhat more collaborative form of information exchange would take place when a professional tests the adequacy of his or her judgment through discussion with persons in other professions.

Perspective exchange is a more collaborative process of interprofessional interaction. In perspective exchange, the care delivery community may be organized to permit more or less frequent consultation among professionals regarding particular clients with whom they each work. Through consultation, professionals inform one another and share their views with respect to the assessment of or care for a particular client.

Perspective interaction is the most collaborative process of interprofessional interaction. In perspective interaction, professionals go beyond discussing the convergences and divergences in their own perspectives and begin to develop a new perspective which synthesizes the contributions of their individual professional paradigms. Perspective transformation occurs best when professionals engage in sustained interaction with one another.

If perspective transformation is the ultimate goal of truly collaborative interprofessional interaction, how might continuing professional education providers encourage it? To address this question we describe briefly some forms which interprofessional continuing education has taken at The Ohio State University and then propose one way we might collaborate to develop a national infrastructure for such kinds of continuing education.

Examples of Interprofessional Continuing Education: The Ohio Experience

The Commission on Interprofessional Education and Practice has been governed, since its inception, by representatives of the cooperating schools of The Ohio State University, the three theological schools in central Ohio, and the corresponding state professional associations (the Ohio Medical Association and the Ohio State Bar Association). These representatives determined that an important element of the Commission's work should be to offer experience in interprofessional collaboration through continuing professional education activities.

A continuing education committee, comprised of both faculty and practitioners, was formed to design these activities. This mix has made possible considerable interaction between the faculty members of the cooperating colleges and schools and the practitioners, allowing genuine issues from the field to be addressed in the Commission's interprofessional credit courses. At the same time, the faculty-practitioner interaction has permitted "quality theoretical guidelines to be employed for reflection and evaluation within the continuing education events" (Browning, 1987, p. 111).

Over the years, the Commission has developed several formats for providing interprofessional continuing education. One format is an annual summer institute which brings together practitioners and preservice students to address interprofessionally such topical concerns as chemical dependency, birth defects, family violence, and childhood disabilities. During June of 1988, for example, more than 100 professionals met for three days reviewing the difficult problems of teen pregnancy and parenthood. Representatives of eight professions attended, some of whom were practitioners, some academics.

Another format has been the interprofessional continuing education conference to which practitioners from the eight participating fields in Ohio are invited. Planned by local academicians and practitioners, these biannual conferences have studied such concerns as AIDS, coping with stress, human sexuality, alcohol and drug abuse, and ethical issues in medical technology regarding decisions about death and the extension of life. National experts serve as resource persons and presenters during the conferences. Several of these conferences have led to the publication of books, providing a comprehensive interprofessional analysis of the conference topic.

A third format for interprofessional continuing education has been the meetings of the Assembly, at which members of more than 40 state professional associations in Ohio come together to address pressing policy concerns. This organization constitutes a unique forum in which professional leaders and practitioners in Ohio share insights and perspectives on state policy. Through the Assembly, policy matters most needing interprofessional consideration and analysis are identified. These lead to the formation of interprofessional policy panels to address a selected concern. Sixteen-member panels are comprised of one practitioner and one academician from each of the eight professions represented. Four such panels have been formed to address policy issues related to alternative modes of human reproduction, break-up of the family, family violence, and health care cost containment. The panels meet each month over a two- to three-year period. The Commission research staff gathers data germane to the policy issue under review and assists in the preparation of reports and other policy documents. Policy panels have produced model legislation on artificial insemination which has become law in Ohio, a national demonstration program of interdisciplinary training on child abuse and neglect, a continuing education video tape on issues related to child abuse treatment, a conceptual matrix for assessing the impacts of any cost containment policy on the quality of health care, and a wide variety of other policy informing products.

The panels also present interim and final reports on their work to Assembly participants, constituting a valuable interprofessional continuing educational event in itself. Assembly forums on policy panel reports often attract 50 to 80 practitioners and academic leaders from across the state. The panel members themselves, of course, experience interprofessional continuing education of the most advanced form and nature through teaching and learning from their fellow panel members.

One of the most exciting formats for interprofessional continuing education has been the National Consortium on Interprofessional Education and Practice. The Consortium emerged following informal meetings in December, 1985, and May, 1986, between Commission staff and leaders of 17 national professional and educational associations. The purpose of these meetings was to explore the opportunities for collaboration at the national level to address societal needs that transcend the resources and competencies of any single profession. Arising out of these informal meetings came the decisions to form the Consortium and to hold interprofessional continuing educational events for national leaders.

The Consortium is governed by delegates designated by the participating national associations. The delegates designed and sponsored the First National Leadership Symposium on Interprofessional Education and Practice in May, 1987, and a second such symposium which took place in June, 1988. The symposia were designed to provide participants and national leaders in the professions "hands-on" experience with interprofessional collaboration.

In the first symposium, participants addressed interprofessionally two complex case studies, one on AIDS and one on Alzheimer's disease. They also outlined factors that affect interprofessional collaboration and identified practical strategies for encouraging colleagues to engage in interprofessional endeavors. In the second symposium, participants discussed interprofessionally policy and practice concerns relating to cases regarding the homeless and teenage pregnancy.

The methods used to provide participants experience with interprofessional collaboration in the symposia are similar to those employed by the Commission in its continuing education conferences and summer institutes. That is, case study materials are developed by an interprofessional team of persons expert in the given subject matter. At the conferences and summer institutes, participants discuss the implications of these cases.

While the interprofessional continuing education activities described above have proved valuable and exciting, the Commission's field research suggests that more needs to be done to encourage human service professionals to collaborate. For example, a series of qualitative follow-up interviews of participants in the spring 1985 continuing education conference, "Children's Fears in a Stressful World," provided important suggestions for improvements in interprofessional continuing education programming, including activities at the grass roots level.

The respondents, the majority of whom were practitioners, were interviewed seven to ten months after the conference. They said that they had enjoyed and valued the conference experience and that it had deepened their appreciation of the need for collaborative interprofessional practice, but that it had not equipped them with practical strategies for developing their own local interprofessional teams and networks. Many respondents said, in effect, "I see a clear need for interprofessional practice, but I do not know how to initiate it effectively in my work. How do I overcome the obstacles to it?"

During December, 1987, and January, 1988, the Commission conducted field research to assess the interest of practitioners and professional leaders from a rural community in assistance with fostering local interprofessional collaboration. Respondents expressed a strong interest in having interprofessional and intraprofessional continuing education programs made available within their communities. They stated the following principles: 1) rural location facilitates interprofessional collaboration, 2) professionals in rural areas are more likely than their urban counterparts to be expected to fulfill civic leadership responsibilities, 3) interprofessional collaboration often occurs informally in a rural community, 4) cost containment initiatives have increased the need for collaboration, and 5) the effectiveness of local professional care and policy making is impeded by the rural community's lack of access to continuing professional education and by gaps in the local availability of professional resources (e.g., in nursing and psychiatry).

Pilot Approaches

A recurring theme expressed by professional practitioners and educators in recent years has been that there are significant impediments to installing interprofessional service delivery systems, but that such systems are decidedly needed. The Commission has identified a number of pilot approaches to address this need. Yet, as we will consider, more systemic change may be warranted, including the participation of national leaders in continuing professional education in the invention and testing of new approaches.

One pilot effort which the Commission is planning is the convening of small groups of practitioners several months after their participation in a Commission-sponsored continuing education event. They will be asked to report and to discuss how applicable the event proved to be given their need for collaborative interprofessional practice. Such meetings will provide a forum, therefore, to bring continuing professional education providers and practitioners together to improve the practical utility of interprofessional continuing educational programming.

Two of the Commission's interprofessional policy panels have determined that they will develop model local interprofessional care systems to address problems related to family violence and family break-up. Soon they will begin implementing these models, assessing how to foster effective collaborative practice and then disseminating recommendations regarding such delivery models through continuing professional education forums.

The National Consortium, meanwhile, is preparing to create study groups to assess pressing national policy concerns and identify coordinated interprofessional policy initiatives at several levels. The national study groups are to work closely with local interprofessional networks and teams so that such policy initiatives are informed by the realities local practitioners face.

While these are promising ideas, we should not limit our imagination to refinements of existing interprofessional endeavors. We may want to think more boldly. What follows is one such vision. It concerns the need to develop a national infrastructure to provide interprofessional and professional continuing education.

The Creation of a National Infrastructure for Interprofessional Continuing Education

One way to foster continuing professional education and provide experience in interprofessional collaboration might be to develop a system similar to that of the Cooperative Extension Service. The nation's Cooperative Extension Service constitutes an effective infrastructure for disseminating useful policy and research information to local citizens. In like manner, an interprofessional extension service might assist local professionals in improving the quality of local care and decision making.

The task of developing such a national interprofessional infrastructure would not necessarily require considerable resources. For the most part, many of the resources already exist to improve local professional care and policy making. Local, state, and national professional associations typically monitor pending legislation; higher educational institutions and other organizations conduct research on the improvement of professional care; continuing professional education organizations regularly provide local practitioners information on new care technologies; and most communities have at least an informal organization for bringing local professional leaders together.

The single greatest hindrance to creating a mechanism for linking these resources may simply be that the various professional organizations have not been accustomed to collaborating with one another. In fact, the linkages between professional associations, higher educational institutions, continuing professional educators, and local professionals have generally been unsystematic and serendipitous. A national interprofessional extension service would need to provide a forum in which these professional organizations could cooperate in a sustained fashion, with the primary purpose of improving the effectiveness of local professional services.

A major justification for the existence of the Cooperative Extension Service is that it provides coordinated educational services in support of local economic development. It has long been recognized in the United States that educators, researchers, policy analysts, farmers, local leaders, economic development experts, business owners, and others need to collaborate to sustain a healthy economy.

The national interprofessional extension service could have three main functions: intraprofessional continuing education, interprofessional continuing education, and policy study. To fulfill these functions, the extension service might engage in activities such as the following:

Brokering, if not itself providing, continuing professional education;.

Monitoring the effectiveness of helping professionals' human services at the community, regional, state, and national levels;

Overseeing equitable access for the disadvantaged to professional services;

Offering career development counseling to professionals;

Encouraging professionals to serve, *pro bono*, in civic leadership capacities;

Facilitating recruitment of promising young adults, particularly minorities, into the professions;

Acting as a third party convener--that is, providing a neutral forum in which diverse constituencies can meet to develop better mutual understanding;

Making interstitial and trans-community observations about community well-being;

Assessing local, state, and federal policy through interprofessional perspectives; and

Fostering greater public awareness about under-utilized existing professional resources through local, statewide, and national educational activities.

There is a wide range of policy concerns which the national interprofessional extension service could monitor, such as the following:

Custody policies affecting children of divorce;

Alternative modes of human reproduction--e.g., surrogate parenthood, artificial insemination, and embryo transplant;

Criteria for qualifying for welfare benefits;

Access to public services, such as health and education providers and libraries;

School policies with respect to teenage parents, discipline, suicide, and gang activity;

Performance of the criminal justice system; Community response to the homeless; and

Impact of large scale economic changes, firm relocations, and other economic dynamics on well-being.

It would not be difficult, of course, to identify examples of professional organizations which now address such matters through continuing education, policy analysis, and pre-service professional education. Unfortunately, examples of collaborative interprofessional efforts are still uncommon. As societal complexity and change intensify, so will the need for sustained collaboration. A national interprofessional extension service could respond to this need effectively and efficiently because it would rely heavily on professional commitment to collaboration.

References

Billips, J. O. (1987). Interprofessional team process. *Theory Into Practice*, *26* (2), 146-152.

Boley, B. A. (1977). *Crossfire in professional education: Students, the professions, and society.* New York: Pergamon

Browning, R. (1987). Continuing interprofessional education. *Theory Into Practice*, *26* (2), 110-115.

Casto, R. M. (1987). Preservice courses for interprofessional practice. *Theory Into Practice*, *26* (2), 103-109.

Childs, J. M., Jr. (1987). Interprofessional approach to ethical needs. *Theory Into Practice*, *26* (2), 124-128.

Cremin, L. A. (1978). The education of the educating professions, *Research Bulletin of the Horace Mann-Lincoln Institute*, *18* (3), 1-8.

Cunningham, L. L., & Dunn, V. B. (1987). Interprofessional policy analysis: An aid to public policy formation. *Theory Into Practice*, *26* (2), 129-133.

Cunningham, L. L., Spencer, M. H., & Battison, S. (1982). Expanding professional awareness: The Commission on Interprofessional Education and Practice. *Mershon Center Quarterly Report*, (4), 1-7.

Cyphert, F. R., & Cunningham, L. L. (1987). Interprofessional education and practice: A future agenda. *Theory Into Practice*, *26* (2), 153-156.

DeYoung, A. J. (1980). Professionalism and politics: Toward a more realistic assessment of the issue. *The Clearinghouse*, *53* (6), 268-270.

Douglas, M. (1988). The effects of modernization on religious change. *Daedalus*, *117* (3), 457-484.

Ducanis, A. J., & Golin, A. K. (1979). *The interdisciplinary health care team: A handbook.* Germantown, MD: Aspen Systems Corporation.

Dunn, V. B., & Janata, M. M. (1987). Interprofessional assumptions and the OSU Commission. *Theory Into Practice, 26* (2), 99-102.

Harbaugh, G. L., Casto, R. M., & Burgess-Ellison, J. A., (1987). Becoming a professional: How interprofessional training helps. *Theory Into Practice, 26* (2) 141-145.

Heiss, A. N. (1970). *Challenges to graduate schools.* San Francisco: Jossey-Bass.

Hooyman, G. (1979). Team building in human services. In B. R. Compton and B. Galloway (Eds), *Social work processes* (pp. 465-478). Homewood, IL: Dorsey.

Houle, C.O., Cyphert, F. R., & Boggs, D. (1987). Education for the professions. *Theory Into Practice, 26* (2), 87-93.

Jacobs, L. A. (1987). Interprofessional clinical education and practice. *Theory Into Practice, 26* (2), 116-123.

Jennings, B., Levine, C., & Bermel, J. (Eds.) (1987). The public duties of the professions. Hastings-on-Hudson, NY: *Hastings Center Report Special Supplement, 7* (1), 1-10.

Mayhew, L. B. (1970). *Graduate and professional education, 1980: A survey of institutional plans,* New York: McGraw-Hill.

McDonnell, P. (1979). A student perspective on nontraditional graduate education. *Alternative Higher Education: The Journal of Nontraditional Studies, 4* (1), 70-76.

McLaughlin, R. T. (1988). Interviews regarding interprofessional collaboration: An internal report. Available from Commission on Interprofessional Education and Practice, The Ohio State University: Columbus, OH.

McLaughlin, R. T., & Rosenberger, J. M. (1988, September 16). Facilitating local interprofessional collaboration: Pre-implementation field research. Paper presented at the Tenth Annual Interdisciplinary Health Care Team Conference, Toledo, OH.

Nisonger Center (1982). Factors affecting an interdisciplinary clinical team. *Nisonger Newsletter Executive Summary, 6* (4), 1.

Snyder, R. (1987). A societal backdrop for interprofessional education and practice. *Theory Into Practice, 26* (2), 94-98.

Spencer, M. H. (1984). *Impact of interprofessional education on subsequent practice,* Unpublished doctoral dissertation, The Ohio State University, Columbus, OH.

Spencer, M. H. (1987). Impact of interprofessional education on subsequent practice. *Theory Into Practice, 26* (2), 134-140.

Part 2:

The Process of Continuing Professional Education

Information Overload, the Knowledge-Added Economy, and Continuing Professional Education

Christopher J. Dede

Just as agricultural societies are based on developing natural resources and industrial economies on manufacturing goods, economic systems in post-industrial nations increasingly center on producing, acquiring, and applying knowledge. The professions exemplify this intensifying focus on knowledge creation, capture, transfer, and utilization. In complex webs of legal precedents, attorneys use higher order cognitive skills and advanced information technologies to find patterns which build a rationale for why their clients should prevail. Physicians sift through a mass of clinical information to develop diagnoses of their patients' illnesses, then use their expertise in physiology to prescribe treatments from a range of potential therapeutic interventions. Educators master a body of knowledge, then select from the spectrum of pedagogical strategies an effective mix of instructional approaches to match the needs of learners. In all the professions, the research practitioners who add to the knowledge base of that field are "first among equals" to their colleagues.

To fuel economic growth, countries are allocating large amounts of resources to producing knowledge. This development has created both opportunities and challenges for the professions. On the one hand, more knowledge increases the effectiveness of professionals and the value of their services to society. Expanding knowledge facilitates the creation of new knowledge in an exponentially growing fashion, building a nation's ability to compete in the global marketplace and improving the overall quality of life for civilization.

On the other hand, many fields are advancing so rapidly that mastering and maintaining a professional knowledge base is becoming very difficult for practitioners. Increasingly, students feel overwhelmed by the volume of knowledge they must absorb and the years they must spend to attain initial certification in a profession. Educators express concern about a crowded, expanding professional curriculum so dense in information that the pedagogical process threatens to collapse under the weight of instructional material. Lest their hard-won skills become obsolete, professionals find that a growing proportion of their time must be spent keeping current with new developments in their fields. Many practitioners are barely able to master the "information explosion" they face and find that, like Alice in Lewis Carroll's *Through the Looking Glass*, they must "run faster and faster to stay in the same place." As discussed in both Grotelueschen's chapter and Nowlen's first chapter, for many professionals the risk of premature obsolescence is substantial and growing.

This situation has created both benefits and difficulties for continuing professional education. Expanding, rapidly changing knowledge increases the demand for instructional services, as professionals seek help in learning leading-edge developments in their fields. However, the volume of continually shifting information to be communicated challenges the ability of educators to maintain a coherent, updated curriculum. Fitting an ever growing body of knowledge into the limited time professionals can give to educational experiences is also becoming very difficult. Moreover, like other professionals, practitioners in continuing education are overwhelmed by the material they must master to keep their methods state of the art. Too often, these challenges combine to make continuing education more a part of the problem in professionals' information explosion than an effective solution.

This chapter discusses emerging concepts in artificial intelligence and cognitive science that may improve the ability of continuing professional education to cope with expanding knowledge. First, the scale of society's information explosion will be delineated; and the relationships among data, information, knowledge, and wisdom will be defined. Then, a forecast of an emerging evolution from data processing to knowledge transfer will be presented, and its consequences for professionals' roles in the post-industrial economy discussed. Finally, the implications of these developments in creating a desirable future for continuing professional education will be assessed. In the context of this book, the chapter presents ideas relevant to three major themes: an understanding of the changing economic environment, new methods in continuing professional education, and ways that advanced technology can facilitate communication among professional fields.

Increasing Information and Expanding Ignorance

The expansion of knowledge may well be limited by an explosion of information that makes keeping up with new developments virtually impossible. Just in the scientific and technological fields, information is stored in over 1,000 computerized data bases which are searched at least 2,000,000 times per year, as well as in over 500 bibliographic data bases with more than 70,000,000 citations (Molnar, 1982). Moreover, scientists are expanding this base of information by producing more than 5,000 reports per day. We are reaching a time in the history of science when it may be easier to repeat an experiment than to search for it in the literature (Molnar, 1987). Marien (1971) argues that we risk becoming an "ignorant society." He believes that professionals have responded to the information explosion by narrowing their areas of specialization. The long-term result of such a trend would be "experts" who know a great deal about very little and almost nothing about anything else. As discussed in Azzaretto's chapter, "real world" problems do not fall neatly into discipline-based specialities, but instead require multiple perspectives and diverse mental models. A collective ignorance caused by specialization could render the professions inadequate for evolving solutions to the complex problems civilization now confronts, especially given the barriers to interprofessional collaboration Cunningham and McLaughlin's chapter delineates.

How can professionals cope with the information explosion, which is an inevitable consequence of society's investments in expanding knowledge? Researchers in artificial intelligence and cognitive science are developing approaches which seem promising for managing the overwhelming volume of data we are creating. Computers have been responsible in part for creating the sea of information in which we are drowning, so a necessary component of the solution centers on how we use these devices.

A New Paradigm

A new paradigm is emerging for how to use the information technologies. Originally, computers were seen as number-crunching machines; with time, their data processing capabilities were recognized. Now, the strengths of integrated computer and telecommunications devices for all forms of individual and group symbolic manipulation are being explored. Just as data bases have empowered a richer way of conceptualizing reality than reducing everything to numbers, so have humanity's many symbol systems provided the potential for deeper, more meaningful representational media than data structures. For example, an instructor's conception of a student's learning style is not easily reducible to fields of information on standardized forms aggregated into data files. The capability of representing and manipulating the conceptual gestalt of learning styles in a computational device tailored to complement human intelligence could greatly improve pedagogical effectiveness.

The conceptualization of information technologies as symbolic manipulation devices is leading to research on ways data and information can be converted to knowledge and wisdom (Dede, Sullivan, & Scace, 1988). Common usage of these terms conveys a sense of increasing complexity and utility, but a delineation of their subtle differences is more difficult. For the purposes of this chapter, "data" will be defined as input gathered through the senses and "information" as integrated data which denote a significant change in the environment.

Information is converted to "knowledge" by interconnecting it with known concepts and skills as part of achieving a goal. (Note that knowledge has an attribute of purpose, which implies the existence of an intelligent agent--human or computational--in transforming information into knowledge.) "Wisdom" adds dimensions beyond individual cognition: the strengths and limits of personal knowledge, its interrelationship with the knowledge of others, and the ethical and affective issues that Adelson's chapter discusses.

To illustrate, for a physician, the existence of a new therapeutic intervention would be data; an understanding of its attributes and what diseases it affects would be information; comprehension of how to use the treatment in therapeutic situations would be knowledge; and mastery of when to use the intervention and of its effects on overall medical practice would be wisdom. Comparable analogies can be constructed for other types of task performance in the professions.

Past generations of information systems have used advances in hardware and software to increase the amount of data available on the assumption that individual and institutional wisdom would thereby increase. In practice, however, beyond a certain level, additional data overwhelm people; they become unable to decide which information is important, to interconnect new information into existing knowledge, or to recognize overall patterns of meta-knowledge. Future generations of information systems--and instructional systems--must instead use increases in power to deliver environmentally meaningful, contextually targeted interconnected data (knowledge). Otherwise, using inexpensive computational devices to increase the amount of information in every aspect of task performance will degrade organizational effectiveness rather than augment individual and institutional knowledge.

From Data Processing to Knowledge Transfer

How can society shift from a focus on increasing information to transferring knowledge? Researchers in artificial intelligence and cognitive science believe that advanced information technologies offer the promise of pre-processing data and information. This change would allow users to interact with these devices at the level of knowledge, where the volume of input is more manageable. Such an advance necessitates enormous amounts of low-cost computational power, which fortunately is now becoming available because of a long-term trend in hardware characteristics.

For about four decades, the power per unit cost of the information technologies has been increasing exponentially (Dede, 1988). All the performance characteristics of computers and telecommunications--speed, memory size, bandwidth--have been repeatedly doubling every several years at constant cost. This trend is expected to continue for at least another decade before fundamental physical limits (the speed of light, entropy, quantum mechanics) pose significant barriers to further advances.

To illustrate how rapid these increases have been, 10 years ago $3,500 could buy an Apple II™ microcomputer with an eight-bit, one-megahertz processor, 48 Kilobytes (K) of RAM, 8K of ROM, a 40-character by 24-line upper-case display, high-resolution graphics (280 by 192 lines of resolution, 16 colors), two 140K disk drives with controller, and a Radio Frequency (RF) Modulator to connect with a television set. Adjusting for 10 years of inflation, an equivalent amount of purchasing power today is $6,800. For that price, one can buy a Macintosh II™ with a 16-megahertz, 32-bit processor, one megabyte of RAM, 170K of ROM, two 800K disk drives with controller, a 20 Megabyte hard disk, and a 640 by 480 RGB display with 256 colors. The microprocessor handles 4 times the information at 16 times the speed, total internal memory is about 20 times larger, total external memory about 75 times larger; and the display is now included--with 7 times the resolution and 16 times the number of colors. Comparable figures can be cited for machines from other vendors.

Exponential growth is explosive because each successive doubling of power adds an equivalent amount of capability to all that has historically existed. As these trends continue, by early in the twenty-first century we can expect all the microcomputer power available now to double, double again, and again and again and again. Users' demand for this power has increased as rapidly as it has become available. For example, in the mid-1960s, IBM was debating whether to use 6-bit or 8-

bit channels for its largest computers (which were considerably less powerful than today's Macintosh II). Those arguing for 6 bits maintained that the extra capacity would never be needed, since users would never want lowercase alphabetic capability on their machines! Those early line-editor applications for text have been displaced by word processors and now by desktop publishing, and professionals are continuing to push the limits of current microcomputer hardware.

Users can easily forget how rapid this advance has been, for our civilization swiftly absorbs new technologies and alters institutional patterns into instant traditions. For example, spreadsheets are now a commonplace modeling tool in information-based occupations; yet this type of application was created only a decade ago. The natural tendency which both professionals and educators must overcome is that of conceptualizing additional power solely in terms of existing functions (e.g., more rapid searches through data bases) rather than visualizing the evolution of innovative capabilities, such as storing information in associative networks (discussed below under "cognition enhancers").

This tendency to underestimate how the emerging power of low-cost information technologies can empower new types of professional and educational applications is a general problem for individuals and organizations. Typically, new information devices have their impact on institutions in four sequential stages (Coates, 1977):

Stage One: The new technology is adopted by an institution to carry out existing functions more effectively.

Stage Two: The institution changes internally (work roles, organizational structure) to take better advantage of these new efficiencies.

Stage Three: Institutions develop new functions and activities enabled by additional capabilities of the technology. As the roles of different types of institutions expand, new competitive relationships emerge.

Stage Four: The original role of the institution may become obsolete, be displaced, or be radically transformed as new goals dominate the institution's activities.

Professionals' workplace tools are entering Stage Three for the early 1980s generation of microcomputers and are in Stage One for the 32-bit generation of machines now emerging. Educational institutions, generally slower to adapt, are reaching Stage Three for the 8-bit personal computers of the late 1970s. Comparable statements can be made about recent telecommunications technologies. As Hofstader and Munger discuss in their chapter, a vital emerging role for continuing professional education is to speed the transfer of new functionalities from advanced information technologies into professional practice.

In summary, information technology's trend toward increasing power at decreasing cost empowers symbolic manipulation, the essential step for moving from data to knowledge. How would interacting with a knowledge base differ from current usage of data bases? Educational illustrations will be used as examples in answering this question, as these 1) are typical of professional applications in general, and 2) build a foundation for understanding the potential implications of knowledge bases for continuing professional educators.

Cognition Enhancers

One way of comprehending some advanced emerging functionalities of knowledge bases is through the concept of *cognition enhancers* (Dede, 1987b). The concept underlying a cognition enhancer is that of using the complementary cognitive strengths of a person and an information technology in partnership. For example, computers have large short-term memories (megabytes of RAM), while human beings are limited to an immediate storage capacity of less than 10 chunks of information (Anderson, 1983). Computers can also execute complex algorithms (precise recipes for solving one class of problem) more rapidly than people can. For tasks involving manipulation of successive symbolic results (e.g., involved mathematical calculations), these two cognitive attributes give a computer an advantage over a human being.

In general, computers are becoming superior at all forms of complex standardized problem solving, which has historically comprised a major portion of professionals' skills. For example, expert systems are now matching highly skilled human performance in narrow, well-structured domains (e.g., finding oil under salt domes, diagnosing pulmonary problems). As will be discussed later, this trend may "deskill" many jobs and automate substantial parts of present occupational roles.

However, people have other types of cognitive strengths which computers currently cannot match. For example, we store symbolic information in rich "semantic networks" containing webs of associationally related textual, temporal, and visual imagery. As an illustration, in a human memory the word "apple" conjures up religious, corporate, computational, botanic, and gustatory dimensions. At present, computers are much more limited in how their information can be interrelated, as anyone who uses a data base knows!

The cognitive attributes of human beings give them an advantage over computers at applying peripheral "real world" knowledge to ill-structured problems (such as diagnosing the source of a student's motivational difficulties). In general, people are still much better than computers at problem recognition, at metacognition (thinking about thinking), and at non-standardized problem solving. All of these are major components of professional knowledge that go beyond routinized problem solving.

The complementarity of human and machine intellectual capabilities offers the potential of productive partnerships between people and intelligent tools. As powerful--but inexpensive--information devices emerge, cognition enhancers designed to combine the strengths of humans and computers are evolving rapidly. These tools are still in their infancy, but so far three kinds seem to be emerging.

Empowering environment. This type of cognition enhancer uses the computer's strengths in structured symbolic manipulation to empower human accomplishment by a division of labor: The machine handles the routine mechanics of a task, while the person is immersed in its higher order meanings. For example, I once took an oil painting course. My goal was to faithfully convey to a canvas the images in my mind so that viewers could share my experiences and emotions. However, rather than pondering form and composition and aesthetics, I spent my time trying to mix colors that remotely resembled my visualizations, trying to keep the paint from running all over the canvas, and trying to keep the turpentine out of my hair.

Now, I can use a graphics construction set on an inexpensive desktop computer to choose from a huge palette of colors to alter, pixel by pixel, the contour of an image, to instantly "undo" my failures. I am involved with the deep symbolic semantics of art, while the empowering environment handles the mechanics. (However, my accomplishments are still ultimately limited by my own talents and knowledge as an artist.)

Primitive empowering environments are beginning to be used in education. A word processor with spelling checker, thesaurus, typing tutor, and graphics tool is the beginning of an empowering environment for writing. Even the early versions of this type of cognition enhancer have an interesting property: their usage by a person unconsciously alters the style of task performance!

For example, as a result of using a word processor, I can no longer write well with paper and pencil. Formerly, I composed a sentence by thinking for a couple of minutes and setting down a final version that was about 90% of the optimal result. I "took my one best shot" because making changes later would involve massive physical cutting and pasting. Now, I write by thinking for half a minute and typing in a sentence that is perhaps 40% of the optimal result, think for another 15 seconds and make a change (now 50%), another change a few seconds later (65%), and so on. The same amount of time is required to get to the 90% level, but now my psychological momentum is behind revision and polishing, rather than producing a single "finished" product. As a result, no cognitive dissonance bars the sentence from eventually evolving to an optimal level.

However, when I try to write with a pencil using this new, superior strategy--disaster! My eraser wears out much faster than the graphite in the pencil. Most people who use word processors (music tools, databases, spreadsheets) experience the same unconscious shift in style. In a world of intelligent empowering environments, the ways in which professionals accomplish tasks may necessarily alter.

The skills required for many occupations are shifting because of the use of empowering environments in the workplace: word processors and desktop publishing applications for jobs involving writing, data bases for information storage and retrieval, spreadsheets for modeling and simulation, computer-assisted design and manufacturing work stations for production. As practitioners' roles increasingly involve using job performance aids based on intelligent tools, continuing professional education will need to prepare its clients for utilizing these empowering environments. Readers interested in exploring the concept of educational empowering environments in greater depth will find further examples in Brown (1985).

Hypermedia. Even with a sophisticated empowering environment for desktop publishing, I can still get writer's block. A second type of cognition enhancer is needed. Hypermedia is a framework for interconnected, web-like representation of symbols (text, graphics, images, software code) in the computer. As discussed earlier, long-term human memory is stored as associational semantic networks; I can know everything I want to write, but not have my ideas in the linear "stream" required for written or oral communication.

I need an "idea processor," a way of creating externally a multi-dimensional construct which mirrors the concepts and links forming the symbolic representation of material in my memory. With my knowledge externalized into a hypermedia system, I can then traverse this network along alternative paths through nodes and links, seeking the right sequential stream for my intended content, audience, and goals. The computer is working in cognitive partnership to eliminate the overload involved in transferring long-term to short-term memory. Moreover, a person's access to long-term memory may be enhanced by the process of building and using hypermedia.

Hypermedia is a general tool that can be used in several different ways. In addition to serving as an externalized associational memory for an individual, hypermedia could be an alternative representational system for a large, shared data base (such as an integrated textbook series for the entire curriculum). Such an approach would encourage group interdisciplinary exploration by explicitly interconnecting similar ideas in different subjects. In addition, hypermedia as a knowledge representation format empowers instructional design based on cognitive principles of learning, such as active structural networks, schema theory, web teaching, and generative learning (Jonassen, 1986).

Hypermedia "documents" are beginning to appear in workplace settings. For example, physicians may soon be using hypermedia-based, electronic medical manuals to diagnose problems. The doctor will trace initial symptoms through a series of linked tests to reach a final judgment on what is wrong, then follow a web of nodes which map the different steps of the treatment. An educational version of such a manual would incorporate "trails" through the hypermedia network which guide the user through a series of structured, sequenced learning experiences. Comparable applications can be cited for other types of task performance throughout the professions.

The emergence of primitive hypermedia systems on personal computers is likely to unleash a variety of new ideas for using this type of cognition enhancer. For example, a hypermedia version of this chapter would place each fundamental concept in a separate node; links would tie related concepts together (e.g. the material on semantic nets in the "cognition enhancers" section and in the "hypermedia" section). Such modularity and juxtapositions might increase comprehension over the forced linearity of textual presentations. Perhaps new styles of remembering and knowledge transfer will evolve as well. For readers interested in further exploring this concept, the Intermedia System at Brown University (Yankelovitch, Meyrowitz, & van Dam; 1985) illustrates work on educational applications of hypermedia.

Microworlds. This third type of cognition enhancer allows the user to explore and manipulate limited "artificial realities." As discussed in

Cervero's chapter, a problem that learners constantly experience is integrating theory and practice: how to relate abstract, formal knowledge to specific real world situations. For example, if I were teaching how Einstein's theories of general and special relativity had altered our understanding of gravity, I could approach this task by explaining the appropriate equations and formulas to my students. However, even if they had the logical reasoning skills and the background in physics and calculus to understand my exposition, few would be able to link their abstract comprehension to "real world" applications (such as why water swirls down drains in opposite directions in the Northern and Southern hemispheres).

What I need is a "microworld," an artificial reality in which I can vary gravity's fundamental properties. The students could use the computer to explore some activity (say, baseball) at the earth's gravity, then at the Moon's gravity, then at Jupiter's gravity, even a very short game at zero gravity! Altering one item at a time, we could work through the constants and variables in the equations, changing each in turn to see how the game of baseball would change. Now, students would have both a formal and an applied knowledge of the theories underlying gravity.

The concept of microworlds extends to "surrogate travel" and "surrogate experience." Taking advantage of the emerging synthesis between telecommunications and computers, interactive videodiscs could allow an individualized "trip" to be taken to the Louvre in Paris. The student could "walk" through the museum examining art objects in any order, at different angles, for any duration, with or without commentary, using hypermedia links to related subjects. This experience would not be the same as actually visiting the Louvre, but would be far more instructive and motivating than group viewing of art history slides.

Or surrogate experience could be gained in a profession (say, medicine) by having the student use an interactive videodisc to interview a "patient," make a diagnosis, and prescribe a therapy. This experience would be far different from a structured problem at the back of a textbook chapter. The student would need to spot visual cues, elicit information essential to the diagnosis, and determine the accuracy of the patient's responses. As with computational microworlds, key variables could be manipulated in surrogate travel and experience to encompass the range of situations in which a particular chunk of symbolic knowledge is useful.

Simulations have been a valuable instructional tool in continuing professional education (Barrows & Tamblyn, 1980). Now, with increasing computational power available, microworlds are beginning to appear in workplace situations, both for training and task performance. Pilots accumulate substantial amounts of flying experience--including first-hand knowledge of how to handle emergency situations--through interacting with elaborate, realistic microworlds. Workers operating flexible manufacturing systems use microworlds to compare alternative scheduling patterns and to analyze possible causes of defective production. Salespeople use microworlds to practice refining their presentation to different types of customers. In continuing professional education, microworlds can enhance the quality of training for all those professions that require mastery of complex processes and sophisticated, rapid performance.

Users find microworlds motivating; in fact, researchers are studying videogames as an example of artificial realities to determine what makes some so addictive. When this reinforcement is understood, its motivational power can then be generalized to educational situations (Malone & Lepper, 1985). For readers interested in further exploring this type of cognition enhancer, the work of Smith (1987) on the Alternate Reality Kit illustrates an educational microworld. Users can manipulate the laws of physics and experience how natural phenomena change.

In summary, new modalities for cognitive partnerships between professionals and intelligent tools are emerging, based both on the increasing power of low-cost information technologies and on advances in artificial intelligence and cognitive science. How will these advances empower professionals to move beyond scanning massive amounts of data and information into acquiring knowledge?

A Scenario: Use of a Knowledge Base

The following scenario shows a user interacting with a knowledge base as an example of intelligent tools accelerating knowledge transfer (Dede, 1987a). The situation is typical of tasks performed in many professions.

Hypothetical Exchanges Between an Intelligent Knowledge Base and a NASA User

A decision maker needs to determine whether a particular application of space technology has the potential to be economically profitable in 1999. An intelligent knowledge base is being used as a source of information and expertise in resolving this issue. This job performance aid serves as a clearinghouse on the commercial development of space, presenting to users current and historical data on technological capabilities, business trends, and societal developments which could affect the space-related market.

The information supplied is continuously updated and evaluated by a sophisticated environmental scanning process. In addition, users of this service can interact with each other and with NASA experts, creating an international electronic forum for the exchange of ideas. The system serves as an empowering environment for this task, with embedded hypermedia representations and microworlds.

This intelligent knowledge base communicates with its user via images on the monitor (photographs, computer graphics, text) and speech synthesis; hard copies of output are produced as needed. Decision makers can query the knowledge base through the keyboard, touch-screen, and mouse, using a restricted form of natural language. When interacting with other people through a network, both computer conferencing and direct voicecommunication are possible.

A session is midway in progress; the monitor shows blueprints of the interior of the space station, with a computer graphic overlay indicating equipment which could be installed and giving descriptions of each component.

1)   *User*: What is the maximum level of gravity at which this type of crystallization is possible?

2)   *KB*: [invokes knowledge based system which specializes in this area] This type of crystallization initiates at 0.2 g.

3)   *User*: Have any experts estimated the likelihood by 1999 of technical advances which would allow production at earth gravity?

4)   *KB*: [calls up internal record] Last year's Delphi panel estimate on this issue indicated a 40% probability of this type of process becoming feasible at 1.0 g in the next five years.

5)   *User*: What technologies are thought to be the potential source of such an advance?

6)   *KB*:   [consults with expert system; displays animated graphic of alternative production process with textual description superimposed]

7)   *User*: What experimental yields have been realized so far?

8)   *KB*:   [displays vertical histogram of yields from different research projects]

9)   *User*: Show me these figures in a table.

10)   *KB*: [displays yield data in tabular form; device notes user preference as a default format for future requests]

11)   *User*: Who are three experts working on this new approach?

12)   *KB*: [searches research index; three listings appear on the screen] Here are the names you requested. You have no previous record of contact with Drs. Jones and Smith. You did interact with Ms. Brown on 6/17/90; the topic of the discussion was crystalline impurities. None of these experts are on line at the moment. Would you like to send a message to them?

13)   *User*: Yes.

14)   *KB*: [this user's standard format for initiating contact appears on the screen for editing; the knowledge base automatically sends the messages when the user has finished]

15)   *User*: How much would such a technical advance lower the unit cost of production?

16)   *KB*: [searches network of causal relationships] Relevant macro-factors include: Probable State of Global Economy, Projected Demand for Pharmaceuticals, Space Station Cost Forecasts, Estimated Crystallization Equipment Costs.

17)   *User*: Show micro-factors for Crystallization Equipment.

18)   *KB*: [concludes from incoming physiological data and historical patterns of user's concentration span that his / her attention is wandering] Would you like to take a break first?

19)   *User*: Yes. While I'm on break, conduct a ten minute search for information added in the last three days which deals with the topic of venture capital for space investments.

20)   *KB*: [initiates associational search through hypermedia network]

This hypothetical example illustrates some of the capabilities an advanced intelligent knowledge base might offer. Response-by-response, a few functions of the device are delineated below:

Response 2 : The knowledge base contains specialized expert systems.

Response 4 : The computer can search through a set of references based on key words derived from a naturally phrased user query, can identify which item is of most immediate relevance, and can determine the approximate level of detail expected in its response--all in a manner transparent to the user.

Responses 6 through 10 : The device can present data in a variety of formats.

Responses 10, 14 : The machine models the cognitive style of the user and tailors its responses accordingly.

Response 12 : Users can access a sophisticated communications network through the computer.

Response 16 : The knowledge base incorporates causal relationships and can present a hierarchical menu of factors.

Response 18 : The device senses changes in the user's consciousness and suggests ways to maximize job performance.

Response 20 : The machine has hypermedia representation capabilities which allow the creation of user-specific definitions of "meaningful," based on individual interests and previous query patterns.

Using Gregory Bateson's definition (1975) of "information" as "any difference that makes a difference," the ultimate purpose of an intelligent knowledge base is to enable users to refine progressively information from data, knowledge from information, and wisdom from knowledge.

A system this complex would require elaborate hardware and software, so its likelihood as a common professional tool in the next decade is low. However, this scenario does provide a sense of where advances in intelligent knowledge-based devices are leading. For the reader interested in additional annotated scenarios of sophisticated "learning while doing" task performance aids, an intelligent tutor and coach are described in Dede (1987a), and a scenario for computer-supported cooperative learning is given in Dede et al. (1988).

Timetable

To give a sense of the speed with which these diverse capabilities might emerge in continuing professional education, table 1 is presented. For different functionalities, table 1 estimates commercial availability at prices comparable to advanced personal computer costs today. These projections have significant margins for error, since widespread adoption depends on many more factors than technical feasibility.

Table 1: Timetable for Availability of Functions

Functionality	Uses	Time Frame
Hypermedia	Interlinking of diverse subject matter; easier conceptual exploration, training, collaboration	Late 1980s
Cognitive audit trails	Support for finding patterns of suboptimal performance	Late 1980s
High quality voice synthesis	Auditory natural language output	Late 1980s
Advanced manipulatory input devices	Mimetic learning which builds on real world experience	Early 1990s
High-bandwidth fiber-optic networks	Massive real time data exchange	Early 1990s
Synthesis of computers, telecommunications	Easy interconnection; realistic simulation	Early 1990s
Standardization of computer and telecommunications protocols	Easy connectivity, compatibility; lower costs	Mid 1990s

(continued...)

Functionality	Uses	Timeframe
Optical-disc systems with multiple read/write and mixed-media capabilities	Support of large data and knowledge bases; very cheap secondary storage; facilitation of artificial realities	Mid 1990s
Sophisticated user interface management systems	Easier development of instructional applications; reduced time for novices to master a program	Mid 1990s
Intelligent, semi-autonomous agents	Support for user-defined independent actions	Mid 1990s
Computer-supported cooperative work (collaborative design, collective problem solving, group decision support), including WYSIWIS (What You See is What I See)	Mastery of team task performance	Mid 1990s
User-specific, limited-vocabulary voice recognition	Restricted natural language input	Late 1990s
High-resolution color monitors with 3-D graphics	Vivid simulation of reality; easy reading of text	Late 1990s
Microworlds	Experience in applying theoretical information in practical situations	Late 1990s
Consciousness sensors	Monitoring of mood, state of mind	Late 1990s

(continued...)

Functionality	Uses	Timeframe
Information utilities	Access to integrated sources of data and tools for assimilation	Late 1990s
Current mainframe performance on microcomputers	Sufficient power for advanced functionalities	Late 1990s
Knowledge processing and knowledge base management systems	Goal-oriented, context-specific mastery of concepts and skills	Late 1990s
Intelligent tutors and coaches for restricted domains	Models of embedded expertise for greater individualization	Year 2000+
Artificial realities	Intensely motivating simulation and experience	Year 2000+

Of course, whether these technical capabilities are rapidly implemented in education will depend in part on whether buying collectives are formed to present sophisticated demands to vendors. One likely means of dissemination would be that military and industrial training needs would drive the emergence of sophisticated instructional workstations, which would then gradually "trickle down" to educational institutions.

In summary, the emergence of powerful, low-cost information devices, the evolution of cognition enhancers, and the development of intelligent knowledge bases are empowering a widespread transformation from data processing to knowledge transfer. This shift will have profound implications both for the skills professionals need to keep abreast of their fields and for the methods continuing professional educators use to communicate this knowledge. In particular, the evolution of computer-supported cooperative work (CSCW) may empower increased interaction among professionals, including inter-field collaborations (Krasner, 1986). Such advances are crucial because of the increasing utilization of professionals in an organizational team context, as discussed in Hofstader's and Munger's chapter.

Professionals in the Knowledge-Added Economy

The technological advances discussed above create the potential for a massive shift to a workplace built on cognitive partnerships between people and intelligent, knowledge-based tools (Dede, 1985b). Such an evolution would be driven by the global marketplace now emerging. In this new economic "ecology," each nation is seeking a specialized niche based on its financial, human, and natural resources. Developed countries, which no longer have easily available natural resources and cheap labor, cannot compete with rising Third World nations in manufacturing standardized industrial commodities (President's Commission on Industrial Competitiveness, 1985). The advent of biotechnology will speed this erosion of traditional sources of economic strength. However, a nation with considerable technological expertise, an advanced industrial base, and an educated citizenry might seek to develop an economy which uses sophisticated professionals and information tools to produce customized, value-added products (Reich, 1983).

One way of understanding the impact of these changes on occupational skills is to contrast how information technology has changed the job roles of the supermarket checker and the typist. Many supermarkets now have bar code readers. Rather than finding the price on each item and punching it into the register, the checker needs only to pass the goods over the scanner. Efficiency and productivity have increased; but the food you buy tastes the same as before, and fewer skills are needed to do the job.

In contrast, substituting a word processor/information networking device for a typewriter completely alters a secretary's function. To use the information tool to its full capability of customizing a single template to the individual needs of a variety of recipients, the clerical role must shift from "keyboarding" to utilizing data bases, desktop publishing, communications, and graphics applications. The job now demands higher order cognitive skills to extract and tailor knowledge from the enormous information capacity of the tool, and the occupational role shifts to the new profession of "information manager."

A comparable evolution of job skills is taking place in all the professions (Zuboff, 1988). As work stations become more intelligent, through embedded models of skilled performance in specialized domains (e.g., coaches, expert decision-aids), the thinking skills required of the human role in the partnership become even more sophisticated. Creativity and flexibility become more vital as the standardized aspects of problem solving skills are absorbed by the machine.

As discussed earlier, current work in cognitive science suggests that computers and people have complementary intellectual strengths; each can supply what the other lacks. The technological advances forecast above, while significant, are unlikely to enable intelligent machines to surpass human performance in recognizing and solving unusual problems in unstructured situations (Woods, 1986). Refining these skills in professionals so that they can work productively with intelligent tools will require a shift in the present educational paradigm toward the intensive use of knowledge transfer devices. Moreover, because the routine parts of work are being automated, a greater proportion of professional decisions will require ethical choices. As advanced information technologies increase the effectiveness of professionals, the latter's ethical responsibilities expand. Greater power leads to more control over events; in turn, this control necessitates confronting new ethical dilemmas. Responses to standard professional situations will be routinely accomplished through intelligent tools, freeing practitioners to spend more of their time on non-routine matters. This increased freedom may increase occupational stress, since professionals will find their working time dominated by challenging situations demanding complex and creative ethical judgments (wisdom).

As discussed in Cervero's chapter, complex work roles involve a mixture of structured and unstructured decisions; and partnerships between people and intelligent tools seem central to jobs which create value-added, customized products and services. Professional services are a paradigmatic example of this type of occupational role. Current trends in office and factory automation (as well as national problems with debt and balance of trade) make the emergence of economic development policies which would promote a knowledge-added workplace a plausible alternative future (Ayres, 1984).

Massive investments in continuing professional education would be vital to drive such a societal evolution. Moreover, the learning experiences professionals receive would increasingly be oriented to knowledge transfer rather than the assimilation of information. These two developments combined would necessitate major changes in current instructional practices.

However, the forecast above is not meant to imply that this transformation of work and education will be inevitable or universal. On the contrary, advanced technology eliminates jobs as well as creates them; and, in an automated workplace, many of the occupations which survive may require only low level skills (Burke & Rumberger, 1987). In every developed nation, significant uncertainty currently exists about fundamental questions such as the following:

How many jobs will be available in the early part of the next century?

What will be the mix of skilled and unskilled positions?

Will sufficient "middle class" occupations (e.g., the professions) be available to prevent a polarization of wealth in society, or will most such jobs be deskilled by intelligent machines?

What will be the implications of these technological and economic shifts for equity?

Fundamental disagreements among experts on these issues are creating difficulties for educators, who are unsure as to what types of knowledge their clients need to be prepared for the future (Spenner, 1985).

In addition, the role technology should play in instruction and the efficacy of the present educational paradigm are currently topics of debate among practitioners and the general public. While of great importance, a thorough discussion of these issues is beyond the scope of this chapter. A reasonable assumption seems that, in developed nations, economies will evolve so as to retain a significant proportion of "knowledge-added" professional roles. In such a context, through using knowledge transfer devices as an intrinsic part of the overall educational model, how might the practice of continuing professional education change?

Implications for Continuing Professional Education

The two most common errors in technology assessment are over-estimating the speed of diffusion of an innovation and underestimating its eventual consequences and side effects. These devices may arrive more slowly than expected, since the primary limits on adoption of a new technology are social, economic, and political; but the impact of knowledge bases on the traditional instructional paradigm will be profound. To stimulate ideas about the consequences of knowledge transfer technologies for continuing professional education, illustrative potential effects of the widespread, long-term usage of cognition enhancers are listed below (Dede, 1988b):

1. Human strengths in partnerships between people and cognition enhancers involve skills such as creativity, flexibility, decision making given incomplete data, complex pattern recognition, information evaluation/synthesis, and holistic thinking. Such higher order mental attributes might

become a new definition of human "intelligence," as basic cognitive skills would increasingly shift to the tool's portion of the partnership. Polishing professionals' mastery of complex standardized problem solving would be like grooming John Henry to compete with the steam engine!

2. Methods of educational assessment would alter from charting mastery of descriptive knowledge to evaluating attainment of higher order skills. Fortunately, cognition enhancers can aid in collecting the detailed individual data necessary, as well as empowering more sophisticated empirical educational research. This capability would greatly aid the development of better methods for assessing individual professional needs, as discussed in the chapter by Smutz and Queeney. The ability to evaluate professional "proficiency" (as defined in Knox's chapter) would also be very useful.

3. "Learning-while-doing" would become a more significant component of education, as combined computer and telecommunications technologies allow delivery of instructional services in a decentralized manner. To allow credit for occupational accomplishments, professionals' tools may include intelligent devices that act as job performance aids, while simultaneously collecting a cognitive audit trail of user skill improvements, creating increasingly informal systems of credentialization. Occupational roles would alter rapidly as the evolution of information technologies drives the knowledge-added economy, and adults might become a much larger clientele of educational institutions (Office of Technology Assessment, 1984).

4. Interlinked "educational information utilities" which supply access to a variety of data, tools, and training might emerge (Dede, 1985b). For example, a device may soon be marketed that combines the attributes of the telephone, radio, television, videotape, computer, copier, and printing press. If I correctly heard an item of interest while watching the nightly news, pushing a function key could output articles on that topic from major newspapers. Scanning those might produce keywords of interest; another keystroke would trigger a knowledge base search.

5. From the list of articles which resulted, I might identify the name of a researcher active in this field; yet another

command would enable dialing that person's work number. If no one answered, a final keystroke could send an electronic mail message. All this integration may seem merely a gain in speed, but from that perspective the airplane is "just" a faster version of the automobile. Such a device (a less powerful version of the intelligent knowledge base in the scenario earlier) could be accessible inexpensively to a wide range of users.

6. Productivity gains from a mature, technology-intensive educational approach could yield a higher overall ratio of learners to teachers, but smaller class sizes for group instruction, through supplementary use of intelligent technologies (Melmed, 1986). Instructor salaries would be higher, and the total educational workforce would increase because of a wider range of clients. Given equivalent expenditures, instructional outcomes would be significantly higher.

7. Long term, the effects of intelligent technologies on cognitive style, personality, and social skills may be profound (Turkle, 1984). The television and the computer have each demonstrated the capability to shape the attributes of youngsters immersed in their usage. The deliberate tailoring of individualized, knowledge-intensive environments could produce a generation radically different in its characteristics from any previous one. For example, a technology-supplemented instructional model could incorporate interactive learning situations designed to build the affective skills of cooperation, compromise, and group decision making essential in a knowledge-added economy. However, unless these devices are carefully implemented, they could intensify the imbalance between cognitive and ethical perspectives described in Azzaretto's chapter.

Although the full range of cognition enhancers will not be widely available for another decade, much can be done to prepare continuing professional education for a paradigmatic shift from communicating information to transferring knowledge. The conceptual and political barriers to such a change are at least as profound as technical and economic constraints. The work of innovative groups in continuing education (as typical of professionals in general) to develop models for acquiring, transmitting, and using their own knowledge will be crucial to a successful transformation.

For example, with the help of the Kellogg Foundation, The University of Georgia is pioneering approaches by which professionals can overcome information overload. A prototype environmental scanning system is collecting and manipulating large amounts of environmental data to refine institutional knowledge (Morrison, 1987). A Personal Adult Learning Services Lab allows professionals access to early generations of empowering environments for education. Efforts such as these are vital building blocks for creating the conceptual understanding of professionals' knowledge transfer needed to actualize the intelligent tools now in development.

Conclusion

The potential implications for civilization of moving from transmitting information to transferring knowledge could be profound. The next generation of information technologies could become history's first "knowledge medium": humanity's conscious mechanism to tailor its cognitive evolution (Stefik, 1986). For example, biologist Richard Dawkins (1976) suggests that ideas (he calls them "memes") are like genes. This opens up a myriad of analogies: meme pools, mimetic drift, mutation, and displacement--even recombinant memes.

At any particular moment, an individual or organization has a certain cognitive ecology of ideas--a meme pool. As the external environment changes and new information is added, "survival of the fittest" alters the balance of different species (types of ideas) in the ecology--mimetic drift. New ideas are mimetic mutations; some survive and prosper, replacing old ideas--mimetic displacement. A creative person or institution may deliberately manipulate this cognitive ecology--recombinant memes. (Of course, such a "survival of the fittest" environment may be functional or dysfunctional, depending on organizational climate.)

If this vision is accurate, over the next generation, civilization may be profoundly shaped by two types of scientific advances: genetic and mimetic manipulation. The professions would be on the forefront of this latter frontier, as professionals' abilities for mimetic manipulation are the heart of their value to society. From this perspective, a major challenge for continuing professional education is aiding its clients to move from scanning large amounts of data to acquiring environmentally meaningful, contextually targeted, interconnected knowledge. Intelligent instructional tools will be central to accomplishing this goal.

However, we as educators must always remember that our primary mission is to help professionals increase their wisdom. Using intelligent tools to aid with knowledge transfer is a vital advance, but a preoccupation with knowledge to the exclusion of affective and moral concerns would be unfortunate. As discussed earlier, partnerships with powerful, automated tools will increase the ethical demands on practitioners . To keep a balance, continuing professional education must develop non-technological innovations to aid in building emotional and ethical skills.

References

Anderson, J. R. (1983). *The architecture of cognition.* Cambridge, MA: Harvard University Press.

Ayres, R. U. (1984). *The next industrial revolution.* New York: Ballinger.

Barrows, H.S., & Tamblyn, R.M. (1980). *Problem-based learning: An approach to medical education.* New York: Springer.

Bateson, G. (1975). *Steps to an ecology of mind.* New York: Ballantine.

Brown, J. S. (1985). Process versus product: A perspective on tools for communal and informal electronic learning. *Journal of Educational Computing Research, 1,* 179-202.

Burke, G., & Rumberger, R.W. (Eds.). (1987). *The future impact of technology on work and education.* New York: Falmer Press.

Coates, J. F. (1977). Aspects of innovation: Public policy issues in telecommunications development. *Telecommunications Policy, 1* (3), 11-13.

Dawkins, R. (1976). *The selfish gene.* New York: Oxford University Press.

Dede, C. J. (1985a). New information technologies, the knowledge based economy, and education. *Educational Media International, 15* (2), 2-9.

Dede, C. J. (1985b). Assessing the potential of educational information utilities. *Library Hi Tech, 3* (4), 115-119.

Dede, C. J. (1986). A review and synthesis of recent research in intelligent computer assisted instruction. *International Journal of Man-Machine Studies, 24* (4), 329-353.

Dede, C. J. (1987a). Artificial intelligence applications to high technology training. *Journal of Educational Communications and Technology, 35*(3), 163-181.

Dede, C. J. (1987b). Empowering environments, hypermedia, and microworlds. *The Computing Teacher, 15* (3), 20-25.

Dede, C. J. (1988). Emerging information technologies of interest for postsecondary occupational education. In K. M. Back, C. J. Dede, P. R. Fama, & O. W. Markley, *Education planning for economic development:* Vol. 29, (pp. 10-78). Austin, TX: Coordinating Board, Texas College and University System.

Dede, C. J. (in press). The probable evolution of artificial intelligence-based educational devices. *Technological Forecasting and Social Change.*

Dede, C. J., Sullivan, T. R., & Scace, J. L. (1988). *Forces shaping the evolution of electronic documentation systems.* Houston, TX: Johnson Space Center, NASA.

Jonassen, D. H. (1986). Hypertext principles for text and courseware design. *Educational Psychologist, 21*(4), 269-292.

Krasner, H., (Ed.). (1986). *Proceedings of CSCW '86.* Austin, TX: Microelectronics and Computer Technology Consortium.

Malone, T. W., & Lepper, M. R. (1985). Making learning fun: A taxonomy of intrinsic motivations for learning. In R. E. Snow & M. J. Farr (Eds.), *Aptitude, Learning, and Instruction: Vol. III. Cognative and affective process analysis* (pp. 223-254). Hillsdale, NJ: Lawrence Erlbaum.

Marien, M. (1971). The discovery and decline of the ignorant society: 1965-1985. In T. Green (Ed.), *Educational Planning in Perspective: Forecasting and Policy-Making* (pp. 80-89). Guildford, Surrey, England: IPC Science and Technology Press.

Melmed, A. (1986). The technology of American education: Problem and opportunity. *T.H.E. Journal, 14* (2), 77-81.

Molnar, A. R. (1982). The search for new intellectual technologies. *T.H.E. Journal, 10* (9), 104-112.

Molnar, A. R. (1987). *Education and the 21st century.* Washington, DC: National Science Foundation.

Morrison, J. L. (1987). Establishing an environmental scanning/forecasting system to augment college and university planning. *Planning for Higher Education, 15* (1), 7-22.

Office of Technology Assessment, U.S. Congress. (1984). *Computerized manufacturing automation: Education, employment, and the workplace.* Washington, DC: U.S. Government Printing Office.

President's Commission on Industrial Competitiveness. (1985). *Global competition: Vol. II. The new reality.* Washington, DC: U. S. Government Printing Office.

Reich, R. B. (1983). *The next American frontier.* New York: Penguin.

Smith, R. B. (1987). Experiences with the alternate reality kit: An example of the tension between literalism and magic. *Proceedings of CHI+GI 1987.* New York: ACM.

Spenner, K. (1985). The upgrading and downgrading of occupations: Issues, evidence, and the implications for education. *Review of Educational Research, 55,* 125-154.

Stefik, M. (1986). The next knowledge medium. *The AI Magazine, 7*(1), 34-46.

Turkle, S. (1984). *The second self: Computers and the human spirit.* New York: Simon & Schuster.

Woods, D. D. (1986). Cognitive technologies: The design of joint human-machine cognitive systems. *The AI Magazine, 6* (4), 86-92.

Yankelovitch, N., Meyrowitz, N., & van Dam, A. (1985). Reading and writing the electronic book. *Computer, 18* (10), 15-30.

Zuboff, S. (1988). *In the age of the smart machine: The future of work and power.* New York: Basic.

Chapter 8

A Model of Professionals as Learners

Ronald M. Cervero

All educational activities for professionals are based on beliefs about how professionals know and incorporate knowledge into practice, under what conditions they learn best, and what role prior experience plays in learning. Although these beliefs are generally not made explicit, they shape the design of continuing professional education in powerful ways. As systems of continuing education for the professions develop and mature, we will continue to see educational programs based on a variety of models of professional knowledge and learning.

The model that currently dominates the provision of continuing education for professionals assumes that professions are service-oriented occupations that apply a systematic body of knowledge to problems that are highly relevant to the central values of society. This viewpoint stresses the functional value of professional activity for the maintenance of society. The key concept in the functionalist viewpoint is expertise. As described by Schon (1983), "Professional activity consists in instrumental problem solving made rigorous by the application of scientific theory and technique" (p. 21). The two key assumptions are that practice problems are well formed and unambiguous and that these problems are solved by the application of scientific knowledge. Thus, professionals are seen as applying a high degree of specialized expertise to solve well-defined practice problems.

The need for well-defined practice problems is crucial. As Moore (1970) states:

If every professional problem were in all respects unique, solutions would be at best accidental, and therefore have nothing to do with expert knowledge. What we are suggesting, on the contrary, is that there are sufficient uniformities in problems and in devices for solving them. Professionals apply very general principles, standardized knowledge, to concrete problems....(p. 56)

With well-defined problems to solve, a systematic knowledge base can be developed more easily and applied with greater effectiveness and efficiency. Practice is rigorous to the extent that it uses "describable, testable, replicable techniques derived from scientific research, based on knowledge that is objective, consensual, cumulative, and convergent" (Schon, 1985, p. 61). Armed with this knowledge, professional practice is seen as essentially technical. The best means (expertise) are selected to solve well-defined problems.

Although the model of professional knowledge based on the functionalist viewpoint accurately represents some forms of learning, there is an emerging viewpoint which accounts more effectively for how professionals learn. The purpose of this chapter is to describe this viewpoint and indicate how it could be implemented to build a more desirable future for continuing professional education. First, the conceptual underpinnings of the critical viewpoint are described and contrasted with the functionalist approach. Next, sources of evidence that support the critical viewpoint are reviewed from 1) the field of cognitive psychology, 2) Schon's writings on the "reflective practitioner," and 3) studies of expertise in the professions. Finally, a model of the learner based on the critical viewpoint is offered.

The Critical Viewpoint

In the past 10 years, a new viewpoint has crystallized in reaction to the functionalist approach. Where functionalism sees well-defined problems, the critical viewpoint assumes that professionals construct the problem from the situation. Because professionals often make choices about what problems to solve as well as how to solve them, this approach stresses the need to be critically aware of these choices and their implications.

The key concept in the critical viewpoint is dialectic. Professionals interact with situations of practice. The ends and means of practice are characterized by a dynamic inner tension and are interconnected, like a web. This view stands in contrast with the separations and consequent linear relationships between knowing and doing, professional and client, and means and ends implicit in the functionalist viewpoint. This linear view of professional practice is challenged on two major counts: the notion of a fixed and unambiguous problem and the basis of professional knowledge.

One often hears professionals claim that most of the problems they see are "not in the book." For example, physicians say that many of their patients' symptoms do not fit into familiar categories of diagnosis and treatment. Thus, the most difficult part of their practice is to decide which of several problems needs to be solved. Once this decision is made, a treatment can be prescribed or a referral made to a specialist. Schon (1987) considers this oft-repeated observation to be central to understanding professional practice:

> In the varied topography of professional practice, there is a high, hard ground overlooking a swamp. On the high ground, manageable problems lend themselves to solution through the application of research-based theory and technique. In the swampy lowland, messy, confusing problems defy technical solution. The irony of this situation is that the problems of the high ground tend to be relatively unimportant to individuals or society at large ... while in the swamp lie the problems of greatest human concern. (p. 3)

Professionals conduct most of their practice in the swamp of the "real world" where problems do not present themselves as well- formed, unambiguous structures, but rather as messy, indeterminate situations.

In the swamp, the practitioner must find or construct problems from ambiguous situations. Thus, problem setting rather than problem solving is the key to professional practice. Practitioners are always in a dialectical relationship with situations that are characterized by uniqueness, uncertainty, or value conflict. Consider the example of the teacher whose student is having difficulty learning how to read. He may not have had a student with this particular set of problems before, so he looks upon this case as unique in many important respects. The teacher may also be uncertain about how to think about the cause of the problem: Is there a neurological problem, is the student not applying himself fully, is a different language spoken at home, or is the student simply developmentally delayed? The teacher may be torn between a variety of value conflicts in the situation. For example, in choosing how to teach reading to this child, he may be torn between the views of his teacher colleagues, his graduate school advisors and textbooks, and his own personal experience. Should he not seek counsel from other teachers because of the fear that the student will be labeled as a slow learner? What if the student is a member of a minority group? Does the teacher worry about evaluating students using culturally biased forms of criteria? This teacher is not simply selecting means to clear ends but also must "reconcile, integrate, or choose among conflicting appreciations of a situation so as to construct a coherent problem worth solving" (Schon, 1987, p. 6).

The second distinguishing characteristic of the critical viewpoint is the nature and source of professional knowledge. Where this knowledge does not come from is clear. At the end of his comprehensive study of the relationship between knowledge and power, Friedson (1986) concludes, "To assume that textbooks and other publications of academics and researchers reflect in consistent and predictable ways the knowledge that is actually exercised in concrete human settings is either wishful or naive" (p. 229). He argues that the formal, research-based knowledge is finally expressed in practice in a way that is considerably modified or even contrary to its original form.

So what is the source of professional knowledge? Schon (1983) argues, "The practitioner has built up a repertoire of examples, images, understandings, and actions" (p. 138). When a professional is trying to make sense of a situation, she sees it as something already present in her repertoire. This knowledge from her repertoire is not applied in a rule-like fashion, but rather functions as a metaphor or exemplar for helping to define the new situation. From her experience as a teacher, Walizer (1986) claims that practitioners "tend to think in terms of specific cases and to make decisions about practice and judgments of individuals based on comparisons with previous, similar experiences" (p. 524). For example, if you ask a teacher how she teaches a concept or handles a classroom problem, you are likely to hear a story about a particular class or student.

The thesis of this chapter is that the critical viewpoint offers a useful way to think about the processes by which professionals learn. Although it does not account for all forms of learning, the critical viewpoint needs to be taken seriously by those who provide leadership for the continuing education of professionals. As Dede points out in his chapter, professional creativity will become even more important in the future as the standardized aspects of problem solving skills are absorbed by intelligent machines. The remainder of this chapter is devoted to a review of the evidence supporting the critical viewpoint and a statement of the model of the learner based on this viewpoint.

Theoretical and Empirical Support for The Critical Viewpoint

Psychologists have always been interested in how people learn. During the early 1970s, the dominant orientation in psychology began to change from behavioristic to cognitive, moving from a focus on observable behavior to the study of mind and how it functions (Shuell, 1986). Much of this research has been conducted with children and with computers (in the field of artificial intelligence) and relatively less with adults. Across these different populations, however, a new consensus has begun to emerge on the nature of learning (Resnik, 1987), a consensus that has a direct bearing on how professionals learn and can be taught most effectively.

Theories and research from cognitive psychology can provide a basic understanding of how professionals develop expertise by describing how the mind works. There is general agreement that in order to understand expertise, one must clearly account for what knowledge is and how it is learned (Glaser, 1984; Glaser, 1985; Sternberg, 1985). In the cognitive conceptions of learning, the focus is on the acquisition of knowledge and knowledge structures rather than on behavior. The model of the learner within the cognitive approach is based on the following premise: Learning is an active, constructive, and goal-oriented process that is dependent upon the mental activities of the learner. This view, of course, contrasts with the behavioral orientation that focuses on behavioral changes requiring a predominantly reactive response from the learner to various environmental factors (Shuell, 1986, p. 415).

Cognitive psychologists use schema theory to explain knowledge (Glaser, 1984). This theory describes how acquired knowledge is organized in the mind and how cognitive structures facilitate the use of knowledge in particular situations. In this kind of theory, schemata represent knowledge that we experience, interrelationships between situations and events that normally occur. Schemata are prototypes in memory of frequently experienced situations that people use to construct interpretations of related situations. Schemata can be thought of as internal models that professionals use as they face new situations.

Cognitive psychologists have identified a variety of types of knowledge structures or schemata. One of the most fundamental distinctions is made between declarative and procedural knowledge, the former being *knowledge that* and the latter being *knowledge how* (Shuell, 1986). Declarative knowledge is our knowledge about things and is represented in memory as an interrelated network of facts (such as, 2 + 2 = 4) that exist as propositions. Procedural knowledge is our knowledge about how to perform (such as, producing the correct sum when given an addition problem). There is open debate about which kind of knowledge is learned first. The answer has important implications for one's model of the learner. If one believes that knowledge in a new domain always begins as declarative knowledge (Anderson, 1983), then the transmission of information about a given topic to learners is clearly the method of choice. A contrasting viewpoint is that all knowledge is properly considered as *knowledge how* and individuals can sometimes transform this knowledge into *knowledge that* (Rumelhart & Norman, 1981, p. 343). Thus, knowledge is acquired by doing because "expertise comes about through the use of knowledge and not by an analysis of knowledge" (Neves & Anderson, 1981, p. 83).

A key form of procedural knowledge is the manner in which one represents the problem to be solved. As most cognitive psychologists agree, the way the problem is posed determines the way it will be solved (Getzels, 1979; Glaser, 1984; Sternberg, 1985). Glaser (1984) explains that there "are schemata for recurrent situations, and that one of their major functions is to construct interpretations of situations" (p. 100). Although the processes of problem finding and of problem solving meld into one another, there are differences between the act of thought in problem solving that begins with an already formulated problem and one that must begin with creating the problem itself (Getzels, 1979). This emphasis on problem finding is an important component of professional practice within the critical viewpoint.

The key assumption underlying the acquisition of knowledge is that learning is cumulative in nature; that is, nothing has meaning or is learned in isolation from prior experience (Shuell, 1986). This assumption has a glorious pedigree dating to Dewey (1933), who said, "No one can think about anything without experience and information about it" (p. 34). If people continually try to understand and think about the new in terms of what they already know, then an effective cycle of learning exists. Schemata can be considered as internal models to be used as professionals represent new situations. One compares the schemata with the situation; and if it fails to account for certain aspects, "It can be either accepted temporarily, rejected, modified, or replaced" (Glaser, 1984, p. 100). In this way, new knowledge structures are created through everyday experience.

Educational Implications

The model of the learner and of learning arising from cognitive psychology has important implications for educational interventions in which one wishes to change what professionals know or do. Because learning is an active process, the educator's task necessarily involves more than the transmission of information. The educator must take into account professionals' prior knowledge because their understanding and interpretation depend upon the availability of appropriate schemata. The educational context must be arranged so that professionals can test, evaluate, and modify their existing schemata so that some resolution can be achieved between the learners' knowledge structures and the new one being proposed. Glaser (1984) suggests that an effective strategy for instruction "involves a kind of interrogation and confrontation. Expert teachers do this effectively, employing case method approaches, discovery methods, and various forms of Socratic inquiry dialogue" (p. 101). A major goal of this form of instruction would be to teach learners how to derive schemata that will be useful in practice. The professional learns what questions to ask to construct useful schemata, how to test new schemata, and what their useful properties are. In summary, the most salient concept from cognitive psychology is consistent with much of what has been described as good practice in teaching adults: "Without taking away from the important role played by the teacher, it is helpful to remember that what the student does is actually more important in determining what is learned than what the teacher does" (Shuell, 1986, p. 429).

Schon's Model of Professional Practice

Schon (1983, 1987) has developed a model of professional practice based on detailed studies of several professions, including architecture, town planning, management, and organizational consulting. As identified in the previous section, the two questions central to constructing a model of the learner are: What is professional knowledge and how is it acquired?

Schon (1983) calls the dominant understanding of professional knowledge "technical rationality." In this view, knowledge is conceived as the basic and applied research that is generated within the university setting. Each profession has a systematic knowledge base that has four essential properties: "It is specialized, firmly bounded, scientific, and standardized" (p. 23). The professional selects the appropriate knowledge to apply to situations of practice. This conception of knowledge is the basis of the functional viewpoint. While there is general agreement that some professionals perform in a superior fashion to others, technical rationality does not adequately describe the forms of knowledge that distinguish the excellent practitioner from the merely adequate one. Thus, Schon argues that technical rationality cannot account for the processes that are central to professional artistry.

Schon's solution is consistent with the critical viewpoint in which professional practice is characterized by indeterminate situations that must be transformed into determinate ones (that is, situations that the practitioner knows how to solve). In order to understand the relationship between professional knowledge and artistry, "We should start not by asking how to make better use of research-based knowledge but by asking what we can learn from a careful examination of artistry, that is, the competence by which practitioners actually handle indeterminate zones of practice" (Schon, 1987, p. 13). By studying professional artistry in a variety of professional fields, Schon has identified two forms of knowing that are central to professional artistry: knowing-in-action and reflection-in-action. Because the latter is central to artistry, Schon's new model of professional knowledge is called "reflection-in-action."

In contrast to the model of technical rationality, which views practice as the application of knowledge, Schon's model assumes that knowing is in the actions of professionals. Many of the spontaneous actions that professionals take do not stem from a rule or plan that was in the mind before the action. Professionals constantly make judgments and decisions for which they cannot state the rules or theories on which their decisions were based. Schon (1983) calls this knowing-in-action and describes it as "the characteristic mode of ordinary practical knowledge" (p. 54). This form of knowing has three properties: 1) there are actions and judgments that professionals know how to carry out without thinking about them prior to or during performance, 2) there is no awareness of having learned to do these things, and 3) there is an inability to describe the knowing that the action reveals (p. 54). It is sometimes possible, by reflecting upon actions, to describe the tacit knowing implicit in them. It must be understood, however, that the descriptions of knowing-in-action are always constructions of reality, which need to be tested against observations of actual behavior.

Most situations of professional practice are characterized by uniqueness, uncertainty, and value conflict. Therefore, more often than not, knowing-in-action will not solve a particular problem. Rather, one needs to construct the situation so as to make it solvable. The ability to do this, to reflect in action, is the core of professional artistry. Professionals reflect in the midst of action without interrupting it. Their thinking reshapes what they are doing while they are doing it. The goal of reflection-in-action is to change indeterminate situations into determinate ones, and the key to successfully completing this problem setting activity is to bring past experience to bear.

Through their past experience, professionals have built up a repertoire of examples, images, understandings, and actions (Schon, 1983, p. 138). As practitioners make sense of a situation perceived as unique in several important respects, they see it as something already present in their repertoires. Although the present and past situations are not precisely the same, they are sufficiently similar so that past experience can be used to make sense of the current situation. When practitioners acquire a new way of seeing the present situation, the utility of this new view must be evaluated by asking whether 1) the situation can be framed in such a way as to make it solvable and 2) the results of this problem solving process are valued. This entire process is achieved in the midst of action. Professionals rethink some part of their knowing-in-action, conduct an on-the-spot thought experiment to test its utility, and incorporate this new understanding into immediate action.

The knowing-in-action of practitioners is acquired from the research produced by universities, in industry, and from the reflection-in-action undertaken in the indeterminate zones of practice (Schon, 1987, p. 40). Reflection-in-action can generate knowledge to be used in new situations, not by giving rise to general principles, but "by contributing to the practitioner's repertoire of exemplary themes from which, in the subsequent cases of his practice, he may compose new variations" (p. 140).

Schon (1983) is less certain about how reflection-in-action is acquired and has called for more research regarding how some people learn more effectively than others. In putting forth his hypotheses on this question, he argues that people reflect in action as a matter of course in their everyday lives. Thus, when practitioners learn the artistry of professional practice, they learn new ways of using the kinds of competence they already possess. They bring generic competencies for communication, experimentation, and imitation on which they can build (Schon, 1987, p. 118). These general competences allow one to reflect in action spontaneously; but to improve that ability, professionals must reflect on their reflection-in-action through the act of describing what they did. As professionals can more consciously describe how they reflect and what that teaches them, they can more readily employ that form of knowing in new situations.

Educational Implications

Schon (1987) has written about how this new model of professional knowledge can be used to reshape pre-service professional education. The implications for continuing professional education can be translated from his prescription: "Professional education should be redesigned to combine the teaching of applied science with coaching in the artistry of reflection-in-action" (p. xii). The teaching of applied science, which is standard fare in continuing professional education, needs to be based on a model of the learner consistent with Schon's views. Second, there is a need to focus directly on the acquisition of reflection-in-action.

Schon (1987) believes there is an important role for research as a source for knowing-in-action. However, this applied science must not stand alone but be incorporated with reflection-in-action; otherwise, it has little chance of becoming part of a practitioner's repertoire. Formal continuing education programs should become opportunities for practitioners to "learn to reflect on their own tacit theories of the phenomena or practice, in the presence of representatives of those disciplines" (p. 321) that are related to their practice situations. This is a repertoire-building process that serves the function of accumulating and describing exemplars in ways useful to reflection-in-action. Commonly used ways of teaching in various professions can promote this process. The teaching of "how to think like a lawyer," the use of case method in business education, and the study of case histories in medical education can serve the function of connecting university-based research and theories with practical ways of knowing.

The second implication is to focus on the task of improving professional artistry directly by improving professionals' ability to reflect in action. This is potentially more important, not only because it is the core of professional artistry, but also because reflection-in-action is an important source of knowledge for professionals' repertoires. Reflection on practice must become an explicit part of continuing education. This concern could be addressed by examining the "ways in which competent practitioners cope with the constraints of their organizational settings" (Schon, 1987, p. 322). Professionals would reflect on the frames they intuitively bring to their performance in the presence of instructors who would explain how they would perform under these conditions, demonstrating their own approaches to skillful performance and reflecting with students on the frames that underlie their work.

Theories of Expertise in Three Professions

A body of theory and research which is consistent with the critical viewpoint is developing on the nature of professional expertise (Dreyfus & Dreyfus, 1986; Kennedy, 1987). As this body of research seeks to explain expertise through a careful examination of professional practice, it echoes many themes from cognitive psychology and Schon's writings. In this section, the research from three disparate professional groups (nurses, business executives, and teachers) is reviewed to illustrate current understandings of the development of professional expertise. Three topics are addressed for each profession: the nature of knowledge, the way in which knowledge is acquired, and the resulting educational implications.

Nurses

Benner (1984) has developed a model of expertise in clinical nursing practice based on an intensive study of nurses in actual patient care situations. By uncovering the knowledge embedded in nursing practice, Benner presents "the limits of formal rules and calls attention to the discretionary judgment used in actual clinical situations" (p. xix). In this way, Benner focuses on what cognitive psychologists call procedural knowledge and what Schon identified as the indeterminate zones of practice. The central premise of her theory is: "Expertise develops when the clinician tests and refines propositions, hypotheses, and principle-based expectations in actual practice situations" (p. 3). Her study identified six types of practical knowledge: 1) graded qualitative distinctions; 2) common meanings; 3) assumptions, expectations, and sets; 4) paradigm cases and personal knowledge; 5) maxims; and 6) unplanned practices. These forms of knowledge are acquired as nurses move through a five-stage sequence in developing skills in actual nursing situations.

Expert nurses have the perceptual and recognitional ability to make graded qualitative distinctions in patient care situations. For example, some nurses learn to recognize subtle physiological changes as early warnings to severe medical conditions, such as heart attack or shock. These finely tuned abilities come only from many hours of direct patient care. Nurses working with common issues in patient care develop common meanings about helping, recovering, and utilizing coping resources in these situations. These common meanings, which evolve over time and are shared among nurses, form a tradition. For example, one common meaning is that nurses typically try to develop a sense of "possibility" for their patients, even in the most extreme situations. From having clinical experience with many similar and dissimilar patients, nurses learn to expect a certain course of events without ever formally stating those expectations. These expectations, which generally show up only in clinical practice and not in statements of formal knowledge, determine how clinical situations are perceived and how those situations are handled. Nurses encounter particular experiences that are powerful enough to stand out as paradigm cases. Expert nurses develop clusters of paradigm cases around different patient care issues. These clusters guide their perceptions and actions in current situations. This type of knowledge is more comprehensive than any theory because the nurse compares whole past situations with whole current situations.

Nurses pass on cryptic instructions, which Benner (1984) terms maxims, that make sense only if the person already has a deep understanding of the situation. For example, intensive care nurses cryptically describe subtle changes in premature infants' respiratory status that would make sense only to one who has had a great deal of experience in these situations. The nursing role in hospitals has expanded largely through unplanned practices delegated by the physician and other health care workers. For example, new treatments that must be administered by physicians are frequently left to nurses because they are present at patients' bedsides on a regular basis. This important form of knowledge is often overlooked because it is not a part of nurses' formal roles. Benner concludes, "A wealth of untapped knowledge is embedded in the practices and the 'know-how' of expert nurse clinicians" (p. 11) which is not recognized because nurses have failed to systematically record what they learn from their own experiences.

These six types of practical nursing knowledge are central to skilled nursing practices. This practical "know-how" is the difference between novice and expert nurses and is acquired only through experience, which "results when preconceived notions and expectations are challenged, refined, or disconfirmed by the actual situation" (Benner, 1984, p. 3). In learning any area of practice, nurses pass through five levels of proficiency: novice, advanced beginner, competent, proficient, and expert (Dreyfus & Dreyfus, 1986). These different levels reflect changes in three general areas of skilled performance. One is a movement from reliance on abstract principles to past concrete experience in actual clinical situations. In the second, nurses see the practice situations, more and more, as a complete whole and, less and less, as a compilation of equally relevant bits of information. The third is a movement from detached observer to involved performer.

Novices have no experience in the situations in which they are expected to perform. Without this experience, they must be given general rules to guide their performance. "But following rules legislates against successful performance because the rules cannot tell them the most relevant tasks to perform in an actual situation" (Benner, 1984, p. 21). Advanced beginners can demonstrate marginally acceptable performance because they have coped with enough real situations to learn the recurring meaningful situational components that Benner (1984) terms "aspects of the situation" (p. 22). Competent nurses see their actions in terms of long-range plans of which they are consciously aware. This plan dictates which aspects of the situation are to be considered and which can be ignored. Proficient nurses, in contrast, perceive situations holistically, rather than in terms of aspects, and performance is guided by maxims. Because of this ability to recognize whole situations, the proficient nurse can recognize when the expected normal picture does not materialize and proceed more quickly to reframe the situation in a way that makes it solvable. Expert nurses do not rely on an analytic principle (rule, guideline, maxim) to connect their understanding of the situation to an appropriate action. With an enormous background of experience, they have an intuitive grasp of each situation and "zero in" on the problem without wasteful consideration of a large range of alternative solutions. It must be

emphasized that this developmental model of expertise is situation-specific so that any nurse entering a situation where she has no experience may
be limited to the novice level of performance if the goals and tools of patient
care are unfamiliar to her.

Educational implications. The most important educational implication of this model is that nursing education programs need to promote
clinical knowledge development so that each nurse learns from clinical
experience. It is important to note, however, that different instructional
strategies are necessary for each level of proficiency because knowledge
is acquired differently at each level. Novices are the most difficult to plan
for because they have no experience on which to draw. The best strategy
is to make the "aspects of the situation" as explicit as possible and try
whenever possible to include a clinical component to the program.
Advanced beginners and competent nurses have enough experience to
allow an instructor to focus on "the more advanced clinical skill of judging
the relative importance of different aspects of the situation" (Benner, 1984,
p. 24). Nurses at the proficient and expert levels can benefit most from ex-
changes, clinical case studies, and opportunities to conduct and participate in research on clinical problems. These nurses could provide case
studies from their own practice that illustrate either expertise or a
breakdown in performance. By working through these cases, the learners
would begin to make explicit the practical knowledge available in their
repertoires, as well as the processes by which they frame the situations
they encounter.

Business Executives

There has been an increasing amount of research in the past
several years on the cognitive processes underlying expert performance
among business managers and senior executives (Isenberg, 1984; Wagner
& Sternberg, 1985; Weick, 1983). Although these processes are described
by researchers in different language, such as intuition (Isenberg, 1984),
thoughtful action (Weick, 1983), and practical intelligence (Wagner &
Sternberg, 1985), the common denominator is the effort to understand
expert executives' knowledge and how they use it in "real life" situations.

The next section reviews Isenberg's work (1984, 1985, 1986) to
illustrate some of the conclusions of this line of inquiry. Isenberg shares
with the others a greater emphasis on understanding what knowledge is
and how it is used and a relatively lesser emphasis on the acquisition of
knowledge.

Isenberg (1984) studied 12 senior managers, who were considered excellent performers, in a variety of ways, including conducting

intensive interviews, observing them on the job, and engaging them in exercises in which they recounted their thoughts as they did their work. A major conclusion is that managers seldom think in ways that might be termed "rational." That is, they generally do not formulate goals, assess their worth, evaluate alternative ways of reaching them, and then choose the way that maximizes expected return. Rather, thinking and acting are inseparable. Thinking and acting are linked in what Isenberg calls "thinking/acting cycles" in which managers develop thoughts about their companies, not by analyzing a problematic situation and then acting, but by thinking and acting in close concert. An implication of this cycle is that action is often part of defining the problem, not just of implementing a solution. This observation is consistent with Schon's argument that a practitioner's ability to reflect on actions while doing them is essential to professional practice.

The primary sources of executives' knowledge are mental images, experienced and stored scenarios, rules of thumb, and "repertoires of familiar problematic situations matched with the necessary responses" (Isenberg, 1984, p. 86). These forms of knowledge are acquired through extensive experience in problem solving and implementation and are stored in memory. The major basis for executives' performance in complex situations is to retrieve these possible courses of action from memory as a result of recognizing familiar features of the problem situation. Knowledge is retrieved through a combination of intuition and calculated deductive thinking. Although both cognitive processes are important, Isenberg puts greater emphasis on intuition as central to the expertise of business executives.

Intuition is not the opposite of rationality, nor is it a random process of guessing. Rather, intuition is "an important thought process for senior managers to use that is based on very rapid recognition, categorization, and retrieval of familiar patterns" (Isenberg, 1985, p. 185). Managers use intuition in five distinct ways. First, they can intuitively sense when a problem exists. Isenberg cites the example of a chief financial officer who forecast a difficult year ahead for the company and, based on a vague "gut" feeling that something was wrong, decided to analyze one division. He found out that the division heads were talking about a future that was not going to happen and thus were putting the entire company at risk. Second, managers rely on intuition to perform well-learned behavior patterns without being aware of the effort. This is very similar to what Schon calls "knowing-in-action." A third function of intuition is to synthesize isolated bits of information and experience into an integrated picture. This process is comparable to Benner's description of the proficient nurse who perceives situations as wholes rather than in terms of aspects of the situation. Fourth, some managers use intuition as a check on more deductive and purposeful thinking. Typically, managers work on an issue until they find a match between intuitive and purposeful types of thinking. Finally, managers can use intuition to bypass in-depth analysis and move rapidly to arrive at a plausible solution. Used in this way, intuition is an instantaneous process in which a manager recognizes familiar patterns.

Educational implications. As mentioned earlier, Isenberg and others have paid relatively less attention to how executives acquire their knowledge, and thus they have not been explicit about how their knowledge and skills could be fostered through education. However, given the focus on the experiential basis of executives' knowledge, many of the strategies suggested earlier in this chapter seem appropriate. Strategies that help executives become more aware of their repertoire of "possible courses of action" and the process by which they think in action should be central to the educational processes. Several that have been suggested include case method approaches, simulation exercises, assessment centers, and coaching to help learners acquire the ability to reflect in action.

Teachers

Of the three professions in this section, the research and theory base about the structure and acquisition of teachers' knowledge is the largest. There are several large-scale research efforts to uncover this knowledge (Berliner, 1986; Shulman, 1986) and several major reviews of the literature (Clark & Peterson, 1986; Feiman-Nemser & Floden, 1986; Kennedy, 1987) on this topic. One strand of this literature is consistent with the critical viewpoint and has examined teachers' practical knowledge, that is, those beliefs, insights, and habits that enable teachers to do their work in schools (Feiman-Nemser & Floden, 1986). This viewpoint rejects the notion that researchers have knowledge and teachers have experience. It places teachers' practical knowledge, which is gained through experience, at the center of professional practice. In contrast to academic knowledge, teachers' practical knowledge is time-bound and situation-specific, personally compelling, and directed toward action.

The work of Elbaz (1981, 1983) is used to illustrate some of the major conclusions regarding teachers' practical knowledge. Elbaz sought to describe the content, organization, and acquisition of practical knowledge embedded in the practice of one high school teacher. Sarah, the subject of the study, had about 10 years teaching experience and was a "responsible and respected member of the English department of her school" (1981, p. 56). Elbaz studied Sarah using several clinical interviews and observations of her classroom performance.

For Elbaz (1981), teachers' knowledge is in a dynamic relationship with practice in that it shapes practice and is derived from practice: "Teachers' knowledge is broadly based on their experiences in classrooms and schools and is directed toward the handling of problems that arise in their work" (p. 67). The five content areas of Sarah's practical knowledge are self-explanatory: subject matter, curriculum, instruction, self, and milieu. However, Elbaz's typology of the structural forms of this knowledge (rules of practice, principles of practice, images) provides a particularly useful way to think about professionals' knowledge and its dynamics in use.

Rules of practice are brief, clearly formulated statements prescribing what to do and how to do it in frequently encountered practice situations. Teachers implement these rules by recognizing a situation and remembering the relevant rule. In using a rule of practice, the ends or purposes of action are taken for granted. For example, Sarah has a rule for dealing with a learning disabled student: "He has my full attention after I finish all the instructions" (Elbaz, 1983, p. 133). This description bears a resemblance to Schon's "knowing-in-action" in that there are many situations which are not problematic for professionals.

In contrast, a practical principle is more general than a rule of practice and is used when the situation is uncertain. Thus, a principle requires that a teacher reflect in action on the situation in order to turn the principle into effective action. For example, when Sarah talks of trying to make the kids happy to walk into the classroom, she states a principle that governs a variety of practices ranging from unstructured talk to coaching a student for an upcoming exam (Feiman-Nemser & Floden, 1986).

Images capture the teacher's knowledge at the most general level, orienting her overall conduct rather than directing specific actions. These images are personally held mental pictures of how good teaching should look and feel, expressed by the teacher in brief metaphoric statements. The image of a "window" is used by Sarah to orient her practice. She wanted to have a "window onto her students," and she wanted her own "window to be more open." For Elbaz (1983), images are the most important form of knowledge because they express teachers' purposes. Whereas rules and principles direct action in specific situations, images order all aspects of practical knowledge. Images also "extend knowledge by generating new rules and principles and by helping to choose among them when they conflict" (Feiman-Nemser & Floden, 1986, p. 514).

Teachers' practical knowledge cannot be acquired vicariously (for example in teacher preparation courses), but rather is learned and tested through field experience: "The teacher's knowledge grows out of the world of teaching as he experiences it; it gives shape to that world and allows him to function in it" (Elbaz, 1981, p. 58). Elbaz argues that teachers have no unique, specialized methods by which to develop practical knowledge, but must use their skills of observation, comparison, trial and error, and reflection in practice situations. This view agrees with Schon's in that, when professionals learn the artistry of professional practice, they learn new ways of using competencies they already possess, such as experimentation and imitation.

Educational implications. Although Elbaz does not provide any specific suggestions for educational planning, she does offer several orienting principles. The key suggestion is that continuing education for teachers must build on what teachers already believe about their work. As is true of other professionals, however, many teachers do not know what they know, so that a first step would be to help teachers uncover the rules of practice, practical principles, and images that guide their practice. In those programs in which the focus is on researchers' theories, there should be an experientially-based component whereby the teacher-learners can test (either through actual performance or discussion) the relationship of these theories to their existing store of practical knowledge.

As would be expected when attempting to review several disparate sources, the evidence from cognitive psychology, Schon's work on the "reflective practitioner," and the theories of expertise in the professions differ in language and areas of emphasis. Yet there are many points of convergence in the understandings of how professionals know and the processes by which they acquire their knowledge. In the chapter's final section these understandings are synthesized into a model of professionals as learners.

A Model of the Learner

The choice of which model of the learner to use must be situation-specific because even the proponents of the critical viewpoint recognize the need for professionals to learn what Schon describes as the results of basic and applied science. Indeed, declarative knowledge cannot be ignored in the development of professional artistry. However, we know very little about practical knowledge that is integrated into professionals' know-how, forming the basis of professional artistry. Although it is inappropriate to use a model of the learner based on the critical viewpoint in all situations, it must be used more frequently in order to improve professional artistry.

Directly stated, this model of the professional as a learner is one in which professionals construct an understanding of current situations of practice using a repertoire of practical knowledge acquired primarily through experience in prior "real life" situations. This model has implications for both what is to be learned in continuing education programs in order to develop professional artistry or expertise and how this content can be learned most effectively.

Two forms of knowing must be fostered through continuing professional education. First, the focus must be on what Benner and Elbaz termed practical knowledge and what cognitive psychologists call procedural knowledge or know-how. This form of knowing is contrasted with what is variously termed academic knowledge, technical rational knowledge, or declarative knowledge, which can be characterized as *knowledge that*. Practical knowledge is generally understood as a repertoire of examples, metaphors, images, practical principles, scenarios, or rules of thumb that have been developed primarily through prior experience. Because most professionals are not fully aware of the knowledge in their repertoire, it is as important to help them make explicit this knowledge as to help them to develop new knowledge.

The second form of knowing that must be fostered consists of the processes by which professionals use their practical knowledge to construct an understanding of current situations of practice. This process of thinking in action has been variously called reflection-in-action (Schon), intuition (Isenberg), or problem finding (cognitive psychologists). Unlike practical knowledge, which is unique to an individual professional's practice, the process by which knowledge is used is a universal, human cognitive act. Thus, both Schon and Elbaz argue that professionals use similar skills to construct an understanding of situations both within and outside their practice. The continuing professional educator can help the learner to make these processes more explicit and thereby make them open to evaluation and improvement.

The starting point of developing educational strategies to most effectively foster these forms of knowing must be that they can be learned but cannot be taught. As the cognitive psychologists remind us, what the learner does is more important in determining what is learned than what the instructor does. If one seeks to develop either kind of knowing in the educational context itself, the key is to provide experientially based methods, such as case studies or Schon's examples of coaching, by which learners can uncover or develop their practical knowledge or the processes by which they use it. In Benner's model, the choice of which educational method to use would depend partly on the level of expertise that the learners possess. Educators may also be able to help learners acquire this knowledge in the context of their daily practice. Thus, Benner and Schon call for helping learners become researchers of their own practice. Glaser argues for using discovery methods, which can model for the learner how to ask questions in problematic situations and to test the usefulness of the results of the questions.

There are risks in using this model of the learner that must be understood and avoided. First, educators can glorify professionals' practical knowledge simply because it is the knowledge they use in daily practice. In this way, educators can make the mistake of believing that the way things are is the way they should be. It should be made clear that practical knowledge must be justified on the basis of public criteria rather than private ones. Second, while recognizing the primacy of practical forms of knowledge, educators should not dismiss technical knowledge. Rather, in fostering the learning of technical knowledge, educators must focus on ways of integrating this into professionals' repertoires of practical knowledge.

It is likely that a variety of models of the learner will guide future systems of continuing education. The argument of this chapter is that current efforts have relied too much on a model that does not accurately portray central features of professional practice. Although some continuing education programs are based on the model proposed above, they are not nearly as prevalent as is needed to develop most effectively professional artistry. In order to do so, this new model must become a guiding principle in the maturation of continuing professional education.

References

Anderson, J. R. (1983). *The architecture of cognition.* Cambridge: Harvard University Press.

Benner, P. (1984). *From novice to expert: Excellence and power in clinical nursing practice.* Menlo Park, CA: Addison-Wesley.

Berliner, D. C. (1986). In pursuit of the expert pedagogue. *Educational Researcher, 15,* 5-13.

Clark, C. M., & Peterson, P. L. (1986). Teachers' thought processes. In M. C. Wittrock (Ed.), *Handbook of research on teaching* (3rd ed.) (pp. 255-296). New York: Macmillan.

Dewey, J. (1933). *How we think: A restatement of the relation of reflective thinking to the educative process.* Boston: D. C. Heath.

Dreyfus, H. L., & Dreyfus, S. E. (1986). *Mind over machine.* Oxford: Basil Blackwell.

Elbaz, F. (1981). The teacher's practical knowledge: Report of a case study. *Curriculum Inquiry, 11,* 43-71.

Elbaz, F. (1983). *Teacher thinking: A study of practical knowledge.* New York: Nichols.

Feiman-Nemser, S., & Floden, R. E. (1986). The cultures of teaching. In M. C. Wittrock (Ed.), *Handbook of research on teaching* (3rd ed.) (pp. 505-526). New York: Macmillan.

Friedson, E. (1986). *Professional powers.* Chicago: The University of Chicago Press.

Getzels, J. W. (1979). Problem finding: A theoretical note. *Cognitive Science, 3,* 167-172.

Glaser, R. (1984). Education and thinking: The role of knowledge. *American Psychologist, 39,* 93-104.

Glaser, R. (1985). All's well that begins and ends with both knowledge and process: A reply to Sternberg. *American Psychologist, 40,* 573-574.

Isenberg, D. J. (1984). How senior managers think. *Harvard Business Review, 62,* 81-90.

Isenberg, D. J. (1985). The author replies. *Harvard Business Review, 63,* 185-186.

Isenberg, D. J. (1986). Thinking and managing: A verbal protocol analysis of managerial problem solving. *Academy of Management Journal, 29,* 775-788.

Kennedy, M. M. (1987). Inexact sciences: Professional education and the development of expertise. In E. Z. Rothkopf (Ed.), *Review of research in education, 14* (pp. 133-167). Washington, DC:American Educational Research Association.

Moore, W. E. (1970). *The professions: Roles and rules.* New York: Russell Sage Foundation.

Neves, D. M., & Anderson, J. R. (1981). Knowledge compilation: Mechanisms for automatization of cognitive skills. In J. R. Anderson (Ed.), *Cognitive skills and their acquisition* (pp. 57-84). Hillsdale, New Jersey: Lawrence Erlbaum Associates.

Resnik, L. B. (1987). Learning in school and out. *Educational Researcher, 16,* 13-20.

Rueschemeyer, D. (1964). Doctors and lawyers: A comment on the theory of professions. *Canadian Review of Sociology and Anthropology, 1,* 17-30.

Rumelhart, D. E., & Norman, D. A. (1981). Analogical processes in learning. In J. R. Anderson (Ed.), *Cognitive skills and their acquisition* (pp. 335-359). Hillsdale, New Jersey: Lawrence Erlbaum Associates.

Schon, D. A. (1983). *The reflective practitioner.* New York. Basic Books.

Schon, D. A. (1985). Towards a new epistemology of practice: A response to the crisis of professional knowledge. In A. Thomas and E. W. Ploman (Eds.), *Learning and development: A global perspective* (pp. 56-79). Toronto: The Ontario Institute for Studies in Education.

Schon, D. A. (1987). *Educating the reflective practitioner.* San Francisco: Jossey-Bass.

Shuell, T. J. (1986). Cognitive conceptions of learning. *Review of Educational Research, 56,* 411-436.

Shulman, L. S. (1986). Those who understand: Knowledge growth in teaching. *Educational Researcher, 15,* 4-14.

Sternberg, R. J. (1985). All's well that ends well, but it's a sad tale that begins at the end: A reply to Glaser. *American Psychologist, 40,* 571-573.

Wagner, R. K., & Sternberg, R. J. (1985). Practical intelligence in real-world pursuits: The role of tacit knowledge. *Journal of Personality and Social Psychology, 49,* 436-458.

Walizer, M. E. (1986). The professor and the practitioner think about teaching. *Harvard Educational Review, 56,* 520-526.

Weick, K. E. (1983). Managerial thought in the context of action. In S. Srivastva (Ed.), *The executive mind* (pp. 221-242). San Francisco: Jossey-Bass.

Chapter 9

Professionals as Learners: A Strategy for Maximizing Professional Growth

Wayne D. Smutz
Donna S. Queeney

Across the professions, continuing education has been championed as a means of promoting competency and as a necessity for disseminating new knowledge (Cervero, 1985; Queeney & Shuman, 1988; Young, 1985). Engineers claim, for example, that the future of high technology in the United States is dependent on acceptance of formal lifelong education as an integral part of their profession (Bruce, Siebert, Smullin, & Fano, 1982). Despite this optimistic outlook, however, continuing professional education, as currently structured, cannot be counted on to meet the true educational needs of professionals or to protect sufficiently the interests of the public.

Indicative of this state of affairs is the lack of conclusive evidence of continuing professional education's effectiveness and value to professional practice (Holt & Courtenay, 1985). Importantly, the stakes are too high for this situation to continue. Thus, a strategy is needed for making the most of opportunities offered by continuing professional education if it is to realize its potential and have the maximum possible impact on professionals (Cervero & Young, 1987; Houle, 1983). The following chapter reviews factors relevant to the development of such a strategy and presents a proposal for a comprehensive approach to continuing professional education.

The Challenge to Continuing Professional Education

Continuing professional education is no longer a luxury but a necessity. While in the past continued learning was undertaken on an informal basis through readings and consultation with colleagues, it has become apparent that this approach will no longer suffice. A more formal, coherent continuing professional education strategy is essential. The public's call for competent professionals demands it, professional associations' insistence on standards for their fields requires it, and the individual professional's pride in his or her work should dictate it (Queeney, 1984a).

Such an orientation to continued learning throughout the years of professional practice does not have a long history. Even pre-professional education of past generations was limited. Consider teachers who less than 50 years ago were sent into the classroom with only two years' educational preparation or attorneys of that era who went into practice with a total of four years' postsecondary education as opposed to the baccalaureate-plus-law-school pattern of today. Perhaps understandably, additional education for practicing professionals scarcely occurred to these groups.

Despite Cervero and Young's (1987) claim that professional leaders of the past assumed practitioner participation in learning throughout life, the professional world has only fairly recently arrived at the realization that the young graduate is not prepared to participate for the next half century without the benefit of additional formal education. As the volume and rate of knowledge increased in the past two decades, leaders in those professions perhaps most affected (e.g., medicine, accounting) began to recognize the urgency for practitioners to continue their learning in a more formal manner. Along with increased consumer concern about professional competence, this recognition led to the encouragement, and sometimes the requirement, of continuing professional education within a variety of professions. The concept of continuing professional education subsequently increased in complexity, so that past approaches have now ceased to be appropriate (Niebuhr, 1984).

A New Kind of Education

These changes of the last 20 years suggest that it is time to recognize continuing professional education as a distinctive type of education, for it is neither a simple extension of pre-professional education nor identical to traditional continuing education. Certainly it builds on previous formal education, but it also must take into account the informal learning that accompanies professional practice and the need to integrate new knowledge. The creation of a systematic approach to continuing professional education thus must recognize its unique features, its commonalties and differences with the rest of the education continuum--primary, secondary, postsecondary, pre-professional, and professional education--and its relationship to daily practice.

While continuing professional education is different from pre-professional preparation, a relationship between the two educational levels is critical. Aside from the need for compatibility of content, students preparing for professional practice should come to understand--and even assume--that entry level education is but the first step in what must be a lifelong process of learning in their chosen fields. Faculty members, not only must believe in this concept, but also must imbue their students with this belief and give students tools with which to become intelligent consumers of continuing professional education. But the orientation to and preparation for lifelong learning that should be an integral part of pre-professional education has been slow in coming. Academic institutions across the nation are just awakening to the value of and possibilities for continuing professional education. Much more is needed, however. If not motivated by altruism, higher education should at least be amenable to protecting the institutional reputation. What self-respecting university wants to claim an incompetent practitioner as its graduate?

Distinguishing between continuing professional education and traditional continuing education is also important. Currently, recognition of the differences between the two is limited, perhaps even more so among continuing educators than among practicing professionals. Complete agreement on a commonly accepted definition of continuing professional education remains elusive (Queeney, 1987). While care should be taken to avoid a dispute over semantics, consensus regarding the defining characteristics of continuing professional education is an essential first step in making the distinction. The notion that continuing professional education remediates deficiencies, fosters growth, and facilitates change for professional practitioners (Scanlon, 1985), coupled with the concept that it is related to the application of professional skills in daily practice (Smutz, Crowe, & Lindsay, 1986), may provide some guidelines.

Most significantly, continuing professional education must be effective in helping practitioners enhance their performance. To advocate or mandate participation in continuing professional education accomplishes little if the educational experience does not improve daily practice (Nowlen & Queeney, 1988). Therefore, continuing professional education must be directly related to practice, providing knowledge and skills that the professional can take back to the work environment and integrate into established practice patterns. As is true with pre-professional education, each professional's continuing education should be a cumulative, integrated process directed toward optimum performance, rather than a series of unrelated events. Each professional should select programs that address identified learning needs and that, when viewed collectively, represent a coherent curriculum for learning throughout the professional's life cycle.

Professionals as Learners

Ensuring that professionals pursue continuing professional education in the fashion just outlined represents no small challenge. One premise of adult education dictates that adult learners assume responsibility for their own learning (Brookfield, 1984; Knox, 1986). Professionals, as adult learners, should indeed be able--and in fact encouraged--to adhere to this principle (Nowlen & Queeney, 1988). Some time ago, G. Lester Anderson (1974) observed, "Society allocates to those who practice a profession a great measure of control of the education for it" (p. 3). Yet most professionals understandably have limited familiarity with the educational concepts necessary to identify their learning needs, to select educational programs to meet those needs, and to chart an integrated educational course for themselves. In short, they have little understanding of their roles and responsibilities as self-directed learners (Brookfield, 1984).

Revealing in this regard is research on needs assessment conducted as part of the 1980-1985 Continuing Professional Education Development Project funded by the Kellogg Foundation at The Pennsylvania State University. This study indicated that practitioners typically view new and unfamiliar knowledge and skills within the profession as synonymous with their learning needs. Rarely do they claim deficiencies related to the skills they use in daily practice. Yet, assessments conducted in the Penn State project showed weaknesses in several such skills within a variety of professions. These findings may be indicative of individuals' inability or perhaps reluctance to recognize that they are not performing effectively the tasks of their daily work. The suggestion is that simply asking professionals what they need to learn is not sufficient. Surely individuals' perceived learning needs are valid and deserve attention; however, they differ from needs identified through performance assessment (Lindsay & Crowe, 1984), which also must be addressed if continuing professional education is to have a role in competency maintenance. Thus, it is evident that professionals require guidance and assistance in structuring their continuing professional education so that it will, in fact, benefit their practice.

The Need for Individualization

Another recently uncovered problem has to do with the need for individualization in continuing professional education. The Penn State project referred to above dealt with group assessments--the assessment of groups of practitioners within a profession to identify strengths and weaknesses across the profession. Assessment center methodology was used, evaluating participants' skills through a series of simulations, case studies, trigger films, role-playing activities, and other exercises designed to measure application of knowledge and skills to practice (Queeney, 1984b). Data obtained from such assessments are useful in determining what content should be addressed in continuing professional education programs and in identifying appropriate delivery methods to be used. Programs based on this type of data address identified, practice-related educational needs of groups of practitioners. If the sample assessed is drawn randomly, generalizations may be made to the larger population from which it is drawn.

However, individuals' strengths and weaknesses often are not addressed in group assessments of this type, although professionals participating in the Penn State assessments perceived their own needs differently after completing the assessment exercises (Lindsay, Crowe, & Jacobs, 1987). While group assessment is useful in identifying the needs of a body of practitioners within a particular profession, it does not take into consideration the needs of individual practitioners. Group and individual needs might be quite similar or even identical; yet practitioners frequently tend to view group assessment results as unrelated to their own needs. As a result, they may not be motivated by reports of such assessments to seek educational programming to address the area of weakness identified.

Even if learning needs are identified effectively, practice- oriented programs are then required to address them. Recognition of these programs as different from traditional programs designed simply to transfer knowledge is a critical point long neglected. Practice-oriented programs deliver knowledge, of course, but their focus must be on application of knowledge to the tasks of daily professional practice. Thus, practice-oriented programs should utilize a variety of learning formats and delivery modes, emphasizing opportunities for participants to simulate application of what is being learned (Knox, 1986). Programs intended to teach skills require different formats, often including opportunities for "hands-on" experience, interaction with peers, or development of a "product" to be reviewed. Unfortunately, such learning experiences are available infrequently.

What continuing education programs are most appropriate for which professionals? And how will they know? Although advising and counseling services are common at other educational levels, comparable assistance is not readily available to professionals. If continuing professional education is to be a coherent learning program, rather than a series of episodic, unrelated events, a strategic learning agenda is required. Leaving individual professionals to develop such plans without expert assistance is inefficient at best and potentially harmful at worst.

No matter how well individual professionals are matched with their continuing learning experiences, the effect on practice frequently is limited without employer support for adaptation in the work setting. Nurses learning innovative ways of preparing patient care plans, for example, have little opportunity to use their new skills if the facility in which they work continues to insist on adherence to traditional practices. Conversely, the failure of individual professionals to consider the relevance of the goals and objectives of their present organization to their professional development activities is likely to affect negatively the implementation of new knowledge and skills. For these reasons, involvement of employers in the development and delivery of continuing professional education is crucial. Employees bring a pragmatic orientation to the process; without this viewpoint, educators' understanding of the potential for practical application of program material can be severely lacking. In addition, on-site reinforcement of learning following continuing professional education participation, while critical to implementation, too often is ignored. Individual professionals should not be isolated learners; encouragement and support from peers, employers, or supervisors seem necessary to overcome the haphazard application of new knowledge and skills.

This discussion suggests that continuing professional education faces a number of challenging problems. Both the field's relative infancy and the difficulty of clarifying its unique qualities have contributed to the current state of practice. Yet, the problems must be addressed if progress is to occur and if the dichotomy between professionals as self-directed adult learners and learners in need of expert assistance is to be reconciled. While focus on group needs has merit, specific efforts also must be applied to help individual professionals grow and develop. Strategies are needed to assist professionals in overcoming the notion that passive reception of information is the optimum--or only--type of formal continuing education experience. The effectiveness of continuing professional education must be addressed both by focusing on individual learning needs and by attending to long-term, instead of only short-term, growth. Finally, integration of learning into the practice context in a timely and efficient manner can no longer be ignored.

A comprehensive approach is required to address these problems of continuing professional education. Understanding of the field's unique qualities must be an integral part of this approach, including the recognition that continuing professional education is a multi-dimensional education issue, not simply one of program provision. Within this context, development of a broad array of learning resources also requires consideration. Such an approach hinges on rethinking the very nature of continuing professional education, a topic to which we now turn.

Self-Managed Professional Development: A Comprehensive Strategy for Continuing Professional Education

A comprehensive strategy for continuing professional education requires reconceptualization of the roles and goals of professionals as learners. A perspective of continuing professional education as self-managed professional development may represent a step in the right direction. Rather than viewing professionals as independently self-directed in their learning activities, self-managed professional development suggests that they effectively utilize multiple educational resources (e.g., needs assessments, learning plans) to guide their activities. From this perspective, professionals are neither entirely independent nor entirely dependent in the learning situation (Brookfield, 1986). Instead, appropriate external expertise and assistance are utilized, while the individual simultaneously maintains ultimate control over the learning process. Under such circumstances, the learner's role is transformed from one of making countless (and often uninformed) decisions regarding learning needs, appropriate programs, and effective strategies of implementation to one of making fewer but more knowledgeable choices, thereby enhancing potential for long-term development.

The use of external expertise is critical from another perspective as well. Many professionals spend their entire working lives as employees of organizations. More and more, the sole practitioner is an exception. For example, accountants, architects, and lawyers gravitate to firms; and physicians join group practices or health maintenance organizations. Thus, the context of professional practice has become quite varied. The nature of that context is absolutely critical, however, in considering the appropriateness of available continuing professional education opportunities. Decisions need to be informed, not only by the professional as an individual professional, but by the perspectives of the larger entity of which the professional is a part.

Update and Competence Frameworks

Self-managed professional development also suggests a change in the goals of professionals as learners. The update and competence frameworks that have guided continuing professional education have an explicit, short-term orientation (Nowlen, 1988). Although they imply that updating and rectifying deficiencies must continue throughout a career, they often focus on only immediate problems. Unfortunately, their implicit assumption that piecemeal, episodic involvement in learning activities will lead to long-term growth is misconceived. Indeed, the perspective that continuous involvement in learning is necessary only to the extent that it maintains competence has the potential for creating a passive orientation toward ongoing learning, thereby affecting motivation.

The update and competence frameworks also suffer from a rather narrow, profession-specific focus. If quality performance is the ultimate goal for all professionals, then attending to the fundamentals of a profession (old and new) may be necessary, but not sufficient, to guarantee such an outcome. As Nowlen (1988) has pointed out, a variety of factors can affect performance, including interactions with other professions and in one's personal life. Ignoring such factors can result in an overly restrictive orientation to what must be learned if one is to be a productive professional.

A More Positive Orientation

In contrast to these traditional frameworks, the concept of professional development represents an alternative and more positive orientation to continuing professional education. The focus is on producing a qualitatively different professional and a more effective career practitioner. Two particular elements within the concept of professional development can promote this orientation. The first involves determination of the types of learning activities that should be undertaken on the basis of a combination of wants, needs, and goals. In this context, "wants" are what the professional desires to learn; "needs" are necessary additions to a professional's knowledge and skill repertoire, based on the expert assessment of professional peers and/or employing organizations; and "goals" are career expectations as defined by the individual professional. Through integration of goals, wants, and needs, professionals can build on their strengths and address their deficiencies. Such an orientation can motivate individuals' ongoing learning because the focus is on attainment of maximum potential, rather than on the maintenance of minimal competence.

The second element embodied within professional development has to do with coherence and integration of learning activities. For too long, continuing professional education has been characterized by a "cafeteria style" approach to programs. If long-term, cumulative growth is the goal, learning activities must be interrelated over time. Establishment of such relationships certainly is a responsibility of program providers, but individual professionals also share responsibility. Professionals' design and implementation of individualized, developmental tracks with assistance and guidance from others may represent one effective approach to this matter. Professional development so construed would not denote simply a series of activities but the achievement of individualized long-term goals through participation in cumulative learning experiences.

The Need for Reconceptualization

Acceptance of the self-managed professional development concept requires rethinking what continuing professional education is and should be. It suggests, not independence or even isolation, but management of resources and expert assistance. At the same time, it draws attention to long-term integrated development, not short-term remediation; that is, to comprehensiveness in ongoing learning that enhances performance. One implication of this reorientation is the need to bring structure to continuing professional education. For example, a long-term orientation to professional growth suggests a need for careful planning. Also, the potential availability of numerous learning resources suggests a need for guidelines to help professionals make choices. In other words, a guiding framework for self-managed professional development is needed.

Figure l delineates just such a process. It identifies key issues that professionals, educators, and employers of professionals must address to create a systematic, comprehensive approach to professional development. Many elements of the process are familiar, representing aspects of a basic seven-step problem-solving strategy. However, experience suggests that few professionals explicitly follow such a systematic process in their continuing professional education activities. Each of the seven steps is described briefly in the following paragraphs.

Step 1 pertains to helping individuals acquire a *Professional Development Framework.* Essentially this means preparing professionals for continuing education by providing grounding in the structure of their profession, by facilitating understanding of the organizational context in which work occurs, where relevant, and by developing the dispositional mindset and learning skills necessary for effective ongoing learning.

Step 2 involves *Assessment.* It requires the use of multiple devices to help professionals uncover practice deficiencies, identify immediate professional interests, and outline future goals and directions. Only through such systematic assessment can individuals eventually design professional development plans that concurrently maintain their competency and enhance their ability to reach maximum potential within their professions and employing organizations.

Figure 1
Self-Managed Professional Development Process

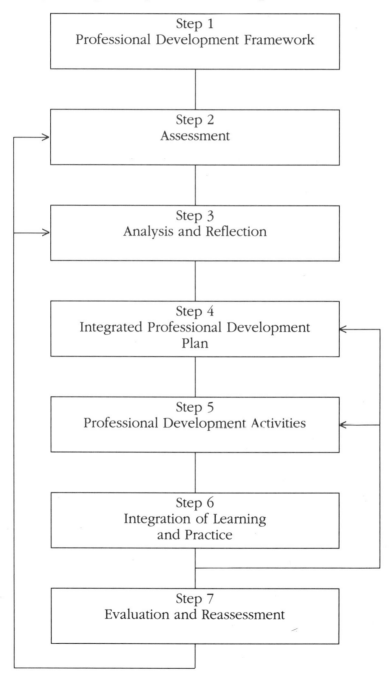

Step 3, Analysis and Reflection, focuses on the need for professionals to step out of the practice context and consciously consider how they want to use their professional development time. Through analysis of individual assessment results (needs, wants, and goals), professionals can clarify their professional development priorities in the context of their profession, their employing organization, and their personal lives.

Step 4, Integrated Professional Development Plan, provides for the design of an action agenda to address systematically the learning priorities identified in the former step. It involves identifying and/or devising appropriate learning activities, specifying their relationships to short- and long-term goals, and outlining a desired sequence.

Step 5, Professional Development Activities, requires participation in continuing professional education. Learning experiences may be formal or informal; undertaken individually or with fellow practitioners; and focused on knowledge, skills, or both. However, they should be selected in the context of the individual development plan designed in Step 4.

Step 6, Integration of Learning into Practice, pertains to application of new knowledge and skills to the practice situation. Sometimes this phase occurs naturally and easily. Often, however, conscious effort must be given to determining what elements from a learning experience can and cannot be integrated into practice. Without such structured consideration, new learnings are too easily forgotten. In addition, efforts to integrate may uncover new professional practice issues which must be addressed. Such information ideally may be fed back into the professional development process at several points, thereby leading to readjustments in the overall approach to professional development.

Step 7, Evaluation and Reassessment, requires periodic consideration of progress made toward accomplishment of professional development goals. Importantly, such an evaluation should include assessment, not only of progress toward professional development goals specified in the learning plan, but also of progress toward effective self-management of the professional development process.

As outlined, the proposed self-managed professional development process appears as a lock-step procedure with little room for deviation, which need not be the case. While proceeding from step to step in a linear fashion may have value in some situations, the process can-- and preferably should be--a dynamic and flexible one. For example, analysis and reflection have value, regardless of whether or not formal assessment procedures have been undertaken. Similarly, actively working to integrate new learnings into practice will prove beneficial, regardless of whether or not a professional development learning plan is operational. In essence, then, the process provides a guiding framework, identifying key issues that must be considered if continuing professional education is to be systematic and comprehensive.

Three Key Elements in a Collaborative Approach

The proposed self-managed professional development process is complex, demanding, and potentially time consuming. The ultimate reason for advocating such a process is to enhance the effectiveness and efficiency of professionals' ongoing learning. To make the process manageable, individual professionals must receive assistance. Fortunately, considerable educational expertise can be applied to the preparation of individuals for ongoing learning and to development of a broad array of learning resources. That expertise must come, not only from higher education, but likewise from professional associations and employing organizations as well. Working collaboratively, all concerned can begin to build the organizational support structure necessary for effective development and use of learning resources. Attention to these three key elements--the individual, learning resources, and organizational support-- is critical if a comprehensive approach to continuing professional education is to succeed.

The Individual: Continuing Professional Education "Mindset" and Learning Skills

The challenge of continuing to learn throughout one's professional life raises legitimate concerns regarding proper identification of individual needs, optimum selection of programs or experiences, effective use of different modes of learning, integration of new knowledge and skills over the career life span, and implementation of learning in the practice environment. Activities that can be pursued informally and independently further complicate the role of the learner.

Because individuals' contributions are critical to this level of education, professionals must be prepared for their responsibilities. It is unlikely that the understanding and skills to effectively and efficiently manage their ongoing learning are developed during pre-professional preparation. Professional curricula are almost always based on well-defined goals provided for students by faculty members (Allan, Grosswald, & Means, 1984). Because of this orientation to the educational experience, it is unrealistic to assume that students socialized to a dependency role in education will automatically and immediately be transformed upon beginning professional practice into independent learners. No doubt there are exceptions. Professionals who, for whatever reasons, can conceptualize and put into practice effective procedures for continued development. Generally, however, professionals need assistance in three tasks: understanding continuing professional education as a distinct level of education, developing a dispositional "mindset" toward it, and acquiring the learning skills necessary to be effective participants.

Professionals' development of a dispositional mindset toward continuing professional education requires that they understand two issues. The first is the structural features of their chosen profession. This entails acquaintance with the profession's knowledge and skills, responsibilities and tasks, division of labor (e.g., management versus practice), and various career stages. Familiarity with a profession at this conceptual level enables individuals to place their overall continuing educational challenge within a broader context than immediate needs. Second, professionals need to understand better the nature of the educational task and the complexity of the challenge posed by continuing professional education. They need to become acquainted with key elements of this level of education: short-term and long-term professional development; the contribution of informal and formal learning activities; the relevance and interrelationship of needs, wants, and goals; the integration of learning into practice; and more. Ultimately, only by understanding structural and educational matters will professionals have the background necessary to develop individualized, integrated professional development plans.

Initiatives for Action

In addition to becoming disposed toward continuing professional education, professionals must acquire appropriate learning skills. Certainly some skills are useful at all levels of education, but continuing professional education poses unique learning challenges and opportunities. Some of the required skills include recognizing deficiencies, consciously utilizing the practice situation for new insights, learning from colleagues, effectively extracting meaning from programs delivered through different media, and integrating learning into practice through different strategies. Only through the development of such skills, few of which receive attention at other educational levels, can professionals make the best use of their learning time.

Practice descriptions. Several initiatives can be undertaken to address issues of dispositional mindset and learning skills that ultimately will help professionals complete Step 1 of the self-managed professional development process. Two factors should be considered with respect to assisting professionals in understanding the comprehensive structure of their professions. The first is encouragement of professions to develop practice descriptions or role delineations that detail the responsibilities and tasks of their members. While the professional school experience imparts some knowledge of the overall profession, explicitly mapping it for all members to use as a yardstick against which to evaluate practice would help professionals better grasp the range of issues they must consider when thinking about their own professional development.

Curricula. Second, some effort should be given to designing continuing professional education curricula for different professions. Such curricula could attend to content (knowledge and skills), methods (effective ways of learning), learning sequences, and appropriate contexts for learning so that more coherence could be brought to the professional development process. Some may question the value of such curricula, but it seems highly reasonable that expertise be used to help individual professionals understand better the scope of content they need to learn, the point in their careers at which they need to learn it, and the degree of depth to be mastered. There indeed may be content that forms the core of a continuing professional education curricula. In this volume alone, Adelson's discussion of the need for professionals to better attend to the ethical dimensions of their work, Cunningham and McLaughlin's analysis of the need for interprofessional education and action, and Azzaretto's focus on the need to reclaim a public service orientation in the professions, all suggest types of content that might form the foundation for continuing professional education curricula. Certainly steps must be taken to guard against any single continuing professional education curriculum being used to rigidly control professionals' learning efforts. At the same time, however, the general guidance such a document could provide, especially if periodically revised, would be invaluable to those trying to bring order and meaning to their learning.

Orientation programs. Beyond the creation of these types of resources, attention should be given to developing continuing professional education orientation programs that focus on the structure of professional practice, configuration of knowledge and skills underlying professional practice, demands and skills of ongoing professional development, and relationships among those three issues. Not only must such programs be offered for students preparing for professional practice, but it must be recognized that the number of practicing professionals who have not been exposed to such orientations is substantial. Finally, increasing mobility of professionals in many fields from private practice settings to organizational environments suggests the need for orientation programs for those responsible for learning in the organizational context. The creation of understanding and supportive environments for continuing professional education within organizations would do much to enhance its effectiveness.

Learning Resources: Tools for Systematic Professional Development

Movement away from professionals as relatively isolated learners to a self-managed professional development process requires the development of learning resources. Such resources are tools that individuals can use to structure and guide their development (Cross, 1978). While all professionals must be responsible for their own growth, this responsibility is a matter of degree. The development and use of educational resources to reduce the current educational burden on professionals is necessary for two reasons.

Efficiency. The first has to do with the issue of efficiency in professional development. In an era of increasing specialization, is it reasonable to ask professionals who are necessarily concerned with their profession-specific expertise also to be totally responsible for the configuration of their ongoing learning? If professionals must acquire and implement the extensive educational expertise necessary to pursue continuing professional education independently, where will they find time, given the demands of their chosen professions? Providing assistance and support to individuals through the design and implementation of education processes that make the challenge of continuing professional education more manageable, if not easy, offers the possibility of helping professionals make more productive use of time committed to continuing professional education.

Expertise. The second reason the provision of learning resources to professionals is important relates to the nature of expertise in the realm of professional affairs. Even though continuing professional education is a segment of continuing and adult education, it has a special character that should not be, but often has been, overlooked. In the areas of continuing and adult education, emphasis on responding to the public's demands and providing choices is well placed. Adults have a level of understanding and indeed the right to select, pursue, and utilize information, knowledge, and skills as they see fit. But this opportunity is, at least in part, based on the premise that any positive benefits or negative consequences that derive from the choices made will fall primarily to the individual adult learner. This is not to say that society does not benefit from adults' ongoing learning--only that society is not the primary beneficiary.

The issue is not so clear in continuing professional education. In the world of professions, standards of practice are developed and

198 Visions for the Future of Continuing Professional Education

expected modes of behavior identified based on the principle that expert knowledge and skills must inform practice. At least in part, this process is used because the public is the recipient and beneficiary of professional services. Because of the power and privileges entrusted to professionals, it is expected that the most relevant expertise will be applied to problems. Professionals' obligation to society is governed by the concept of expertise. Thus, for continuing professional education, the conceptual foundations of continuing and adult education, which attend to individuals' demands and choices, must be somewhat modified. Professionals may not always have the liberty to learn only what they choose, because they may not have the necessary expertise or level of understanding to realize what they do not know or what they cannot do. If the educational choices made by individual professionals affected only them, this issue would not assume such significance. However, the educational choices have potential to affect seriously the public and hence to affect the professional's legal liability in today's litigious society. For that reason, educational expertise has a legitimate contribution to make in terms of the content and educational methods of continuing professional education. It is appropriate and even imperative, therefore, to develop educational processes that guide professionals in their ongoing professional development. To continue to conceive of the professional as a totally independent learner without recourse to advice, suggestions, guidance, and direction is to undermine the very foundation of professionalism--its acceptance of expertise--and to risk propagation of a laissez-faire attitude toward professional knowledge and skill.

Learning Resources for Continuing Professional Education

Given the importance of learning resources to continuing professional education, what types are needed? Noted below are some that may facilitate individuals' efforts to navigate the various steps of the self-managed professional development process. (This list represents an initial attempt to identify types of resources that are needed and in no way should be viewed as definitive.)

Step 1: Professional Development Framework

Integration of continuing professional education into pre-professional and professional curricula to facilitate aspiring professionals' consideration of lifelong learning's role in their careers.

Orientation programs on continuing professional education for experienced professionals to introduce them to the professional content and learning skills necessary for effective lifelong learning.

Accessible role delineations or practice descriptions to facilitate individuals' understanding of their professions.

Profession-specific continuing professional education curricula that provide guidance with regard to appropriate content, learning contexts, and methods.

Step 2: Assessment

A practice profile questionnaire that will enable professionals to map the dimensions of a particular practice. Such an instrument will provide practitioners with insights into how they actually spend their time and help them make decisions about possible changes in practice.

Self-administered needs assessment instruments that clarify what professionals want to learn and what they need to learn. Such instruments must focus on the knowledge and skills of professional practice and address professionals' perceptions of their learning needs, peers' expert determinations of profession-based deficiencies, and where appropriate, employers' judgments regarding areas in need of attention.

Procedures to help professionals better understand their own practice behavior. As Cervero pointed out when discussing teachers in chapter 8, "A Model of Professionals as Learners," "Continuing education for teachers must build on what teachers already believe about their work. However, many teachers, as other professionals, do not know what they know so that a first step would be to help teachers uncover the rules of practice, practical principles, and images that guide their practice."

Practice-based peer evaluation instruments that provide professionals with information about how others view their professional performance.

Evaluation procedures that enable individuals to analyze practice situations (in real time or retroactively) to identify deficiencies or obstacles that hinder optimal performance.

Goal assessment procedures that enable individuals to map future career directions.

Step 3: Analysis and Reflection

Counselors to help professionals interpret assessment results.

Procedures to help professionals clarify their professional development priorities through systematic reflection and through consideration of relevant factors such as the organizational context.

Strategies to help professionals identify and prioritize their learning goals.

Step 4: Integrated Professional Development

Procedures to guide professionals through the development of an extended learning plan. Assessment results, continuing professional education curricula, and consideration of the employing organization's goals and objectives should be integral parts of such procedures.

Regional learning activity data banks that catalog available formal continuing professional education programs for different professions.

Computerized procedures for matching individual learning plans with learning activities cataloged in the data banks.

Step 5: Professional Development Activities

Continuing professional education programs that are directly related to practice. Although programming generally has been well attended to by continuing professional education, the three matters noted below need additional attention.

Programs that concentrate, not on information transfer, but on skill development and/or on "clinical knowledge development" as noted by Cervero in the chapter "A Model of Professionals as Learners."

Programs for relatively new practitioners addressing issues related to the transition from student to practitioner. Such programs are necessary because there are knowledge and skills in most professions is either not addressed by professional curricula or best learned when actual practice experience can be applied.

Programs that help practitioners understand the interprofessional nature of many practice problems and enhance the likelihood of future interprofessional collaboration, as noted in the Cunningham and McLaughlin chapter.

Step 6: *Integration of Learning into Practice*

Learning reinforcement exercises for use during and following participation in formal continuing education programs. Such exercises should assist participants in extracting meaning from program content and aid them in designing strategies for implementing new learning.

Peer or colleague learning reinforcement networks that can serve as support systems for individual professionals attempting to implement new learnings into the practice setting.

Employer commitment to provide resources for integration of learning into practice.

Step 7: *Evaluation and Reassessment*

Formative and summative evaluation procedures to assist professionals in making judgments about the usefulness of their extended learning plans.

Organizational Infrastructure: Support for Comprehensive Continuing Professional Education

The learning resources outlined above are necessary tools to assist professionals in systematically addressing continuing professional education. In and of themselves, however, they are not sufficient. Such resources must be deployed in a context of broad-based organizational support for ongoing professional development. Often individuals take cues from organizations about what is important and what is not. In the case of those organizations that have a stake in continuing professional education--higher education, employing organizations, and professional associations--those cues have occasionally been ambiguous. Certainly there has been no dearth of pronouncements about the value of continuing professional education from each, but actions speak louder than words. And in terms of actions, the commitment of these organizations to continuing professional education, beyond the offering of programs, has not always been clear. This apparent ambivalence to continuing professional education has indicated to some that major social changes may be on the horizon. For example, in "Education and the Workplace: An Integral Part of the Development of Professions," Hofstader and Munger's contribution to this volume, it is suggested that a totally new type of institution may have to be developed to fill the continuing professional education void created by current organizations. Similarly, Mawby (1988) has warned, when criticizing the failure of land grant universities to attend appropriately to their public service function, that "new systems will be established to replace those which disappoint."

Implementation of a fully developed self-managed professional development process clearly will not be without challenges and difficulties. The cost of educational services, for example, is always an issue. It is conceivable, however, that the funds currently being expended on fragmented continuing professional education could be applied more productively to a comprehensive system and that extraordinary increases in financial resources would not be necessary. Other critical questions at this time are: Who will develop the various learning resources and how will a self-managed professional development process be maintained? A totally new educational institution should not be necessary. While present institutions and systems may not have delivered as effectively as needed, neither have they fully disappointed in the professional development arena. They have much to contribute to creating a supportive environment. Higher education institutions possess the educational expertise to design and implement many of the educational resources noted earlier. Professional associations have the capacity to influence professionals' perspective on the need for ongoing growth and development and the authority to establish standards of performance. Organizations employing professionals have considerable influence over their motivation to pursue professional development and a unique opportunity to affect implementation of learning in the practice context (Green, Gunzburger, & Suter, 1984). If these multiple organizations join together to provide support, acceptance of a systematic approach to self-managed professional development is well within reach.

Organizational support can be provided in a variety of ways. One is through the independent development of learning resources by organizations. To illustrate, colleges and universities might use their expertise and opportunity to prepare students to be effective lifelong learners as part of their preprofessional and professional education. Such preparation is no less vital than preparation in professional techniques or ethics and can easily be integrated into the curriculum.

Independent action by other relevant organizations also is important. Some organizations have begun to chart new courses for themselves and their members. The American Institute of Certified Public Accountants (1986), providing leadership for its members to establish a systematic approach to professional development, has produced a continuing professional education curriculum that identifies the range of knowledge and skills necessary for ongoing effective practice. This type of guidance is critical in any comprehensive system.

Organizational support also can be provided through collaborative development of necessary learning resources by relevant organizations. For example, creation of practice descriptions and needs assessment instruments depends on input from professional associations, employing organizations, and higher education institutions. Only if the expertise and perspectives available within these groups is integrated collaboratively into the development of learning resources will these tools have the legitimacy necessary for acceptance on a broad scale.

Much has been written about the structuring of and needs for collaboration in the design and delivery of continuing professional education (Bruce et al., 1982; Cervero & Young, 1987; Lindsay, Queeney, & Smutz, 1981; Nowlen & Queeney, 1988; Queeney, 1984a; Smutz, 1984), and earlier collaborative work in the field has been encouraging (Office of Continuing Professional Education, 1985). Certainly collaboration is not a simple task, but the challenge can be met if those concerned with maintaining integrity within the various professions, protecting the public served by professional practitioners, providing education to enhance professional practice, and serving society through the provision of goods and services begin to address the issue aggressively.

One example of the type of collaboration that can occur is a project undertaken by the American Institute of Architects (AIA) and Penn State's Office of Continuing Professional Education. Starting in 1987, the two organizations began to develop jointly a series of self-assessment instruments for use by architects in identifying their individual learning needs. Architects may complete the assessment instruments in their homes or offices, then submit them for scoring, and receive not only their scores but a list of suggested educational opportunities to address their weaknesses, enhance their skills, and develop new skills. Eventually, instruments will be available to cover the full range of responsibilities and tasks included in architectural practice. Such a collaborative effort presents a number of complex issues for the participating parties pertaining to who pays for what, who does what, and who gets what. Progress on this AIA/ Penn State joint venture to date suggests, however, that such difficulties can be overcome as long as there is a strong commitment to the ultimate goal.

Organizational support also can be provided by devising new ways to implement learning resources. If self-managed professional development is to become an integral part of individuals' professional lives, it must be infused throughout the range of their professional activities. There is no reason, for example, that continuing professional education "orientation" programs cannot be delivered in professional association and/or organizational practice settings, as well as in higher education locations. Needs assessment can be administered and feedback from counselors can be provided at annual professional meetings or within the work context. And certainly, learning reinforcement efforts cannot be isolated but must be embedded within the practice setting.

Finally, organizational commitment is important. It is imperative that all units and levels of the relevant organizations be intimately involved in continuing professional education issues if the necessary organizational support is to materialize. Professional development matters simply cannot be segmented into a single, human resources unit within an organization. To illustrate, in the case of employing organizations, not only employees, but also supervisors must have a fundamental grounding in the means and ends of professional development. With respect to higher education, lifelong learning issues must become a part of the pre-professional and professional curricula as well as the continuing education operation.

Systematic self-managed professional development will become a reality only if organizational support is evident through the development, provision, and ongoing maintenance of learning resources. Such a challenge represents no small task, but acceptance and adoption of a comprehensive approach to continuing professional education is not possible without that level of commitment. Importantly, cooperation and collaboration among professional associations, regulatory agencies, higher education institutions, and employers of professionals appear to be the key to the future of a comprehensive approach. For existing organizations, independent action certainly is necessary but no one of them can independently "own," produce, facilitate, or fully support the range of learning resources needed. Nor should they. Each brings to continuing professional education its own limitations and biases, which would only be exacerbated if left unchecked. Ongoing, effective cooperation and collaboration are necessary to insure a systematic approach to professional development. It is time to commit the resources and energy necessary to make it happen.

Summary

The challenges posed by continuing professional education are impressive, but not insurmountable. From our perspective, preparing the individual, providing learning resources, and building an organizational infrastructure through cooperation and collaboration are the key ingredients necessary to facilitate adoption of systematic, self-managed professional development. The time has come for such a comprehensive approach if we truly expect to enhance the performance of individual professionals throughout their careers. Indeed, those concerned with continuing professional education ought not strive for anything less.

References

Allan, D. M. E., Grosswald, S. J., & Means, R. P. (1984). Facilitating self-directed learning. In J. S. Green, S. J. Grosswald, E. Suter, and D. B. Walthall (Eds.), *Continuing education for the health professions* (pp. 218-241). San Francisco: Jossey-Bass.

American Institute of Certified Public Accountants. (1986). *National curriculum: A pathway to excellence.* New York: Author.

Anderson, G. L. (1974). *Trends in education for the professions.* (ERIC/ Higher Education Research Report No. 7). Washington, DC: American Association for Higher Education.

Brookfield, S. D. (1984). *Adult learners, adult education, and the community.* New York: Teachers College Press.

Brookfield, S. D. (1986). *Understanding and facilitating adult learning.* San Francisco: Jossey-Bass.

Bruce, J. D., Siebert, W. M., Smullin, L. D., & Fano, R. M. (1982). *Lifelong cooperative education.* Cambridge, MA: Massachusetts Institute of Technology.

Cervero, R. M. (1985). Continuing professional education and behavioral changes: A model for research and evaluation. *Journal of Continuing Education in Nursing, 16* (3), 85-88.

Cervero, R. M., & Young, W. H. (1987). The organization and provision of continuing professional education: A critical review and synthesis. In J. C. Smart (Ed.) *Higher education: handbook of theory and research,* (Vol. 3, pp. 402-431). New York: Agathon Press.

Cross, K. P. (1978). *The missing link: Connecting adult learners to learning resources.* New York: College Entrance Examination Board.

Green, J. S., Gunzburer, L. K., & Suter, E. (1984). Interaction of continuing education clients and providers: Increasing the impact of education. In J. S. Green, S. J. Grosswald, E. Suter, and D. B. Walthall (Eds.), *Continuing education in the health professions* (pp. 115-131). San Francisco: Jossey-Bass.

Holt, M. E., & Courtenay, B. C. (1985). An examination of impact evaluations. *Continuum, 49*(1), 23-35.

Houle, C. O. (1980). *Continuing learning in the professions.* San Francisco: Jossey-Bass.

Houle, C. O. (1983). Possible futures. In M. R. Stern (Ed.), *Power and conflict in continuing professional education* (pp. 254-264). Belmont, CA: Wadsworth.

Knox, A. B. (1986). *Helping adults learn.* San Francisco: Jossey-Bass.

Lindsay, C. A., & Crowe, M. B. (1984). Relationships between clinical psychology practitioners' expressed needs and demands for continuing professional education. Paper presented at Lifelong Learning Research Conference, College Park, MD.

Lindsay, C. A., Crowe, M. B., & Jacobs, D. F. (1987). Continuing professional education for clinical psychology. In A. Edelstein and S. Berler (Eds.), *Evaluation and accountability in clinical training* (pp. 331-363). New York: Plenum Press.

Lindsay, C. A., Queeney, D. S., & Smutz, W. D. (1981). *A model and process for university/professional association collaboration.* University Park, PA: The Pennsylvania State University.

Mawby, R. G. (1988, October). Unfinished business. Paper presented at the annual John W. Oswald Lecture, The Pennsylvania State University, University Park, PA.

Neibuhr, H. (1984). *Revitalizing American learning.* Belmont, CA: Wadsworth.

Nowlen, P. M. (1988). *A new approach to continuing education for business and the professions.* New York: Macmillan, NUCEA, American Council on Education.

Nowlen, P. M., & Queeney, D. S. (1988). *The role of colleges and universities in continuing professional education.* Washington, DC: National University Continuing Education Association.

Office of Continuing Professional Education (1985). *An overview: Continuing professional education development project.* University Park, PA: The Pennsylvania State University.

Panel on Continuing Education (1985). *Engineering education and practice in the United States: Continuing education of engineers.* Washington, DC: National Academy Press.

Queeney, D. S. (1984a). The role of the university in continuing professional education. *Educational Record, 65* (3), 13-17.

Queeney, D. S. (1984b). Using assessment center methods to identify practice-oriented learning needs of professional practitioners. Paper presented at 12th International Congress on the Assessment Center Method, Lincolnshire, IL.

Queeney, D. S. (1987). Continuing professional education: A responsibility of higher education. *Journal for Higher Education Management, 2* (2), 27-33.

Queeney, D. S., & Shuman, S. B. (1988). *Professional and occupational practice requirements* (4th ed.). University Park, PA: The Pennsylvania State University.

Rockhill, K. (1983). Mandatory continuing education for professionals: Trends and issues. *Adult Education, 33,* 106-116.

Scanlon, C. L. (1985). Practicing with purpose: Goals of continuing professional education. In M. Cervero and L. Scanlan (Eds.), *Problems and prospects in continuing professional education* (pp. 5-19). San Francisco: Jossey-Bass.

Smutz, W. D. (1984). *Formal boundary spanners and organizational change: Establishing university/professional association interorganizational relationships.* Unpublished doctoral dissertation, The Pennsylvania State University, University Park, PA.

Smutz, W. D., Crowe, M. B., & Lindsay, C. A. (1986). Emerging perspectives on continuing professional education. In C. Smart (Ed.), *Higher education: Handbook of theory and research* (Vol. 2, pp. 385-430). New York: Agathon Press.

Stern, M. R. (1988, October). Continuing professional education: The learning landscape. Paper presented at the National Conference on Continuing Professional Education, University Park, PA.

Young, A. & Company (1987). *Review of California's continuing education program.* Sacramento, CA: California Department of Real Estate.

Chapter 10

Ethics in Professional Practice: Some Issues for the Continuing Professional Educator

Yolande C. Adelson

Introduction

This chapter is not primarily about the rampant self-interest, sleaze, greed, and white-collar crimes that fill the pages of our newspapers and journals and that dominate the "news" reported via the electronic media.

Certainly there is evidence of a decline in public confidence in the ethicality of some public officials and some of the professions traditionally held in high regard. The September 22, 1980, edition of *Chemical Engineering* published the results of a survey in which its readers rated 14 occupational groups on a scale of 1 (extremely unethical) to 7 (extremely ethical). The professionals included engineers, physicians, lawyers, clergymen, "newspaper reporters," chemists, and corporate managers.

Some five years later, the December 9, 1985, *U.S. News & World Report* (McBee) conducted a similar poll of its readers and compared the results against a 1983 Gallup Poll. In all three studies, the clergy, engineers, and physicians were regarded as the most ethical professionals, and lawyers and reporters were rated the lowest.

Remitz (1983) quotes Robert Ingle, senior vice president and executive editor of the *San Jose Mercury News*, as saying, "Why the need [for a written ethics code for journalists]? The primary thing is that the press...has suffered a loss of credibility in the last couple of decades. I think we all know that 30 or 40 years ago some ethics standards were not very high" (p. 38).

It seems reasonable to assume that public trust in so highly esteemed an institution as the Getty Museum in Malibu, California, was diminished by the discovery, in 1984, that its curator, a widely revered scholar, had traded inflated appraisals for donated antiquities. According to the *Los Angeles Times* (Muchnic, 1988) the curator retired in the wake of the disclosures.

Equally serious is the cynicism that is growing around the legislative process. The national presidential race and many state and local campaigns for elective office in 1988 were widely regarded as reflecting a low point in American politics. In California alone, expenditures on 29 propositions on the November 8, 1988, ballot topped $130 million more than tripling the previous all-time high of $33.4 million spent in 1984. The stakes were extremely high for a variety of interest groups; and for months new charges of bribery, misleading and deliberately false advertising, and corrupt political practices dominated the news.

It may be that America has lost its sense of moral direction and that "survival of the fittest" is all that will determine whichof us is destined to survive and in what kind of jungle we will live. Some commentators, however, regard the continuous exposés of unethical and criminal behaviors in business, the professions, and public agencies as evidence of a revival of public interest in morality and expect the outcry against abuses of public trust to result in much needed reform.

In any event, we need to keep clearly in mind the distinction between the role of law enforcement, which addresses issues of crime and punishment; and that of education, which must, ultimately, work only through the free and open mind, emotion, spirit, and will of the individual or the group. It seems reasonable, therefore, to suggest that protecting the public against abuse by those who regard their own "self-interest" as the first law of nature is not fairly made the charge of ethics and ethics education.

To test this hypothesis, I put the following question to several professionals: If you could determine public policy, what would you do to prevent professional, legislative, and/or institutional violations of the public trust? The following responses were typical:

- Offer very large rewards for whistle-blowing and provide strong (legal) protection against retaliation.

- Increase the penalties substantially. A fine of a few thousand dollars against a corporation that has millions at stake is laughable. The corporation can simply regard this as the cost of doing business. Make the penalty commensurate with the sought-after gain.

• Mandatory jail sentences for white-collar criminals.

One respondent gave me an article published in the January 1987 *California Business* (Elliott) entitled "How To Teach Shame: the Hester Prynne...Scarlet Letter...Sanction." According to this article, at the University of Southern California's Business School, some critics of traditional ethics courses claim that what is needed is moving beyond guilt (which can be expiated by recourse to the checkbook) to shame (evidenced by the compulsion to hang one's head and hide one's face, driven by a sense of loss of self-worth.)

This "Scarlet Letter" theme was reflected in the suggestions of one respondent who, not having seen this article, suggested independently that the names and affiliations of persons proven guilty of violations of public trust be carried prominently in daily newspapers and displayed on television until the offenders made some significant acts of retribution to the public. No one suggested ethics education for willful and gross offenders of the public trust. What good, then, is ethics? What is the point of ethics education?

Ethics education is of most benefit to people who want to be good. If that seems too limited an audience, remember the considerable evidence that most people regard themselves as basically good and want to be honorable. They acknowledge, however, that they are often confronted by situations in do not know what is the "right" thing to do and by dilemmas created by values in conflict. The hard choices are not between good and evil, but between competing goods or, even worse, competing evils. (Can anyone who saw the movie, *Sophie's Choice*, in which a mother had to condemn one of her babies to a Nazi gas chamber in order to save the other, fail to understand the concept of "tragic choices" as that phrase is used by Calabresi and Bobbitt in their 1978 book with that same title?)

This chapter may incidentally provide some clarity and perhaps even suggest some directions for persons charged with protecting society against willful wrongdoers. However, it is written primarily for continuing professional educators willing to consider whether they have given too much attention to technical competencies and too little to professional behavior and whether, as charged by some, American educators in particular have failed to exercise their special obligation and responsibility to relate ethical values to the meaning and purpose of learning.

Case Study

On Thursday evening, May 5, 1988, one of the tallest buildings in Los Angeles, the First Interstate Bank building, built without sprinklers before passage of the 1974 law requiring them, caught fire on the twelfth floor. Before the fire was extinguished, five floors had burned totally, one man who re-entered the building to help others died horribly in a service elevator, and 42 building maintenance workers -- many of whom spoke no English and so were at greater risk because they could not understand the rescue instructions being sent in to them -- were rescued, many heroically.

A direct loss of hundreds of millions of dollars was sustained. Additional costs of unknown size have since been incurred through displacement of tenants, traffic congestion in the area, lawsuits, and lost productivity. Had the fire, which was controlled in only three and one-half hours, continued for one half hour more, the flame-resisting material applied to the structural members during construction would have burned through, and the huge tower could have collapsed with much graver consequences.

Installing sprinklers in a new building adds about $1 per square foot to its costs. This amount would have added over a million dollars to the original cost in this case. Industry statistics show that fires of all kinds occurred in "only 4%" of high-rise structures last year, and most of them were not designated serious fires. Those that were serious, however, incurred inestimable costs in human terms.

Consider the following issue. In failing to equip the First Interstate Bank building with sprinklers, the licensed professionals (architects, lawyers, engineers) broke no laws and violated no rules, and all were involved in implementing a "rational" business decision. But was the decision a "good" one? Is there an ethical issue in this case? Would there have been if the building had never burned? How might such questions be approached?

From the practitioner's perspective, were there higher professional standards with respect to public safety than were required by law? If not, are professionals expected to possess a personal morality that compels them to perform according to extraordinary standards of judgment and conduct? To whom is duty owed? Who are the primary stakeholders, the rightful objects of the professional's "caring?"

With these questions in mind, hypothetically change the facts to the following scenario:

The architect's firm has been seriously affected by a building slump and badly needs the contract just to stay alive. Nevertheless, the architect, regarding the *users* of the building rather than the *client* as the ones to whom first duty is owed, insists on sprinklers, with their attendant expense *to the client.* The client decides to award the contract to a different architect who is willing to build without sprinklers.

Query: So long as the architect stays within the law and exercises at least the minimum degree of care for the public required by his profession, does not she/he have an obligation, as a creative, competent, and responsible professional, to stay in business, providing services to clients and insuring the welfare of employees, employees who in turn will be able to buy goods and services from the community at large and continue living as responsible members of their respective communities? How does one make such choices? How should one? By rules of reason? By rules of the heart?

Some Implications for Continuing Educators for the Professions

In the months following the First Interstate fire, other, lesser fires in high rises occurred around the nation. Assume that during the extended public discussion that followed those fires, various state licensing agencies, faced with growing public concern, asked continuing educators for the professions for guidance on the advisability of making ethics education mandatory for licensed professionals. What considerations would arise? Whether mandatory continuing education were deemed appropriate or not, might continuing professional educators consider urging professional associations to include ethics education in their definitions of competency?

Continuing professional education can positively affect work performance; and mandatory continuing education, while it means only a minimal commitment to educational enhancement for the life of the professional's license, can be shown to improve competence and performance (Phillips, 1987). The Grotelueschen chapter in this book makes this same point.

Are there compelling reasons for exempting the study of morality and ethics from regulation of any kind -- legal, administrative, or professional? If so, is ethics education, nevertheless, sufficiently valuable that professionals should be encouraged voluntarily to give some priority attention to it? In their chapter of this book, Smutz and Queeney describe a plan for self-managed professional development that "lead[s] the individual to seek attainment of maximum potential rather than simply to maintain minimal competence." Should ethics education be included in such a plan?

Professionalism and Ethics: Indivisible Concepts

To speak of professionalism is to speak of trust, and trust is an ethical issue. In a very general sense, a profession is an area of practice that has qualifying standards of education, experience, and ethical practice. As pointed out in the Cunningham and McLaughlin chapter, professions began to become important in American life when organizations and occupations grew more and more specialized, and it became difficult for others to assess the quality of the specialists' services to them. They remind us that the professions "provided assurances that experts were service-oriented and, therefore, trustworthy."

Vickers (1974) identifies six elements which "distinguish the professional from the mixed class of client-employer on the one hand and from the rest of the self-supporting populace on the other" (pp. 168-169). The professional has: special skill in understanding (some types of situations); special skills in designing (new situations within prescribed limits); special value and authority as an advisor (based on ability to understand and design); special skills in operating (in the sense of having mastery of technique and technology, the special ability to "do"); special knowledge (which is related to the others but which, alone, would not make the professional a good advisor); and special responsibilities (to the lay client and, sometimes, conflicting ones to the lay public). Because of these special elements, Vickers asserts that the professional "invites a more than usual degree of trust, so he has a more than usual responsibility to exercise his function rightly" (p. 169).

The idea that the professional has obligations to the public that must, under certain circumstances, be given priority over obligations to one's own practice or the wishes of one's client, is a source of controversy, one that is likely to grow in importance in the coming decade.

The parameters of this debate are compellingly addressed by Jennings, Callahan and Walt (1987). In reviewing the changes that have been taking place over the last 50 years in the discourse between the professions and their various publics, they assert that the focus has broadened to include, in addition to issues that emerged in the sixties and seventies pertaining to the ethics of professional/client relationships, "systemic issues of public policy, equitable access to services, and the allocation of scarce technological or institutional resources" (p. 1). Before going on to review profession-specific issues, they note generally that, "Each of the professions is undergoing, to some degree, a process of intellectual ferment, social transformation, and ethical redefinition. No longer does any profession enjoy uncritical admiration or implicit trust from its clientele or the public at large. The new 'social contract' between society and the professions that is in the offing will require that the professions take their duty to serve the public interest and the common good much more seriously than ever before" (p. 1).

Implications, Definitions, and Concepts

In considering the implications of all these issues for continuing professional education, several closely related terms--*morality, values,* and *ethics*--which are frequently used interchangeably, deserve separate attention.

Morality

Morality pertains to *human behavior* that can be characterized as "good or bad," "right or wrong," "righteous or evil." That it is human behavior to which we are referring when we discuss morality needs to be kept in mind. The black widow spider who kills her mate after copulation is not immoral. Only human conduct is to be characterized as moral or immoral. Philosophically, morality pertains to "the good life." The importance of the search for "the good, the true, and the beautiful" and the meaning of those concepts can be found, in some form, in the art and customs of all peoples. Every community has a morality which is central to its well-being, and which defines, for it, "the good life."

The complexities of what might appear as a fairly straightforward concept--morality--are revealed when we try to identify what it is that all human beings regard as "good" and when we seek to judge whether their efforts to attain those "goods" may be deemed moral or immoral. Grisez' "goods" (in Velasquez & Rostankowski, 1985) are:

1. Life itself, including physical and mental health and safety.

2. Activities engaged in for their own sake (e.g., games and hobbies) including those which also serve an ulterior purpose (e.g., work performed as

self-expression and self-fulfillment, which also has a useful and economically significant result).

3.   Experiences sought for their own sake (e.g., aesthetic experiences and watching professional athletic competitions).

4.   Knowledge pursued for its own sake (e.g., theoretical science and speculative philosophy).

5.   Interior integrity--harmony or peace among the various components of the self.

6.   Genuineness--conformity between one's inner self and his outward behavior.

7.   Justice and friendship--peace and cooperation among men.

8.   Worship and holiness--the reconciliation of mankind to God. (p. 57)

Grisez asserts that no purposive human action that is really final can be found that is not contained in these "goods." Regarding all deliberate human choice as a pursuit of some good, we are positioned to better understand the action; only after we have sought to understand the purpose of an action (i.e., the sought-for good) are we positioned to judge the action of another as moral or immoral.

What might be our criteria for "morality?" Grisez (in Velasquez & Rostankowski, 1985) joins Kant and other philosophers who regard morality as a function of attitude, of the "good will":

What divides moral good from moral evil? The answer is that moral goodness and evil depend upon the attitude with which we choose. Not that any and every choice would be good if only it were made with the proper attitude, for some choices cannot be made with the right attitude. But if we have the right attitude, we make good choices; if we have the wrong attitude, we make evil ones. (p. 58)

For Grisez, then, the criteria for a "right moral attitude" includes (a) recognition of a primary obligation to realize human goods in ourselves and others; (b) an appreciation of the "entire ambit of human good," which compels us to contribute to others when help is needed; (c) recognition of the effects of changing one of the goods or all other goods; (d) fidelity to commitments made in view of the good to be achieved.

Value and Values

In a moral context, *value* and *values* can be said to pertain to that which is treasured, prized, or desired by human beings, whether for its intrinsic worth, or instrumentally, as a means to a desired end. The dictionary defines *values* as "the ideals, customs, institutions, etc. of a society toward which the people of the group have an affective regard... these values can be positive, as cleanliness, freedom, or education, or negative, as cruelty, crime, or blasphemy."

Values can also be positive in one context but experienced as negative in another. The basic American business values of initiative, competition, hard work, and freedom are the very values which many regard as providing rationalizations for much of the malaise within our social order today.

The concepts of morality and value come together cogently in writers who regard morality as pertaining to the values of the "good person in the good society." Velasquez and Rostankowski (1985) regard morality as having to do with "actions freely performed that significantly benefit or harm ourselves or others"(p. xi). An even larger frame of reference is being offered by those who want to extend our value systems, our morality, to bring all aspects of nature, including human and non-human animals and the environment, within the scope of our caring.

Ethics

Ethics requires still fuller comment. Ethics is about morality; and in the dominant ethical traditions of Western culture, morality is grounded in principles and committed to reasoned methods of moral decision making. Accordingly, "right decisions," "good choices," "morally sensitive judgments" are arrived at not by appeal to emotion, but to reason (Velasquez and Rostankowski, 1985). The major ethical systems, utilitarianism, universalism, natural law, and social contract, are cognitive philosophies and contrast sharply with those Shklar (1964) identifies as moralities of the "inner light -- the morality of sentiment, of authenticity, and of self-realization" (p. 57).

Rationalistic ethics. The lay person typically thinks of ethics only as the norms by which behavior is judged, the "shoulds" and "oughts" of conduct. The continuing professional educator, however, needs to understand the concept's larger philosophical dimensions.

There are three primary approaches to ethics:

1. *Descriptive ethics* concerns itself with what people do and how they differ in what they do, recounted without judgment as to rightness or wrongness, morality or immorality.

2. *Analytic ethics* or *metaethics* concerns itself with what people say about what they do or ought to do, and with the questions people ask about moral meanings, justifications, and values.

3. *Normative* or *prescriptive ethics* concerns itself with what people should and should not, ought or ought not do.

Writers on ethics may or may not indicate whether the focus of their interest, in a particular instance, is descriptive, analytical, or normative. It may actually be some mixture, and which approach they are using at any given moment may have to be inferred.

The importance of being able to make such distinctions when discussing professional behavior can be illustrated by an article, entitled "Bork on Elections and Constitutional Law" in the October 3, 1988, *Christian Science Monitor* (Sitomer, 1988). Judge Robert Bork, whom the *Monitor* described as "the conservative scholar whose nomination was defeated by the Senate last year after a bitter battle over judicial ideology," was quoted as saying, "'You're likely to find a more activist judiciary appointed by Governor Dukakis, one determined to expand a moral and social agenda that is quite liberal'" (p. 6). Then Vice-President Bush, on the other hand, according to Bork, would appoint "'temperamentally conservative [judges] who are more likely to take the court along a path down the center'" (p. 6).

One who took issue with Judge Bork's comment might be interested only in challenging the accuracy of the *factual* assertions, but could also challenge the *normative* assumption, clearly implied, that the Republican's appointee's agenda would be preferable to the Democrat's. One might, however, choose to engage at a meta level, by seeking to determine what system of justice best contributes to the good society.

No changes of heart or mind may result from prior agreement on levels of discourse, but we do need to know what we are talking about.

As Jessup (1949) points out, "Need for agreement is axiomatic: Between persons there can be no rational disagreement, that is, disagreement of the kind that leads to discussion rather than contention, unless there is first agreement" (p. 125).

With respect to rationalistic systems of ethics, then, bear in mind the following: 1) typically references to *ethics* and *ethical systems* are referring to normative ethics, whether or not so designated; 2) the speaker or writer, in most instances, is talking about rules that govern conduct or action, (i.e., rule-based behavior); and 3) the ethical task is that of seeking to determine by *rational* processes, freely chosen, what is the "right" thing to do.

Non-rationalistic ethics. Some moral psychologists contend that the essence of ethics and morality is inherently non-rational. From an educator's perspective, non-rationalistic approaches to morality differ from rationalistic ones in that the latter are by definition primarily cognitive (i.e., pertaining to perception, judgment, and reasoning), while the former are affective (i.e., feelings, values, attitudes/loving, caring/prizing), and conative (i.e., willing, striving, following-through). Quinn (1987) offers a model of the "Humanistic Conscience" that "portrays moral character as a function of the developmental integration of the conative, the affective, and the rational dimensions of the person" (p. 71).

Gilligan (1982) challenged Kohlberg's (1973) "masculine," justice-oriented theories of cognitive moral development and advocated a "feminine" ethic of caring, bringing the cognitive versus affective/conative approaches to moral development and moral education to front and center stage. Shklar (1964), while not discussing the "feminine" ethic in psychological terms of affect and conation, points out that the non-rationalistic ethicists begin by denying the value of rules and rule following, and rejecting the ethics of rules, obligation, and primary adherence to principles. Noddings (1987), for example, says:

> Ethically caring, the relation in which we do meet the other morally, arises out of natural caring--that relation in which we respond as one--caring out of love or natural inclination. The relation of caring is the human condition that we, consciously or unconsciously, perceive as good....Everything depends upon...this realistic picture of oneself as a caring person--for we shall not have absolute principles to guide us. Indeed, I reject ethics of principle as ambiguous and unstable....My attention is not on judgment nor on the particular acts we perform

but on how we meet the other morally....Our efforts must, then, be directed to the maintenance of conditions that will permit caring to flourish. (p. 13)

A different tone, one that does not reject ethics grounded in principle and reason but which, nonetheless, has strong affective and conative components, can be found in the works of Srivastva and Associates (1988) on developing executive integrity. Kolb, a co-author, states:

The concept [integrity] describes a way of knowing that is much more sophisticated than that measured by conventional intelligence tests, encompassing moral judgment, creativity, and intuitive and emotional skills as well as rational, analytic powers. Integrative knowing transcends the timidity of wisdom to encompass coura-geous action. It softens the dictates of justice with the mercy of love....Integrity is not living by principle, but the process of choosing principles by which to live. (p. 68)

Schon's (1987) concept of "reflection-in-action" uses the same approach. Moreover, many people place reliance on revealed truth ("what has been revealed to me as the will of God"), rather than reasoned belief systems, to determine what is right or wrong and for knowing how and what to choose when values conflict. Matthews, Goodpaster, and Nash (1985), and Hosmer (1987) provide two very helpful, although quite different, reviews of these various theories.

Ethics in Practice

If these concepts can be our work tools and if, as discussed in the introduction, ethics is not expected to carry the full burden of maintain-ing a morally integrated society, then ethics can be regarded for what it is--a powerful determinant of morally-grounded professional practice. How ethics plays its unique role and how it relates to the other major systems (primarily legal, administrative, institutional, and professional) which attempt to regulate professional behavior and which are also morality-oriented can best be understood by viewing ethics in juxtapo-sition to those systems. Figure 1 illustrates these relationships.

That many of our laws and standards of practice are grounded in (wrapped around by) concepts of morality is easily demonstrated. Grisez (in Valasquez & Rostankowski, 1985) reminds us, for example, that equality before the law is a moral principle as well as a legal one and

Figure 1. The Practitioner's Environment:
The Morals Wraparound

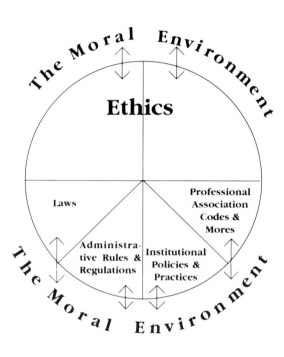

that whether it is ever right for one human being to take the life of another is both a legal and a moral question. The policeman's commitment to a standard of "never employing unnecessary force or violence" is both proscriptive and aspirational. Similarly, the distribution of prescription drugs or financial gain subjects a pharmacist to legal and administrative penalties; but because it is also a source of much needless human suffering, it is by definition also immoral.

The morals wraparound concept reminds us that the "High-Rise Inferno" case, which raises questions about the duties and responsibilities of licensed professionals, must be examined from each system's perspective, independently and in relationship to one another.

The Gray Areas

Ethics, as a moral system, differs from these other morally oriented systems in two important respects.

Enforceable versus self-regulated behaviors. One of the most significant dimensions of morality and ethical practice pertains to the matter of *enforceability.* Most professional codes contain rules that are mandatory, whether they are cast prescriptively (ordered, dictated, required) or proscriptively (condemned, prohibited, forbidden), and the disciplinary consequences of infractions are explicit. Ethics educators need to keep clearly in mind that even though these rules are contained in "codes of ethics," these enforceable dimensions of practice are not the essence of ethics. Ethics needs to be understood as addressing behavior that cannot be enforced and must, therefore, be entrusted to self-regulation. Ethical behavior is by definition freely chosen, self-regulated conduct. This distinction is clearly evident in professional codes, typically referred to as "codes of ethics" or "codes of professional conduct."

The Code of Professional Conduct (1988) of the American Institute of Certified Public Accountants makes this distinction most explicitly in the following assertion:

> Compliance with the Code of Professional Conduct, as with all standards in an open society, depends primarily on members' understanding and voluntary actions, secondarily on reinforcement by peers and public opinion, and ultimately on disciplinary proceedings, when necessary, against members who fail to comply with the Rules...The Principles call for an unswerving commitment to honorable behavior, even at the sacrifice of personal advantage. (p. 3)

Similarly, The University of California Faculty Code of Conduct (1974) distinguishes "ethical principles" which affirm the highest professional ideals, from "types of unacceptable conduct" which are mandatory in character and state "minimum levels of conduct below which a faculty member cannot fall without being subject to University discipline" (p. 5).

Some codes distinguish between *canons, ethical standards*, and *rules.* The condensed statement of the Preamble of the Code of Ethics and Professional Conduct of The American Institue of Architects states:

> Members of The American Institute of Architects are dedicated to the highest standards of professionalism, integrity and competence. The Canons are broad prin-

ciples of conduct intended as guidelines for members in fulfilling those obligations. The Ethical Standards are more specific goals toward which members should aspire in professional performance and behavior. The Rules of Conduct are mandatory, the violation of which is grounds for disciplinary action by the Institute. (unpaginated)

Figure 2 distinguishes self-regulated conduct (a matter of the individual conscience and, thus, the domain of ethics) from mandated conduct, which is the domain of law, administrative regulation, and the professional associations and institutions to which many professionals now belong.

Figure 2. Mandated vs. Self-regulated Domains of Professional Practice

This analysis suggests that the licensed professionals who made the decision not to install sprinklers in the First Interstate Bank building were clearly acting within the law and most probably the rules of professional practice. However, determining whether they acted ethically (i.e. whether their behavior can be judged as moral) requires grappling with questions that go beyond mandated laws, rules, and regulations.

Rule-based ethics versus aspirational principles. Having been shown to pertain partly to voluntary conduct, the codes can further be seen as treating ethical behavior from both rationalistic (i.e. cognitive), and non-rationalistic (i.e., affective and/or conative) perspectives. The former is found in provisions regarding roles, relationships, and behaviors which, while not mandated, are specifically delineated. This is the domain often referred to as "rule-based ethics." As discussed earlier, it is regarded by some as derived from justice-oriented theories of cognitive moral development.

Many of the codes clearly go beyond rules, emphasizing values, attitudes, and feelings (the affective domain), and calling for conduct in terms that are aspirational, often even inspirational, and fully dependent on personal strivings and commitment (the conative domain).

One university campus law enforcement code of ethics [no reference available] contains the following:

> As a Law Enforcement Officer, my fundamental duty is to serve mankind; to safeguard lives and property; to protect the innocent against deception, the weak against oppression or intimidation, and the peaceful against violence or disorder; and to respect the Constitutional rights of all men to liberty, equality and justice....
>
> I will never act officiously or permit personal feeling, prejudices, animosities or friendships to influence my decisions. With no compromise for crime and with relentless prosecution of criminals, I will enforce the law courteously and appropriately without fear or favor, malice or ill will, never employing unnecessary force or violence and never accepting gratuities....
>
> I recognize the badge of my office as a symbol of public faith, and I accept it as a public trust to be held as long as I am true to the ethics of the police service. I will constantly strive to achieve these objectives and ideals....

Similar distinctions between rule-based ethics and non-rationalistic ethics are found in the American Bar Association's Model Rules of Professional Conduct (1983). In addition to the "rules of reason" (p. 3), some of which, according to the preamble, are imperatives, others of which are permissive, the Code also contains comments which "do not add obligations but, instead, provide guidance for compliance with the Rules" (p. 3). The practitioner is advised that:

> The Rules do not, however, exhaust the moral and ethical considerations that should inform a lawyer, for no

worthwhile human activity can be completely defined by legal rules. The Rules simply provide a framework for the ethical practice of law. (p. 3)

Figure 3 reflects the distinctions which can be made between behaviors which reference rule-based norms, typically cast in rationalistic terms, and those that are related more to the affective and/or conative domains.

It can be seen, then, that as ethics influences the law, so law and other external forces influence ethics. Further, and of primary interest to the ethics educator, the commitment to live by principle, the ability to make sound moral judgments, and the fortitude that ethical follow-through requires are all internal to the person and will depend, in the last analysis, on the human will.

Figure 3: The Domains (Affective, Conative, Cognitive) of Professional Practice

Where Does the Professional Educator Begin?

It may be true, as some assert, that you cannot teach a professional to be ethical; but ethics *can* be taught, and professionals struggling to know and to do what is right have much to gain by studying ethics for guidance. Appreciation of the moral significance of many aspects of the practitioner's environment strongly suggests that before the decision is made to offer courses in ethics for any profession, careful thought be given to some of the realities of the professional's work environment.

Situational Analysis

If we acknowledge that instruction aims to bring about change, we are ethically required to ask, first, "What's going on that needs changing?" and then, "Will instruction help?" (Adelson, 1986).

The "Can't-do's": Systemic immoralities. Individuals who fail to act according to some identified ethical norm may not need or may not benefit from a course in ethics. Experience informs us that there are often systemic obstacles to ethical performance that individuals find very difficult to overcome, no matter how motivated or committed they may be. For example, the Institute of Electrical and Electronic Engineers (IEEE) Code of Ethics for Engineers (1974) states, in Article III, that "Engineers shall, in their relations with employers and clients ... inform their employers, clients, professional societies or public agencies or private agencies of which they are members or to which they may make presentations, of any circumstance that could lead to a conflict of interest" (unpaginated). Such prescriptions are now commonly referred to as "whistle-blowing"; but without strong protections against reprisal, such mandates are often left blowing in the wind. A "good person" may do a quick cost/benefit analysis and decide that the collective good is not worth the individual risk.

Many individuals experience conflict stemming from organizational goals that are perceived as ethically incompatible with each other. Consider the manager who had an opportunity to hire a clearly excellent ethnic minority candidate but who was required by organizational policy to accept through the transfer system a satisfactory non-minority employee who had been laid off. Rather than bring into a critically important job an employee whom the manager learned, unofficially, was satisfactory but only minimally so, the manager withdrew the position until the laid-off employee had been recalled by another division. Is the problem the personal ethics of a manager or the ethics of the system that the manager experienced as inflexible?

Harder, even tragically difficult conflicts are posed daily in the fields of medicine and bio-ethics. Health professionals and families who are forced to keep hopelessly ill and suffering patients alive through the use of life-support systems during protracted and costly legal proceedings may themselves be regarded as victims of unethical systems. It would be a mistake for ethics educators to approach such problems purely from the perspective of personal ethics. Systemic immorality is a meta-reality which should not be ignored.

The "Won't-do's": Motivation. A second class of cases in which ethics education is likely to be irrelevant involves individuals who knowingly choose to defy the rules. These may be individuals whose personal goals, needs, or values are not compatible with the goals of the profession or institution. For example, as Queeney and Smutz explain in this volume, the desire for money, power, and position may be stronger, at some phase in the professional's development, than the desire to serve the public as required by the profession's code of ethics. Self-serving behaviors, such as those evidenced by insider trading cases, represent clear cases of "won't-do" behavior.

From a different perspective, the professional who is feeling alienated because of lack of adequate recognition, for example, may lose interest in the profession's goals, especially those that are aspirational, and may do nothing more than is minimally required.

Perhaps the clearest example of "won't-do" attitudes or behaviors is found in the military. Confronted by their commanders' orders to kill, some individuals have always refused to obey, based on personal concepts of morality which were in conflict with their duty to obey superiors. For such persons, "goodness" requires, in Grisez's language, genuineness and interior integrity. DeGeorge (1984) suggests that concerns about the morality of war are growing in the military and espouses development of a mini-code of ethics for officers to supplement the Uniform Code of Military Justice. DeGeorge first points out that the only morally justifiable military mission is keeping the peace and fighting only defensive wars. In that context, he calls for a six-point code that requires, among other things, the officer to obey "all legitimate orders, but only legitimate orders" and to remember that those beneath the officer are "moral beings worthy of respect" and never to command them to do that which is immoral (p. 23).

Again, if ethics education is to be at all relevant, it must be designed with the meta-realities of the prospective student's life circumstances in mind. Figure 4 demonstrates the relationship between instruction and the extant situation.

Figure 4: Will Instruction Help? A Situational Analysis

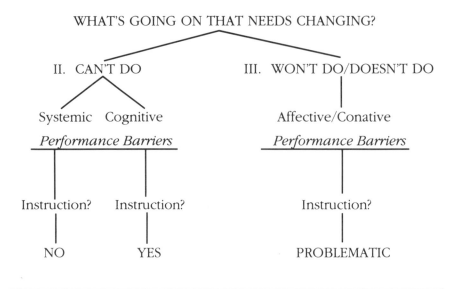

I. THE PROBLEM:

WHAT'S GOING ON THAT NEEDS CHANGING?

II. CAN'T DO   III. WON'T DO/DOESN'T DO

Systemic   Cognitive   Affective/Conative

Performance Barriers   *Performance Barriers*

Instruction?   Instruction?   Instruction?

NO   YES   PROBLEMATIC

Such an analysis suggests that continuing educators for the professions may be in position to influence how and where professional ethics can be incorporated into the professional's continuing learning and development plans. It also suggests that educators who would do more than help professionals meet minimal standards of compliance with external regulations or who would not elect to offer ethics education as a buffer or substitute for needed systemic changes may be faced with the ethical dilemma of either offering something or else offering nothing. The educator's own standards will have to provide guidance for such a circumstance.

Continuing educators for the professions who have not had formal training in ethics are likely to find the subject complex and controversial enough to warrant seeking advice and help. Those who have not previously programmed in this area could do no better than to become familiar with the Hastings Center Project, *The Teaching of Ethics in Higher Education* (1980). Their first nine monographs and a subsequent one by Jennings, Callahan, and Wolf (1987) are widely regarded as the seminal work in the field. In addition, *Ethical Issues In Adult Education* (Brockett, 1988) contains approaches to adult education that will be immediately transferable to the ethics education of professionals.

Continuing professional educators will typically find faculty in their schools' departments of philosophy and/or religion rich sources of guidance, reference, and participation. Other departments and extra-university sources should be looked to as well. Perhaps in no subject more than ethics is the need for interprofessional collaboration more easily demonstrated, and many excellent models are now available for study.

Instructional Goals as an Ethical Issue

The decision to design courses or curricula requires the educator to make decisions at the outset about instructional goals. This process, as was the case with the analysis of the codes, is aided by approaching the development of learning goals from the perspectives of the cognitive, affective, and conative domains and introduces an important educational controversy.

The issue is whether ethics education should focus exclusively on cognitive goals, such as acquisition of knowledge, development of moral judgment, and ability to engage in moral reasoning; or whether affective/conative goals, such as interest, valuing, appreciating, and commitment, should also be addressed. At the undergraduate and graduate levels, while the importance of values and ethics education is widely acknowledged, fear of indoctrination and intrusions on personal freedom causes many educators to be extremely cautious about trying to teach values, develop character, or directly influence conduct.

Goals language found in materials associated with ethics courses is often fuzzy, making it difficult to know what the goals of instruction actually are. Some educators and policy makers feel that it is entirely appropriate to promote a sense of moral integrity and a commitment to ethical conduct, but their methods may be entirely cognitive (i.e., stressing knowledge, skills and intellectual abilities; avoiding direct efforts to affect or measure attitude, values, or behavior change). Rosen and Caplan (1980), in adapting portions of The Hastings Center Report, *The Teaching of Ethics in Higher Education* (1980), state that many instructors of undergraduates feel that courses in ethics should directly seek to change behavior, which suggests that this intent will be reflected in course designs. The authors take the position that changing behavior of undergraduates should not be an explicit goal for the following reason:

> In order to bring about direct immediate changes in student behavior, professors might well be tempted to pursue highly dubious techniques of manipulation and

coercion; at the least, the temptation to crudely indoctrinate would be very strong. Moreover, an explicit attempt to change student behavior would beg many important moral questions, precisely those questions that ought to be pursued in an ethics course: Just what constitutes good or correct behavior: What virtues are appropriate for human beings: What behavior is right when two or more valid moral principles are in conflict?" (p. 21)

Survey

Wishing to examine issues of instructional goals in courses and programs designed for practicing professionals, I contacted some 75 ethics centers focusing on professional and applied ethics and received materials and course descriptions from over 50 of them. In addition, many respondents wrote personal letters offering encouragement for the project.

Cognitive goals clearly dominated in every profession. Representative goals were: *engineering*, "recognize moral problems likely to arise in the practice of engineering"; *public policy*, "develop an informed awareness of the ethical dimension of public policy issues"; *architecture and city planning*, "provide a sense of the sorts of arguments one might make to defend a moral judgment"; *health care*, "illumination of value questions in medical settings; encourage the careful examination of alternative patterns of thought and explanation."

Examples of affective/conative goals that did emerge included: *engineering*, "foster in students dispositions that will help them deal responsibly with [moral] problems when they arise"; *journalism*, "elevate the standards of journalism"; *interdisciplinary studies,* "help build and maintain the professional's ethical character and commitment; encourage the incorporation of ethical concepts in private and public decision-making; promotion of ethical principles creatively and aggressively; develop a professional conscience."

This small sample illustrates that the desire of ethics instructors to have greater influence, whether directly or indirectly, on the morals and behavior of their students poses serious questions for continuing professional educators regarding methods and goals. Widely read authors (such as Schon, *Educating the Reflective Practitioner* (1987); and Srivastva and Associates, *Executive Integrity* (1988)) may be contributing to the call for something more than the current highly cognitive approaches which some, whether mistakenly or not, see as a passionless, reasoned response to morals conflicts that are ripping segments of our society apart. Others remind us that it is precisely during times of upheaval and stress that reasoned approaches to values conflicts must be carefully protected and honored.

For continuing educators willing to move beyond the traditional and search for methods that maintain the integrity of the instructional process while responding to the changing needs of the professions and professionals, ethics education will likely continue to be grounded in reason. However, the approach will be more integrated, drawing on the multidimensional aspects of the person--mind, emotion, spirit and will-- and, as suggested by Childs (1987), understanding individuals as "historical, social, political, and cultural beings" (p. 124).

From this perspective, ethics, as always, will contribute to problem-solving and decision-making when values are in conflict. It may also be of service to the cause of social moral integration and transformation. While primary tools of ethics will continue to be the informed moral judgment and the sensitized moral conscience, to these may be added, (without regard to gender) love, fidelity to duty, and the caring heart. These challenges, if accepted, suggest the following questions:

To what extent do teachers of ethics limit themselves to primarily cognitive goals because they lack confidence in their teaching abilities in the affective and conative domains? To what extent do they do so because they believe it would be unethical to do otherwise?

To what extent are teachers striving for conative and affective goals covertly? Is such practice ethical?

Should teachers be encouraged overtly to expand into the affective/conative domains? Could they do so without indoctrinating or being seen as indoctrinating? How?

Do these questions suggest special challenges for pedagogy/androgogy with respect to teaching ethics for the professions? How are they being dealt with now, and how might they be?

If "values" are to work their way overtly into the classroom, whose values are they to be, and who is to decide? How? What happens if someone objects, perhaps on the best of ethical grounds?

Substantively, can ethics education hope to be relevant to licensed professionals caught increasingly in existence-threatening dilemmas?

For continuing professional educators whose programs are not encompassing ethical issues in professional practice at all, is it ethical to continue bypassing them?

Whatever one decides concerning these issues, the ethically relevant curriculum must reflect the continuing professional educator's competence and commitment in helping the professions deal effectively with the challenge of living and practicing ethically.

References

Adelson, Y. (1986). *Will training help? The can't-do's and won't-do's of behavior.* Unpublished manuscript.

American Bar Association. (1983). Model rules (unpaginated) of professional conduct. *ALI-ABA course of study materials.* Chicago, IL: American Bar Association.

American Institute of Architects. (1988). *Code of ethics and professional conduct.* Washington, DC: American Institute of Architects.

American Institute of Certified Public Accountants. (1988). *Code of professional conduct* (as adopted January 12, 1988). New York: American Institute of Certified Public Accountants, Inc.

Baum, R. J. (1980). *Ethics and engineering curricula.* Hastings Center Project on the Teaching of Ethics in Higher Education, Vol. VII. Hastings-on-Hudson, NY: The Hastings Center.

Baxter, G.D., & Rarick, C.A. (1987). Education for the moral development of managers: Kohlberg's stages of moral development and integrative education. *Journal of Business Ethics, 6,* 243-248.

Bloom, B.S. (Ed.). (1956). *Taxonomy of educational objectives: Book 1, cognitive domain.* New York: Longman.

Brockett, R.G. (Ed.). (1988). *Ethical issues in adult education.* New York: Teachers College (Columbia University) Press.

Calabresi, G. (1985). *Ideals, beliefs, attitudes, and the law.* Syracuse, NY: Syracuse University Press.

Calabresi, G., & Bobbitt, P. (1978). *Tragic choices: The conflicts society confronts in the allocation of tragically scarce resources.* New York: W.W. Norton.

Childs, J. M., Jr. (1987). Interprofessional approach to ethical issues. *Theory into practice: Interprofessional education. 26* (2), 124-128.

Christians, C. G., & Covert, C. L. (1980). *Teaching ethics in journalism education.* Hastings Center Project on the Teaching of Ethics in Higher Education, Vol. III. Hastings-on-Hudson, NY: The Hastings Center.

Clouser, K. D. (1980). *Teaching bioethics: strategies, problems, and resources.* Hastings Center Project on the Teaching of Ethics in Higher Education, Vol. IV. Hastings-on-Hudson,NY: The Hastings Center.

Cousins, N. (1981). Hutchins believed that history was a succession of open moments. *The Center Magazine*, 14(1), 10-14.

Crittenden, B. (1988). A comment on cognitive moral education. *Phi Delta Kappan*, 69(10), 695-696.

Davies, A. P. (1965). *The temptation to be good.* Boston: Beacon Press.

DeGeorge, R. T. (1987). A code of ethics for officers. *In Military Ethics* (pp. 13-32). Washington, DC: National Defense University Press.

Dwivedi, O. P. (1988). Man and nature: A holistic approach to a theory of ecology. *The Environmental Professional, 10* (1) 32-33.

Elliott, S. (1987). How to teach shame. *California Business, 22* (6), 32-33.

Fleishman, J. L., & Payne, B. L. (1980). *Ethical dilemmas and the education of policymakers.* Hastings Center Project on the Teaching of Ethics in Higher Education, Vol. VIII. Hastings-on-Hudson, NY: The Hastings Center.

Geiger, G. R. (1949). Values and inquiry. In R. Lepley (Ed.). *Value: A cooperative inquiry* (pp. 93-111). New York: Columbia University Press.

Gellerman, S. W. (1986). Why "good" managers make bad ethical choices. *Harvard Business Review, 64* (4), 85.

Gilligan, C. (1982). *In a different voice.* Cambridge, MA: Harvard University Press.

Goodpaster, K. E. (1985). Ethical frameworks for management. In J. B. Matthews, K. E. Goodpaster, & L. L. Nash (Eds.), *Policies and persons: A casebook in business ethics* (pp. 507-529). New York: McGraw-Hill.

Hosmer, L. T. (1987). Ethical analysis and human resource management. *Human Resources Management, 26* (3), 313-330.

Institute of Electrical and Electronic Engineers, Inc. (1974, December 4). *IEEE code of ethics for engineers.* New York, NY: Unpublished manuscript.

Jennings, B., Callahan, D., & Wolf, S. M. (1987, February). The professions: public interest and common good. *Hastings Center Report,* 3-11.

Jessup, B. E. (1949). On value. In R. Lepley (Ed.). *Value: A cooperative inquiry* (pp. 125-146). New York: Columbia University Press.

Kant, I. (1959). *Foundations of the metaphysics of morals.* (L. W. Beck, Trans.) New York: Bobbs-Merrill. (Original work published 1785)

Katz, L. (1987). *Bad acts and guilty minds.* Chicago: University of Chicago Press.

Kelly, M. J. (1980). *Legal ethics and legal education.* Hastings Center Project on the Teaching of Ethics in Higher Education, Vol. II. Hastings-on-Hudson, NY: The Hastings Center.

Kohlberg, L. (1975). The cognitive-developmental approach to moral education. *Phi Delta Kappan, 57* (10), 670-683.

Kolb, D. A. (1988). Integrity, advanced professional development, and learning. In S. Srivastva and Associates, *Executive integrity: The search for high human values in organizational life* (pp. 68-88). San Francisco: Jossey-Bass.

Krathwohl, D. R., Bloom, B. S., & Masia, B. B. (1964). *Taxonomy of educational objectives.* (Vols. 1-2). New York: Longman.

Kuttler, C. M. (1987). Why do we need ethics courses? *Higher Education & National Affairs, 36,* 7-8.

McBee, S. (1985). The state of American values. *U. S. News & World Report, 99* (24), 27-31.

Mill, J. S. (1975). *On liberty: Annotated text; sources and background; criticism.* D. Spitz, (Ed.). New York: W. W. Norton. (Original work published 1859)

Muchnic, S. (1988, November 3). An art world detective story: The Getty's "Head of Achilles." *Los Angeles Times,* 8-9.

Noddings, N. (1987). The mother's voice: The masculine ethics of justice gives way to a feminine ethics of caring. *Business Ethics, 1*(5), 12-15.

Pastin, M. (1986). *The hard problems of management: Gaining the ethics edge.* San Francisco: Jossey-Bass.

Peters, R. S. (1975). A reply to Kohlberg. *Phi Delta Kappan, 57*(10), 678.

Phillips, L. E. (1987). Certifiably educated. *Association Management, 39*(9), 73-75.

Powers, C. W., & Vogel, D. (1980). *Ethics in the education of business managers.* Hastings Center Project on the Teaching of Ethics in Higher Education, Vol. V. Hastings-on-Hudson, NY: The Hastings Center.

Quinn, R. H. (1987, winter). The humanistic conscience: An inquiry into the development of principled moral character. *Journal of Humanistic Psychology,* 27(1), 69-92.

Remitz, E. (1983). To code or not to code. *Feed/back, Society of Professional Journalists/Sigma Delta Chi convention proceedings.*

Roberts, J. S. (Ed.). (1987). *Leadership ethics.* Maxwell Air Force Base, AL: Air Force ROTC.

Rosen, B., & Caplan, A. L. (1980). *Ethics in the undergraduate curriculum.* Hastings Center Project on the Teaching of Ethics in Higher Education, Vol. IX. Hastings-on-Hudson, NY: The Hastings Center.

Rosenberg, J. E., & Towers, B. (1986). The practice of empathy as a prerequisite for informed consent. *Theoretical Medicine, 7*(2), 181-194.

Schon, D. A. (1987). *Educating the reflective practioner.* San Francisco: Jossey-Bass.

Shklar, J. N. (1986). *Legalism: Law, morals, and political trials.* Cambridge: Harvard University Press.

Sitomer, C. J. (1988, October 3). Bork on elections and constitutional law. *Christian Science Monitor*, p. 6.

Srivastva, S. and Associates (1988). *Executive integrity: The search for high human values in organizational life.* San Francisco: Jossey-Bass.

Steiner, G. A., & Steiner, J. F. (Eds.). (1972). *Issues in business and society.* New York: Random House.

Toffler, B. L. (1986). *Tough choices: Managers talk ethics.* New York: John Wiley & Sons.

University of California. (1974). *University policy on faculty conduct and the administration of discipline.* Berkeley: University of California Press.

Velasquez, M., & Rostankowski, C. (Eds.). (1985). *Ethics: Theory and practice.* Englewood Cliffs, NJ: Prentice-Hall.

Vickers, G. (1974). The changing nature of the professions. *American Behavioral Scientist, 18* (2), 164-189.

Walters, K. D. (1975). Thinking ahead. *Harvard Business Review, 53* (4), 26-34.

Warwick, D. P. (1980). *The teaching of ethics in the social sciences.* Hastings Center Project on the Teaching of Ethics in Higher Education, Vol. VI. Hastings-on-Hudson, NY: The Hastings Center.

Wasserstrom, R. (1975). *Today's moral problems.* New York: Macmillan.

Emerging Imperatives for Continuing Professional Education

Alan B. Knox

Much progress has been achieved in continuing professional education through the efforts of talented and dedicated practitioners in the field. However, the foregoing chapters have pointed out how much we can continue to learn from experience in other professional fields and from ideas from various scholarly disciplines. Great improvements could occur from emulating exemplary educational programs already in operation in other professional fields. For these improvements to occur, practitioners must know about such programs and about similarities and differences across specialized fields as a basis for adaptation.

This concluding chapter suggests emerging themes shared by continuing educators in many professional specialties, themes likely to be ever more important for progress as continuing professional education leaders learn their way into the future.

The suggested themes are organized around five of the major topics important to continuing professional education theory and practice reflected in the foregoing chapters. These topics are *participants, society, benefits, collaboration,* and *leadership.* For each topic, three issues are presented from the many that are important to various professional fields. As Houle (1980) and Cervero (1988) have noted, there are important similarities and differences among professional fields regarding continuing education. In this chapter the emphasis is on generic issues. Each issue is phrased as a question to which better answers are required for progress to occur. Each question regarding emerging imperatives is accompanied by a brief rationale that suggests useful sources of answers.

Participants

The people who plan continuing professional education value responsiveness to the clientele. One distinctive characteristic of the professional as learner is having a responsible occupational position based on substantial formal education and ability. Many continuing professional education activities seek to deliver recent information regarding specialized aspects of a complex knowledge base and practice profile. A holistic view of professionals as self-directed and informed consumers of continuing professional education is also desirable. Admittedly, the extent to which this is the case in practice varies from field to field and person to person. However, if this holistic view reflects a desirable and distinctive characteristic, it seems important both to be responsive where the capability exists and to nurture it where it does not. Following are three pertinent questions.

Why Is It So Important That We Help Professionals Become More Informed Consumers of Continuing Education?

As knowledge, technology, practice, and careers evolve, professionals who fail to continue learning soon become obsolete. As Houle (1980) and Cervero (1988) have explained, the foundation of such lifelong learning is the self-directed learning activities of professionals. Professionals who are informed consumers can avoid just reacting to remedial updating programs but instead select personal and organization development activities that advance their careers, field, and service to society.

Planners of continuing professional education can strengthen such a developmental approach by devoting some program time to encouraging and supporting self-directed learning. One example is helping professionals progress to higher levels of understanding (Knox, 1986). At lower levels, learners have a fragmentary understanding of facts or details without central concepts or broad integrating themes; or they comprehend such concepts and themes but without relation to supporting facts and details. A higher level of understanding occurs when learners integrate concepts with facts by identification of both similarities and differences. A still higher level of inclusive understanding occurs when learners use deep processing of integrating themes to go beyond the context of information presented to explore relations among alternative views.

How Much Emphasis Should Be Given to Ethical Issues and Value Judgments by Professionals?

Each professional field contains distinctive conflicts of interests and loyalties as professionals apply knowledge to the action decisions in practice. Preparatory education programs emphasize value neutral knowledge, while actually professional practice is replete with difficult value choices. The contribution of continuing education to actual practice depends on helping professionals deal with value judgments and their resulting ethical implications. However, continuing education providers have discovered how difficult it is to attract professionals to programs on ethical and societal issues. A more effective approach might be to embed sessions on ethical issues in broader programs on practical topics. This approach has the advantage of giving participants practice dealing with the confluence of technical and ethical questions as they actually confront them.

How Can Programs Help Professionals Become More Reflective in Their General Decision Making?

By definition, professionals should know why as well as how (Schon, 1987). Some topics pertain to tasks and influences close to the practice setting. Programs can help professionals reflect on the insights that emerge from that rich firsthand experience. Discussion with peers about personal professional experience can provide a useful vehicle for becoming more reflective practitioners. By contrast, other topics pertain to more remote societal influences that affect the recipients of their services, to laws and regulations, to policies of their professional associations, and to relations with other professional fields. It seems desirable to increase program emphasis on societal influences. Comparative analysis of practice in various settings and interprofessional education are ways to enable professionals to reflect on the assumptions, influences, choices, and implications associated with their practice.

Society

Responding to major societal influences strengthens continuing professional education. In addition to helping professionals identify such influences in their practice, program planners can engage in contextual analysis, in parallel with needs assessment, as the twin bases for learning. North American continuing education tends to depend heavily on information about individual educational needs and to give much less attention to societal trends and issues. In other parts of the world, more emphasis is given to societal expectations. Following are three questions that continuing professional education planners might consider regarding societal influences.

What Are the Realities of Fragmented Professions in a Pluralistic Society?

In most professions there are various specialties and views of the future. Likewise, the United States is pluralistic (compared with many centralized societies around the world) with divisions of responsibility among public and private sectors and national, state, and local levels. Largely uncoordinated relations among similar professions add to this complexity. This pluralism limits the influence of government on professional practice and assumes that professional associations will attend to both the rights and responsibilities of professional practice. Continuing professional education for separate professions or for clusters of professions has the potential to help professionals and policymakers address relationships between the professions and society. In the past, this examination has seldom occurred. Current changes in the roles of professions make this a propitious time for consideration of these relationships (Cervero, 1988).

What Attention Should Program Development Give to Social Change?

The societal context is changing, along with professional roles. A traditional form of continuing professional education is updating to reduce obsolescence. However, much more could be done to use education to help professionals address global trends and policy directions. Environmental scanning and futures forecasting can be used to both guide professional practice and to provide continuing education opportunities. Interprofessional education helps professionals place their own fields in comparative perspective and to recognize societal issues that span many professions. Program planners can also use educational activities to stimulate and guide innovation.

How Should We Move Toward Policies That Strengthen Continuing Professional Education?

There are many views of the professions and their impact on society. Some negative views emphasize abuse of professional power and the need for policies to protect the public. Some positive views emphasize the societal benefits of professional practice and policies to extend those benefits. Continuing professional education planners can also analyze current and potential policies as they affect such educational programs. Consideration of public policy approaches in countries such as Sweden and Japan, where societal benefits have received more emphasis than they have in the United States, can provide a useful international perspective (Knox, 1987a). Part of the content of continuing professional education can be an analysis of the impact of such policies on educational programs.

Benefits

There are many potential beneficiaries of continuing professional education. Included are the professionals who participate as learners in the programs, the associations to which professionals belong, the organizations in which professionals work, the clients of professional services, and the larger society that may receive generalized benefits from professional contributions, such as technological innovations, economic productivity, cultural programs, and improved quality of life. Each of these categories of people can be thought of as stakeholders of continuing professional education who receive benefits and may be expected to help cover the costs (Mitroff, 1983). Following are three questions regarding benefits. Answers to these questions can help program planners make decisions about program financing including who should help pay the costs.

What Portions of Benefits Accrue to Individuals, Organizations, and Society?

The multiple beneficiaries seem evident (Schein, 1978). Personal growth and professional advancement have been used to justify that professionals receive most of the benefits and, therefore, should pay most of the costs. In many professions, increased group or organizational productivity has been used to justify management decisions to subsidize educational programs as an investment. It has been more difficult to specify the program benefits to the people who receive professional services and to decide their extent of program support and their voice in program content. Considering various stakeholders and beneficiaries certainly complicates program planning but has the potential to make continuing professional education a more powerful vehicle for change.

What Types of Benefits or Levels of Outcomes Should Be the Focus of Continuing Professional Education?

Most continuing professional education aims to enhance the knowledge of participants. However, for many programs the ultimate intent is that new knowledge is applied to improved performance to benefit the clients of professional services and society as a whole. Some regulations for mandatory continuing education assume that mere participation will affect performance, especially by the 5 to 15% of members of a profession whose substandard performance places the public at risk. Given the multiple reasons for substandard performance, it seems unlikely that requirements for attendance will provide much protection to the public. The concept of proficiency lies between knowledge and performance and constitutes a more satisfactory focus for many programs (Knox, 1985). Based on combinations of knowledge, attitudes, and skills, proficiency is the capability to perform satisfactorily. Simulations provide an effective means of enhancing proficiencies and encouraging application. A focus on proficiency constitutes one of the most promising ways to strengthen the planning, implementation, and impact of continuing professional education.

How Can Programs Become More Future Oriented?

Many programs are reactive and remedial, with emphasis on merely updating recent developments. It is assumed that professionals who know about new developments elsewhere will translate them into their own practice. It seems desirable to provide more proactive programs that help professionals achieve longer term benefits. Such benefits might be career advancement, professional innovation, or public policy. Achieving these benefits is more likely if programs deliberately address desirable future directions.

Collaboration

In each professional field there are multiple providers--associations, universities, enterprizes, and consultants. Some emerging imperatives pertain to relations among providers. Both societal and professional trends make strengthening collaboration among providers increasingly important. Following are three questions regarding collaboration.

What Are the Distinctive Contributions of Each Type of Provider?

Cooperation is strengthened by recognition of the complementarity of contribution, as well as shared benefits. Interprofessional education can promote cooperation. Recognition of sources of resistance to collaborative efforts can be used to develop more effective future collaboration. Many programs are more effectively developed unilaterally by a provider than through cosponsorship. Program planners should plan individually when appropriate, but collaborate when warranted.

What Influence Is Technology Having on Collaboration?

Technology affects the provision of continuing education as well as professional practice. In each, there are both positive and negative effects. A positive influence is increased productivity and outreach; a negative influence is that technology can widen the gap between large organizations that can afford educational technology and small ones which cannot. Collaboration is one way small providers can narrow that gap.

How Can Desirable Collaboration Be Promoted?

Ways to promote desirable collaboration include helping program planners understand benefits and strategies associated with collaboration (Knox, 1982). Cooperation can also be advanced by reports of research and evaluation studies of collaboration that help planners increase the effectiveness of such cooperation.

Leadership

A distinguishing characteristic of leaders is their future orientation (Bennis & Nanus, 1985; Simerly & Associates, 1987). This principle applies to continuing professional education practitioners and scholars. Use of ideas about goals and trends is aided by a systems view of programs in their societal contexts that helps leaders relate future directions to both past experience and current decisions. Following are three questions regarding leadership.

What Aspects of Continuing Professional Education Should Be Addressed in Program Planning?

Earlier in this chapter, reference was made to desirable proficiencies of continuing education practitioners that build on knowledge bases regarding program development, collaboration, and professionals as learners. However, there are many other aspects that could serve as program goals (Houle, 1980). Included are understanding the distinctive contribution of the profession, public accountability and legal reinforcement, resource acquisition, and program coordination. Continuing education to advance the professions and their contributions should extend beyond dissemination of theoretical and practical knowledge by addressing the dozen additional characteristics of professions.

How Can Sets of Proficiencies of Continuing Professional Education Practitioners Be Used To Strengthen Programs?

People who plan and conduct continuing professional education come from many backgrounds and often with little shared preparation. It would be very helpful to publish sets of proficiencies that reflect the scope of practice of program planners and coordinators (Knox, 1987b). Such a listing could serve as a set of standards for selecting coordinators and as criteria for assessing their performance. In the form of self-assessment inventories, they can help continuing education coordinators identify areas of desirable professional growth. Research and evaluation on such inventories can identify proficiencies associated with success and lead eventually to practice standards.

What Are Desirable Relations Among Continuing Professional Education Practitioners and Scholars?

In most fields, some tension exists. The critique of practice by scholars contributes to this tension as well as serves as a stimulus to improvement. Most of the above imperatives for strengthening continuing professional education call for contributions by both practitioners and scholars. Their concerted efforts can contribute to creative tensions that benefit both practice and scholarship.

Conclusion

One use of the foregoing review of emerging imperatives for continuing professional education is as a curriculum for continuing professional education coordinators. This volume contains details and references to further readings. Such a development would be one of the best means of strengthening the field.

References

Bennis, W. & Nanus, B. (1985). *Leaders.* New York: Harper & Row.

Cervero, R. M. (1988). *Effective continuing education for professionals.* San Francisco: Jossey-Bass.

Houle, C. O. (1980). *Continuing learning in the professions.* San Francisco: Jossey-Bass.

Knox, A. B. (1982). *Leadership strategies for meeting new challenges:* New directions for continuing education (No. 13). San Francisco, Jossey-Bass.

Knox, A. B. (1985). Adult learning and proficiency. In D. A. Kleiber, & M. L. Maehr (Eds.), *Motivation and adulthood,* Vol. 4 (pp. 251-295). *In Advances in Motivation and Achievement.* Greenwich, CT: JAI Press.

Knox, A. B. (1986). *Helping adults learn.* San Francisco: Jossey-Bass.

Knox, A. B. (1987a). International perspectives on adult education (Information Series No. 321, ERIC Clearinghouse on Adult, Career, and Vocational Education). Columbus, OH: The Ohio State University.

Knox, A. B. (1987b). Leadership challenges to continuing higher education. *Journal for Higher Education Management,* 2 (2), 1-6.

Mitroff, I. I. (1983). *Stakeholders of the organizational mind.* San Francisco: Jossey-Bass.

Schein, E. (1978). *Career dynamics.* Reading, MA: Addison Wesley.

Schon, D. A. (1987). *Educating the reflective practitioner.* San Francisco: Jossey-Bass.

Simerly, R. G. & Associates. (1987). *Strategic planning and leadership in continuing education.* San Francisco: Jossey-Bass.